Advertising Age

The Principles of Advertising and Marketing Communication at Work

Esther Thorson
University of Missouri

Margaret Duffy
University of Missouri

SOUTH-WESTERN
CENGAGE Learning

Australia • Brazil • Japan • Korea • Mexico • Singapore • Spain • United Kingdom • United States

Advertising Age: The Principles of Advertising and Marketing Communication at Work, First Edition

Esther Thorson and Margaret Duffy

Vice President of Editorial, Business: Jack W. Calhoun

Publisher: Erin Joyner

Executive Editor: Mike Roche

Developmental Editor: Daniel Noguera

Marketing Manager: Gretchen Swann

Senior Marketing Communications Manager: Jim Overly

Production Manager: Jennifer Ziegler

Senior Rights Acquisition Specialist: Deanna Ettinger

Media Editor: John Rich

Buyer, Frontlist: Miranda Klapper

Senior Art Director: Stacy Jenkins Shirley

Content Project Management: PreMediaGlobal

Production House/Compositor: PreMediaGlobal

Internal Designer: PreMediaGlobal

Cover Designer: Oliver Munday

Cover Image: iStock Photo

Library of Congress Control Number: 2011931568

ISBN 13: 978-1-111-52875-1
ISBN 10: 1-111-52875-6

Student Edition ISBN-13: 978-1-111-97250-9
Student Edition ISBN-10: 1-111-97250-8

South-Western
5191 Natorp Boulevard
Mason, OH 45040
USA

Cengage Learning products are represented in Canada by Nelson Education, Ltd.

For your course and learning solutions, visit **www.cengage.com**

Purchase any of our products at your local college store or at our preferred online store **www.cengagebrain.com.**

Printed in the United States of America
1 2 3 4 5 6 7 15 14 13 12 11

BRIEF CONTENTS

CONTENTS

Esther Thorson

Associate Dean for Graduate Studies and Research and Director of Research,
Reynolds Journalism Institute School of Journalism,
University of Missouri

Esther Thorson, Ph. D., has published extensively on the news industry, advertising, news effects and health communication Along with professors Hari Sridhar and Murali Mantrala she has developed econometric models that link newspaper budget management with revenue/profit patterns. Her scholarly work has won a variety of research and writing awards and she has advised nearly 40 doctoral dissertations. She applies research, both hers and that of her colleagues, in newsrooms and advertising agencies across the US and abroad. She serves on an extensive list of journal editorial boards. Her latest books are (with David Schumann) *Internet Advertising: Theory and Research* (Lawrence Erlbaum, 2007) and (with Jerry Parker), *Health Communication in the New Media Landscape* (Springer, 2008).

Margaret Duffy

Chair, Strategic Communication Faculty School of Journalism,
University of Missouri

Margaret Duffy, Ph. D., chairs the strategic communication faculty at the Missouri school of Journalism. She has extensive professional experience, including serving as an executive for GTE (Verizon) in marketing, advertising and public relations. Her research focuses on new and interactive media, especially with regard to advertising and the news. She is the co-developer of the Media Choice Model and the Health Communication Media Choice Model. Her fellowship at the Donald W. Reynolds Journalism Institute investigated youth advertising, news and media habits. She consults with clients as diverse as the U.S. Army and the Estee Lauder Corporation and has presented research and conducted training with agencies, universities and news groups in the United States, Italy, China, the United Kingdom, Thailand, Australia, and South Africa.

By Rance Crain

The role of our weekly publication, *Advertising Age*, and books on marketing used to be at opposite ends of the spectrum. After all, *Ad Age* for over 80 years has been a hard-driving newspaper, and books on marketing have been based on case histories or theoretical concepts.

This book bridges that divide. The role of *Advertising Age* has actually changed over the years to encompass material that goes beyond news and even news analysis. We now view our job as helping our readers do their jobs, and so many of our articles, available both in print and online, explain the latest ways to use social media, tips on handling the latest corporate crisis or five "surprising facts" marketers should know about the latest census stats.

That's why this new version of the *Advertising Age* textbook is more pertinent than ever. The authors, if I may be so bold to say so, do a superb job of matching theory with practice– and of drawing examples of the astonishing changes that have rocked the advertising, marketing and media business. The need for advertising educators and professionals to work closely together has never been more acute, and it's my view that this book goes a long way toward bringing both sides a little closer together.

The concept of the book is the same as the first version, but perhaps the biggest differences involve extending the scope of what's covered. For example, in the original edition advertising was pretty easily differentiated from sales promotion, publicity and earned media, and media sales. One of the important themes of this book is how these lines have blurred, and the importance of strategic thinking and customer focus over tactical considerations (a television commercial vs. a print ad). The authors summarize a couple of *Ad Age* articles in each chapter to drive home their points and provide links to other of our material.

As our publisher Allison Arden explained, the contents of this book will enable you to understand the underlying principles of advertising that are core to your education as well as provide practical examples of how they work in the real world.

"We have always considered advertising education to be part of our mission," Allison said, "and our content will serve you as a continuously evolving, supplemental text to your studies, and through your career. *Advertising Age* takes advantage of all the new ways we can communicate and connect with our community, and we hope you take advantage of all the tools we now create for you"—including our Ad Age On Campus Program.

Above all, we always keep in mind that advertising is an energizing and energetic business and it's our job to explain some pretty arcane stuff in accessible, intelligent and lively prose. We've made it a priority to be ahead of the curve in what's happening out there, and I think this book reflects our goal of helping you navigate the tricky and unsettled waters of our business.

ACKNOWLEDGMENTS

We are grateful to Rance Crain for his encouragement and support for this book. We were inspired by Rance and his team of topnotch professionals who have provided outstanding coverage and analysis of the advertising world for many years. Rance's *Advertising Age* column offers hard hitting and incisive observations about the achievements and the missteps of people, organizations, and campaigns. He unflinchingly addresses tough issues including political advertising, advertising ethics, and the industry's role in society and the world. Rance has served as a great friend to the Missouri School of Journalism and certainly to the authors. We thank you, Rance.

Allison Arden, publisher of *Advertising Age*, offered excellent advice on the book's form and content and encouraged us in many ways, particularly with her commitment to advertising education. We are most grateful to her.

We are privileged to be faculty members in the Missouri School of Journalism, where there are close and supportive relationships among the strategic communication faculty members and journalism faculty. This is largely due to the leadership of Dean Mills, who has led the School since 1989. Dean is a great supporter of the role of advertising, public relations and strategic communication at the School. He encouraged us with this project as well as many others.

We would both like to acknowledge friend, mentor, and all-time great guy, the late Ivan Preston. Esther, who was trained as an experimental psychologist, learned about the many aspects of advertising from Ivan when she began teaching at the School of Journalism and Mass Communication at the University of Wisconsin. Ivan's work with advertising law and regulation was some of the most important done in the last 50 years. We mourn his too-early passing in 2010.

We're thankful as well for the educators and students at the University of Iowa School of Journalism and Mass Communication, Margaret's alma mater. Their intellectual depth, commitment to scholarship and their mentoring encouraged her to become a teacher and researcher.

We are also grateful to all the undergraduate, masters and doctoral students we have been privileged to work with. We particularly want to mention several students and alumni who constantly challenged us and pointed out interesting new advertising approaches while we were writing the book. This includes Chang Dae Ham, Joonghwa Lee, Eunjin Kim, Janis Teruggi Page, and Saleem Halabash.

We also thank our staff members whose intelligence, positive energy, organizational skills, and hard work make it possible for faculty and students to succeed. Kathy Sharp, Sarah Smith-Frigerio, Martha Pickens, and Ginny Cowell have all played important roles in our completing the book.

Our gratitude goes out to the many professionals and industry leaders who think great thoughts and offer examples of great work that are the basis of our book. We're indebted to the teachers and scholars in the field who help us understand how marketing communication works and generously share their ideas with colleagues and students.

We also thank Mike Roche and Daniel Noguera of Cengage South-Western publishing and Karunakaran Gunasekaran of PreMediaGlobal who offered excellent editorial and design support as did Ann Marie Kerwin of *Advertising Age*.

Esther dedicates her work on the book to her children and children-in-law. Kjerstin Thorson teaches at the Annenberg School at the University of Southern California and her husband Matt Pearson is a knowledge software consultant. Ian Keesey recently finished his doctoral degree in entomology and plant biology, and Kylie Thorson and husband Alex Soucy live in Lacey, Washington, where Alex serves in the U.S. Army. Recent additions to this wonderful group are two grandchildren, Madeline Pearson and Dominic Soucy.

Margaret dedicates her work to her family including her sister and brother-in-law, Carmen and Bill Haberman, the world's best relatives, and to the late Frederick W. Haberman, eminent professor at the University of Wisconsin who first encouraged her to pursue a Ph. D. Her nephew and his wife, Fred and Sarah Bell Haberman, are media and marketing entrepreneurs in Minneapolis who share Margaret's interest in storytelling and brands that contribute to the betterment of communities and individuals at modernstorytellers.com. Her niece, Sarah Haberman, is also a top communication professional in New York City doing development for Jazz at Lincoln Center, supporting this important cultural treasure. Finally, special thanks to Daryl Moen whose unflagging support, advice, editing, and good humor made this book possible.

PREFACE

David Ogilvy, named one of the "100 most influential advertising people of the century" by *Advertising Age*, said this: "It takes a big idea to attract the attention of consumers and get them to buy your product. Unless your advertising contains a big idea, it will pass like a ship in the night."

Advertising Age itself exemplifies a big idea. For more than eighty years, *Advertising Age* has chronicled the day-to-day triumphs and heartbreaks of this dynamic profession. Its talented editors and reporters create compelling, informative stories that aren't only important—they're sharp, literate, and fun to read.

Taking a cue from *Advertising Age*, this book seeks to showcase the lessons and the fun of the business for students. Of course, as the industry suffered the effects of the economic downturn that began in 2007, for many the business became less enjoyable. But *Advertising Age* columnist Marc Brownstein has some encouraging words for us: "working in the ad industry is still fun". (A1) He notes that ad people are hip, forward-thinking problem solvers in a business fueled by creativity.

Advertising Age, the foremost trade publication for the advertising field, has expanded well beyond the weekly magazine. Through AdAge.com, key industry events and conferences and white papers and research tools, *Advertising Age* provides advertising and marketing professionals with the insights, data and information they need to make smart and informed decisions.

G. D. Crain launched the journal in 1930. He needed courage and optimism to start his enterprise in an economy gripped by the woes of the Great Depression. Today, G. D. Crain's son Rance Crain is president of the company that publishes *Advertising Age*, and he writes a column offering his take on current developments. His column explores the critical issues in our field ranging from economic policies to ethics to education. He courageously addresses the toughest issues with key insights and good advice.

Those columns and *Advertising Age* articles were the inspiration for this book. We selected articles that exemplify advertising theories, concepts, and research—and show how relevant they are to real-world, cutting-edge changes in the advertising industry. A secondary goal for the book is to help students keep up with the astonishing levels of change in the profession. Even very recent advertising textbooks (and there are many excellent examples) could benefit from this since by the time they go to press, new technologies, innovations, and practices have emerged.

In addition, the book is designed to offer students access to online updates and examples of video advertising, making their learning experience more interesting and vivid.

We hope this book will help students of advertising get the real-life lessons of *Advertising Age*, building a bridge between the theories of persuasion and advertising and the richness of the profession. In it, students will learn about brands; the companies that pay for, carry, or create advertising; advertising history; the role advertising plays in combination with other promotional efforts such as public relations and sales promotion; as well as more detailed information about account and media planning, creativity, and the regulatory and ethics concerns swirling around advertising.

Guided by their professors, students will learn not only how to persuade, but also how to be more informed and intelligent consumers.

We'd like to thank Rance Crain for his vision and support for this project. In the first version of this book, (1) Mr. Crain wrote in the Foreword of the importance of connecting *Advertising Age* with students and advertising faculty. In fact, thanks to Mr. Crain and others, *Advertising Age* developed a strong relationship with the American Academy of Advertising (AAA). Through this organization, hundreds of advertising professors share their research and interact with professionals as they have since AAA's founding some fifty years ago.

Regarding the importance of *Advertising Age* to students and faculty, Mr. Crain said,

> For many years, *Ad Age* has participated in programs to help put the publication into the hands of faculty and students. We have done this because it helps faculty stay current and helps bring students up to career speed.... Careful study and analysis of the news and features in *Ad Age* serves a continuing supplement to advertising education.

We thank Allison Arden, vice president and publisher of the Ad Age Group, for her excellent feedback about the structure of the book and her work to bring about the publishing arrangements.

We especially want to thank the terrific professors of advertising, public relations and marketing communication. We had the pleasure of reading many of the foundational textbooks in our field which present diverse and complex information in smart, comprehensive, and readable materials. Although we can't recognize all of the outstanding educators and writers in our field, we'd like to acknowledge the following people for their authorship of important texts and their significant commentary on the field:

Chris Allen	Karen King
Craig Andrews	Dean Kruckeberg
Jim Avery	Ron Lane
Christian Arens	Dan Lattimore
William F. Arens	Charles Marsh
Donald Baack	Sandra Moriarty
George Belch	Doug Newsom
Michael Belch	Thomas O'Guinn
John Burnett	Don Parente
Glen Cameron	Tom Reichert
Allen Center	Jef Richards
Glen Broom	Shelly Rodgers
Scott Cutlip	Kim B. Rotzoll
Bonnie Drewniany	Don Schultz
Tom Duncan	Richard J. Semenik
Michael Guolla	Terence Shimp
David Guth	Paul Smith
James E. Haefner	Jonathan Taylor
Chris Hackley	Elizabeth Toth
Steven R. Hall	Judy Turk
Suzette Heiman	Michael F. Weigold
Jerome Jewler	William Wells
Donald W. Jugenheimer	Dennis Wilcox
Larry D. Kelley	

Note

1. Thorson, E. *Advertising Age: The Principles of Advertising at Work.* Lincolnwood, IL: NTC Business Books, 1989.

Article

(A1)   Marc Brownstein. "A Simple Reminder: The Ad Industry Is Still Fun." Published September 21, 2009. Available at: http://adage.com/post?article_id=139160

CHAPTER 1

What Is Advertising and What New Forms Is It Taking?

© AP Images/Ben Margot

In 1995, nobody Googled anything. And certainly few, if any, in advertising and media businesses foresaw that search, along with other digital technologies, would profoundly disrupt their lucrative business models.

Today, Google is not just a company, it's a verb. The story begins at Stanford University when Larry Page, a Ph.D. student, became intrigued with how the web's links worked. Page observed that while pages linked to each other, you couldn't tell what other pages linked back to a page. He was studying backlinks and referred to his project as BackRub.

A key insight was that backlinks alone wouldn't be the whole story—rather, it would be how popular or important those links were. He and fellow student and math whiz Sergey Brin teamed up to create a complex algorithm or set of clearly defined processes for solving a problem. They called their system PageRank, and it brilliantly managed to combine the raw number of links into a site and the popularity of the pages it linked to. Google's site describes it this way:

> PageRank Technology: PageRank reflects our view of the importance of web pages by considering more than 500 million variables and 2 billion terms. Pages that we believe are important pages receive a higher PageRank and are more likely to appear at the top of the search results. PageRank also considers the importance of each page that casts a vote, as votes from some pages are considered to have greater value, thus giving the linked page greater value. (1)

The PageRank system is like a complicated popularity contest. For example, let's assume that a local fellow starts Uncle Bill's Book Nook and even builds a pretty nice website. However, his Uniform Resource Locator (URL) probably won't show up at the top of page rankings because few important sites link to his.

Why does this matter? The algorithms that Google and its competitors use continue to give searchers the opportunity to actively locate the products, services, and information they want. This means that consumers are not passively viewing ads beamed at them from television. Rather, they're in control of what they wish to see and hear. They're able to find and act on information related to purchases, travel, and news, often cutting out the middleman.

Even more significant, consumers have an increasing array of choices available to them for media and services, thus making them far more difficult to reach in traditional mass-mediated channels such as television, newspapers, and magazines.

Of course, the power of Google and the power of search are only one—but important—part of the advertising and promotion landscape today. As you're reading this, it's likely that a media or technology entrepreneur is creating the next Google, iPad, or Facebook. (2)

Chapter 1 provides specific definitions of advertising, marketing, and sales promotions, and of all the different specific subcategories of advertising: direct response, out-of-home, point-of-purchase, public service advertising, and a variety of other terms. In this book, you'll learn all of these terms and how they're used in contemporary marketing. You'll also be introduced to other kinds of promotional tools that can be used as partners to advertising efforts: samples, coupons, sponsorships, events, refunds, contests, and public relations. Advertising is one of a number of tools that communicators use to tell people about ideas and brands, as well as to persuade them to like, buy, or use the ideas and brands. We'll also look at *Advertising Age* stories about many of these concepts to give you a good feel for how important they are in the day-to-day world of advertising.

So Just What Is Advertising?

In 2002, Richards and Curran looked at just about every effort to define advertising. (3) The following is the definition they came up with that seemed to best capture all of the different definitions that had been floated: "advertising is a *paid, mediated* form of *communication* from an *identifiable source,* designed to *persuade* the receiver to take some action, now or in the future." According to this definition there are five criteria for determining whether a message is advertising. We look at each in turn.

First, some person or company has to have *paid* for the advertising—paid to have the message created and paid for the media time or space into which it is channeled to reach people. But even before we agree on "paid," we have to note that some messages that look a lot like "advertising" are not paid in this sense. Public service announcements such as messages from Smokey the Bear about preventing forest fires or McGruff the Crime Dog about taking a bite out of crime are often created and produced free ("pro bono") by advertising agencies, and media such as newspapers and network television stations run the messages without charge. And there's a new kind of advertising that has gotten a lot of play lately. In *user-generated* advertising, nonprofessionals—ordinary people of every type—create advertisements completely on their own and post them in various locales on the Internet (e.g., their own website, YouTube). And in some cases, advertisers create contests in which nonprofessionals compete to create advertisements that will appear in paid media. In view of these exceptions, we say that most of advertising is paid for, but not all.

Second, advertising is carried via media (*mediated*) such as iPads, cell phones, television, newspapers, magazines, and even social networks such as Facebook and MySpace. So when you tell a friend about the great new athletic shoes you just bought, emphasizing that they're on sale and perhaps your friend might want to also buy a pair, you are not advertising. You are simply communicating interpersonally, an activity that the industry calls *word-of-mouth* or *viral* advertising. Advertising travels from a source (i.e., the advertiser) through a medium

Figure 1-1 A Bad Frog

(e.g., television) to people. And usually that mediation is "mass"; that is, the messages are delivered to a large group of people. But we have to admit that the mass-mediated feature is not without exception either. You may have noticed getting more and more of what look like personalized persuasive messages, such as emails that may even address you by your first name. Computers have made it possible to send out "mass" messages that mimic individual messages. But because they are "mass," we'll still consider this to be advertising.

Third, what is a *communication*? The simplest concept of communication is meanings that pass from source to receiver. Some communications are simple and perhaps even nonverbal—such as when another driver "flips you the bird." Advertising communications are much more complex. They are usually carefully designed to have desired specific impacts on receivers. Often thousands of dollars of research and professional thinking go into advertising. The complexity of these communications is endless. There's always a new way to communicate a brand or idea. But you should keep in mind that sometimes advertising does "flip you the bird." Jim Wauldron, president of Bad Frog Beer, explains (http://store.badfrog.com/info.html) that his brand began with T-shirts for a fictitious "bad frog beer"—and in response to people's requests for the beer, began a successful brewing company. As you can see in Figure 1-1, this frog is delivering a significantly negative and aggressive message.

Fourth, we look at *source*. Almost all advertising tells the receiver where the message came from, although the source identification is not always as clear as might be desired. Political advertisements must tell viewers whether they come from a candidate or some other organization. Brand advertisements, however, do not have to indicate the company behind the message. For example, Tide advertisements are made and paid for by Procter & Gamble, but they only identify the brand name. Most adults (but probably not young children) know that brand advertising comes from a company. Sometimes advertising can pose as "news," a form we call advertorials, but if these messages appear in newspapers, they are often labeled "advertisements." Labeling advertorials may be even less common in magazines, which often have looser standards for identifying advertiser-paid content, even though the American Society of Magazine Editors does have clear standards about how editorial content and advertising should be distinguished. Identifying the source of a message is important because people want to know whether there is a persuasive intent in messages. As soon as a person identifies a message as an advertisement, his or her processing of that message changes. As we'll see when we start talking about how people process advertising, identifiable source is an important aspect.

Finally, advertising is *persuasive* in nature. The exact persuasive intent may vary, but the reason the source paid to have that advertisement reach you is either to inform you about something likely to change your behavior (e.g., buy something, quit smoking) or to make you experience emotions that lead you to feel good about a brand or an idea and want to acquire it, learn more, and so on.

Advertising and the Rest of the Promotional Toolbox

The impact that advertising has on people, as well as the millions of dollars spent on it every year, demonstrates how important advertising is for someone with a message to share or a brand to sell. But advertising does have limitations in its effectiveness. This means that those with a brand or an idea to sell will often need to combine advertising with other messaging tools. We can think of any marketing campaign as an organized plan for strategically using a blend of promotional tools such as public relations and sales promotions. Campaigns that employ a variety of kinds of promotions and/or a variety of different media channels are (as you will see in Chapter 19) often called integrated marketing communications (IMC).

In this chapter we explore a sample of the new tools that digital technology and the Internet have enabled recently. The new tools we'll look at here include promotional email, cell phone applications ("apps"), social networks such as Facebook and Twitter, online advertising video, search advertising, and user-generated advertising. There are also new devices that serve as media channels that carry advertising, foremost among them, cell phones, the Internet, and e-readers.

These new tools and channels, which exhibit unceasing invention and change, are accused of seriously disrupting how the advertising industry goes about creating and placing advertising. Certainly the new tools and channels have significantly changed how people learn about ideas and brands. There are now new industries that handle how advertising gets into media channels—advertising networks and exchanges being two primary examples. And there are important changes in how a specific advertisement reaches a person most likely to want or need that message with approaches such as behavioral targeting and search advertising.

The pages of *Advertising Age* allow us to track what's going on with these new promotional tools and channels and approaches—which is important if our understanding of advertising is to be cutting edge. It's hard to believe that only a little more than a decade ago the idea of Internet advertising was born. *Advertising Age* was the first publication to start tracking it as it developed. (4)

A Sampling of Advertising Innovations

Devices as New Media Channels

The big three new media devices that serve as channels are the Internet, cell phones, and e-readers.

Internet Advertising   With the Internet, ads can be anywhere. Natalie Zmuda describes how Macy's, McDonald's, and other companies are now placing advertisements on our online bank accounts (A1; http://adage.coverleaf.com/advertisingage/20100419/?pg=3#pg3). The new company Cardlytics links scores of banks with advertisers who want to plant special offers and advertisements on the pages of online bank statements. Sometimes these messages are so carefully targeted that you'll receive an ad from a restaurant where you charged your lunch last week. There are pros and cons to an advertising delivery channel like this one. Its proponents tout the lack of waste in targeting people who are already consumers because they are much more likely than others to respond to the advertising. But consumer groups worry about companies having access to their purchases. Is this really an invasion of privacy? We look more closely at the issue of privacy versus behavioral targeting in Chapter 4.

Mobile Advertising: Cell Phones   Delivering advertisements to cell phones started as early as 2003, but there were many barriers to its success and there was little growth in the media (A2; http://adage.com/article?article_id=107758). The most significant barrier was that at that time, many cell phone users paid for their service in terms of minutes used. Using expensive minutes receiving an ad was a nonstarter for many. Furthermore, most American phones at that time did not have an Internet connection. As more and more smartphones came into use, their Internet connectivity opened a whole new set of possibilities for delivering advertising on cell phones.

Probably one of the fastest growing product successes in recent times is Apple's iPhone. This smartphone also brought with it applications (or apps). These downloadable programs for the iPhone allow users to create shopping lists, find garage sales, look up recipes, play games, link to Twitter, and do just about every other activity one can imagine. So they provide fertile ground for advertisers. Rita Chang provides examples of what kinds of smartphone applications are working for advertisers and kinds that haven't been particularly successful (A3; http://adage.com/article?article_id=140746). In the success list are Audi's driving game app and Dunkin' Donuts' app for both ordering and telling others that you're at one of their shops. In the not-so-successful list are Charmin's app for identifying public restrooms close by, and Pedigree dog food's program to record your dog's bark. Apps for both iPhones and smartphones with other operating systems are likely to become important players in many advertising plans.

E-Readers and Other Mobile Media   Rita Chang describes how e-readers, computer tablets, and navigation devices have all become important media channels for advertising (A3; http://adage.com/article?article_id=140746).

Mobile Marketing Beyond the Mobile Phone

E-readers, Tablets and GPS Systems are Connecting More People Every Day—
Here's How Marketers Can Benefit

The important takeaway from this article is that marketers are thinking strategically about how consumers are using mobile devices, how they meet consumers' needs and desires and how marketing messages can most effectively be delivered via these devices. In other words, mobile marketing is far more than cell phone advertising.

The author discusses the array of mobile products that connect us to our physicians, our pets, our businesses and our friends. In a world with "cameras on dog collars" and multi-player smart phone gaming, marketers are thinking creatively about how to be persuasive without being intrusive.

The first place marketers and researchers begin is the effort to understand how mobile communication changes people's behaviors. E-readers are mainstream technology today and many of them offer features that go far beyond reading including the ability to interact with other readers, play videos, and submit reviews. Why does this matter? Marketers are imagining how advertisers might sponsor certain content or offer desirable apps in exchange for receiving a persuasive message. The author offers the example of a reader who downloads a book on gardening and then might be offered gardening tips, free apps, coupons or other benefits possibly sponsored by a company that makes fertilizer or pesticides.

Another important category includes tablets of all sizes and capability. Magazine publishers are excited about the opportunity to offer rich content (including color, video, and interactivity) to their readers. Similarly, advertisers are interested in how this rich content can increase consumer engagement with products and services.

Where is all this headed? Some observers think that as mobile devices become more sophisticated, consumers will flock to those with multiple functionality, what some call "one device to rule them all." As smart phones, e-readers and tablets evolve, they are offering music, news, video, navigation and games. It's truly a time for marketer strategic thinking and creativity.

Notice that as recent as this article is (2009), it predates introduction of the Apple iPad, which joined the e-reader group of devices early in 2010. All of these devices will provide ways for advertisers to reach consumers wherever they are. As we'll see in later chapters, these devices can use GPS information so that the advertising can travel directly from a nearby store to the consumer for further strength in targeting. For example, with a cell phone app, Macy's can give you gift points for entering the store and can offer you advertising for perfumes as you pass the Clinique counter.

Social Networks

With the rapid growth of Facebook (an estimated 25 million users in the United States alone), the opportunity to place advertising in this huge social network, as well as the many other highly trafficked sites, is a central focus for both advertisers and site owners. Emily York tells of one of the most successful social network advertising programs to date (A4; http://adage.com/article?article_id=142202). In response to losses in sales, Starbucks employed a number of social network sites. It set up MyStarbucksIdea.com to let people make suggestions. For Facebook's 5.7 million fans of Starbucks, the company provided coupons and music downloads, as well as advertising messages. The Starbucks vice president for online points out that the natural link between the atmosphere at Starbucks stores and the idea of social media sharing made their program successful. Starbucks is also adding iPhone apps to the mix, with the store location and menu information offered, providing an excellent backup to the social media.

Twitter

Josh Bernoff, Forrester Research senior vice president, argues that marketers should give serious consideration to buying advertising tweets (A5; http://adage.com/post?article_id=143257). Early in 2010 Twitter began allowing advertising tweets to turn up in the search process. In the Starbucks example, the company also combined a Twitter feed with their other social networking efforts, quickly amassing 750,000 followers. This suggests that the linkage between consumers and brands can itself become of value.

Online Video Ads

Given advertising agencies' focus on television advertising, it makes sense that there would be great desire to develop online video commercials. The problem is getting people to watch them without annoying them. Although many consumers are willing to watch some commercials in return for a free movie or old television sitcom, linking online commercials with news and other kinds of content is a real problem. Michael Learmonth points out how difficult it has been to figure out a successful way to motivate commercial viewing online (A6; http://adage.com/digital/article?article_id=137606). A group-funded research project called the Pool recently reported that a key to reducing viewer displeasure with online video is to allow consumers to choose which one of several ads they want to watch. Hulu's approach has been to have some programming "sponsored" by an advertiser, just as sponsorships are used in PBS television programming. YouTube is also experimenting with kinds of choices that people can make among video ads and "promoted videos," which are also advertisements. There is still much experimenting to be done to figure out how to effectively move the television commercial to the online environment.

Advertising Networks and Exchanges

Magazines, newspapers, blog sites, and all kinds of other online publications offer display space to advertisers, with much of that space being filled by local advertisements. But in many of these publications, there is significant space left vacant. Advertising networks developed to aggregate remnant space and sell it to advertisers. Most ad networks have contracts with online publications to sell their space. This space is often, but not always, less expensive than space sold by the publication itself. As we see in "Ad Networks and Exchanges 101", the degree of audience targeting that the advertising networks offer varies from almost none to very sophisticated delivery of advertising to those with particular interests indicated either by where in the publication the advertising is located (e.g., sports versus home styles) or by behavioral targeting enabled by data on where in the sites people have spent time (see below) (A7; http://adage.com/adnetworkexchangeguide10/article?article_id=143310). "Confused by Where to Click?" explains in more detail how advertising exchanges work (A8; http://adage.com/adnetworkexchangeguide/article?article_id=126222). The best analogy for them is the stock market, where all available online space is traded in real time by advertisers and publishers. Advertisers can see the prices that others bid for space and respond accordingly. One of the best known of these exchanges was started in 2007 by DoubleClick, a company started in 1996 and bought by Google for $3.1 billion in 2008.

Networks and exchanges are important to advertising because they are entirely new ways for advertisers to get their ads into media channels. These two approaches to media handling will only become more important as online commerce and publishing become more dominant.

New Ways to Target the Right Consumer with the Right Message

Behavioral Targeting

Behavioral targeting uses data about people's online behavior to determine what advertising they will be exposed to. There are lots of ways to do behavioral targeting. It can be done within an individual publication, which will place a cookie on visitors' computers, and then use data from that cookie to see what part of the publication is most visited. Then the publication sells that information to advertisers who want to reach pet owners, sports fans, home remodelers, or any other kind of behavioral pattern linked with what advertisers are selling.

As we see in "Holy Grail of Targeting," more sophisticated behavioral targeting goes beyond people's behavior on a single site to track all of their online behavior, and often these data can be further refined for connecting online behavior with information from credit card purchases, home ownership information, census details, and a wide variety of other information about individual consumers (A9; http://adage.com/digital/article?article_id=142903). As the article points out, while this level of behavioral targeting is truly the "Holy Grail" for advertisers, concerns about invasion of consumer privacy have to be considered.

Holy Grail of Targeting Is Fuel for Privacy Battle

Melding of Online and Offline Info Is Delicate Dance for Marketers, Could Raise Red Flag to Regulators

What do marketers know about you? Well, quite a lot, and this article examines the fine line that marketers are treading in gathering consumer data in order to better target consumers. The author explains that companies gather "offline" data, or information available beyond monitoring a person's behavior. This can include easily available information such as an individual's income, credit rating purchase history, number of children, and home value. Marketers then combine that information with an individual's online behavior to gain consumer preference information that's considered "revolutionary."

The article points out, however, that some regulators and members of Congress consider this revolutionary as well—but not in a good way. Alarmed by the possibilities for invasion of privacy, many interested parties are proposing regulation that could hamstring marketers' use of these data. Although marketers using behavior techniques claim that they remove data that identify individual consumers, regulators have doubts about the security of the information and the intentions of the marketers.

Other consumer watchdog groups argue that people unwittingly give up personal information such as their birthdates and names of friends and families. In addition, their search and purchase behaviors can reveal information about highly personal matters such health conditions or sexual preferences. In addition, since firms are able to make money from individuals' information, other critics argue that consumers should at least receive compensation for it.

Finally, with the massive growth of social networks featuring extensive personal preferences linked to friends and others, marketers are mining that category of online behavior. Bottom line? If marketers want to continue to gather this type of data, they will have to very carefully consider privacy issues and the protection of consumers.

We will look further at the conflict of privacy and behavioral targeting in Chapter 4. Behavioral targeting has the potential to provide far more accurate targeting than advertisers have ever had previously.

Search Advertising

Advertising that greets you as you do a search for anything is called *search advertising*. It is a subactivity of search marketing, the topic of Abbey Klassen's article (A10; http://adage.com/digital/article?article_id=140083). The statistics about search advertising are impressive. Nine out of ten advertisers use what is called organic search optimization, which means that they carefully craft their website language to increase the likelihood that it will pop up high in searches. Fully 70 percent of advertisers use paid search, which means that they pay search engines such as Google and Yahoo to place their websites at the top of the search list delivered to consumers. Search ability has made consumers much more powerful in finding the information they want, when they want it. Some argue that search has robbed advertising of a lot of its power to bring product and idea information to people. But, on the other hand, search advertising has the advantage of being delivered to people who have self-selected themselves as part of the target market. It seems clear that search advertising has damaged the link between publications and advertising, because publications are no longer needed. "The State of Search Marketing: 2009" provides an encyclopedic overview of how search marketing works in general and how search advertising fits into that total picture. (A10)

Where Next?

In the next chapters we will look in detail at the major topics that just about every beginning advertising textbook addresses. But two features will be different and we think will add to your understanding and enthusiasm for advertising. First, every chapter will bring news from the headlines of *Advertising Age* to provide examples of how the advertising industry, advertising researchers, and pundits are dealing with the rapidly innovating real world of advertising. And second, because the field is changing so fast, we will mostly focus on breaking news about how advertising is operating. These chapters will be enhanced by your ability to go online to access each week's *Advertising Age*, look at commercials we have gathered as good examples, and read the *Advertising Age* college materials.

Notes

1. Available at: http://www.google.com/corporate/tech.html
2. Batelle, J. "The Birth of Google," *Wired Magazine*, August 2005. Available at: http://www.wired.com/wired/archive/13.08/battelle.html?pg=2&topic=battelle&topic_set=
3. Richards, J. I., & Curran, M. C. "Oracles on 'Advertising': Searching for a Definition," *Journal of Advertising* 31, no. 2. (2002): 63–77.
4. Thorson, E., Wells, W. D., & Rodgers, S. "Web Advertising's Birth and Early Childhood as Viewed in the Pages of *Advertising Age*," in *Advertising and the World Wide Web*, ed. David Schumann and Esther Thorson (New Jersey: Lawrence Erlbaum, 1999), 5–26.

Articles

(A1) Natalie Zmuda. "McDonald's, Macy's Tap New Ad Medium: Online Bank Statements." Published April 19, 2010. Available at: http://adage.coverleaf.com/advertisingage/20100419/?pg=3#pg3
(A2) Claire Atkinson. "Cellphone Advertising Off to Slow Start." Published March 8, 2006. Available at: http://adage.com/article?article_id=107758
(A3) Rita Chang. "Mobile Marketing beyond the Mobile Phone." Published November 30, 2009. Available at: http://adage.com/article?article_id=140746
(A4) Emily Bryson York. "Starbucks Gets Its Business Brewing Again with Social Media." Published February 22, 2010. Available at: http://adage.com/article?article_id=142202
(A5) Josh Bernoff. "Why You Should Embrace Advertising on Twitter." Published April 19, 2010. Available at: http://adage.com/post?article_id=143257
(A6) Michael Learmonth. "New Formats Give Online Video Ads Potential." Published June 29, 2009. Available at: http://adage.com/digital/article?article_id=137606
(A7) Rich Karpinski. "Ad Networks and Exchanges 101." Published April 19, 2010. Available at: http://adage.com/adnetworkexchangeguide10/article?article_id=143310
(A8) "Confused by Where to Click? We're Here to Help." Published April 14, 2008. Available at: http://adage.com/adnetworkexchangeguide/article?article_id=126222
(A9) Michael Learmonth. "Holy Grail of Targeting Is Fuel for Privacy Battle." Published March 22, 2010. Available at: http://adage.com/digital/article?article_id=142903
(A10) Abbey Klaassen. "The State of Search Marketing: 2009." Published November 2, 2009. Available at: http://adage.com/digital/article?article_id=140083

Business Structures in the Advertising Industry

© AF archive/Alamy

In season one of *Mad Men*, the hit AMC television series about the advertising business in the 1950s, Roger Sterling, advertising agency principal, says to creative but troubled advertising genius Don Draper, "You know what my father used to say? 'Being with a client is like being in a marriage. Sometimes you get into it for the wrong reasons, and eventually they hit you in the face.'" Judging from the exodus of creative executives from American advertising agencies in 2010, the same might be said for the relationships between agencies and many of their creative stars (A1; http://adage.com/article?article_id=145979).

In the past few years, such creative executives as Gerry Graf of Saatchi, Ty Montague and Rosemarie Ryan of JWT, Eric Silver of DDB New York, as well as a number of others left high-paying, high-visibility advertising agencies to strike out on their own, sometimes even to try out new businesses.

The large advertising agency has long been the centerpiece for what advertising means, for great advertising campaigns, and for the veneer of glamour, excitement, and fast-lane living. So why are so many high-placed advertising creative executives jumping ship? As we'll see in this chapter, advertising may be as Kevin Roddy, chief creative officer at Bartle Bogle Hegarty (BBH) New York, says, "getting harder" (p. 28 in A1).

Advertising agencies are not just challenged by the loss of some of their star creative people. Although advertising agencies claim they are the trusted partners of advertisers and their brands, that client–agency relationship is often troubled. For example, in one week in June 2010, Chevrolet, Cadillac, and Mazda all fired their agencies and put their accounts up for grabs—$600 million of advertising. The CEO of BBH first heard about his agency's firing from reading about it in *Advertising Age* (A2; http://adage.com/agencynews/article?article_id=144700).

In this chapter we look at advertising agencies, advertisers, and the media to try to understand some of the complexities of their structures and how they relate to each other.

Advertising Agencies

Many of you will spend at least part of your career in one or more advertising, media, PR or marketing communication agencies. Most advertising and promotion originates in agencies. Since 1944, *Advertising Age* has tracked the world's agencies—their consolidations and breakups, their total expenditures on media, and their client lists. In the late 1800s when the first advertising agencies appeared, they were small and most started with a single individual. During the 1900s agencies came to employ hundreds and provide a full spectrum of services—creating advertising, managing brand accounts, researching consumers, and buying media placements for the advertising. By 2000 there had been huge mergers of individual advertising agencies, with Dentsu, a Japanese-based company, the largest. "Agency Report" notes that Dentsu is now the fifth largest company, with WPP, Omnicom, Publicis, and Interpublic heading the list (A3; http://adage.com/agencynews/article?article_id=143467). Although advertising agencies started in the United States, three of the top five companies are now headquartered abroad. In the United States, the top five agencies are McCann Erickson, BBDO, JWT, Y&R, and Leo Burnett, although each of these agencies belongs to one of the five top worldwide agencies.

The year 2009 was a bad one for agencies, with U.S. revenue falling 7.5 percent. That may not sound like a lot, but in terms of revenues and the financial health of the agencies, it's huge. All of the four kinds of agencies lost revenues: traditional agencies, media agencies, direct customer agencies, and public relations agencies. The only area of advertising that rose was digital, and the change was very small: a half percent.

As a student of advertising and marketing communication, you probably ask yourself, what makes working at an agency fun and fulfilling? Lots of people have tried to figure out just what makes agencies successful. Most agree that ad agencies have "personalities" and that you can see them reflected in the advertising that they do. Another way to look at life at ad agencies is in terms of their "culture." Agency culture is crucial for attracting talented professionals who can produce great ads (A4; http://adage.com/article?article_id=143477). Many argue the importance of treating ad professionals well. Check out the list of things that some agencies are doing to make sure their culture is a winning one.

In Adland, the Best Culture Lures the Best Talent

As Hiring Freezes Thaw, Expect Fun, Contemporary Agencies to Have an Easy Time Attracting and Retaining Quality Staffers

As a student of advertising and marketing communication, you've probably thought about what it's like to work in communication at an agency, a corporate office, or perhaps for a charitable organization. This article can give you some ideas about what to expect. One of the most important things for you to consider is the culture of the organization you may join. You'll not only want good working conditions, good pay, solid and ethical management, and other characteristics—you'll want a good fit with your personality and work style.

The article points out that the most successful agencies have a "defined" culture that stays true to the vision of the founders of the agency. Some corporate cultures may be buttoned up, structured and formal and that is often a very successful approach and may be where you're happiest. Other corporate cultures are successful with a more organic, informal and unstructured style. There's no "right" corporate culture, but there's likely a "right" culture for you.

Here's a summary of some tactics agencies use to foster the kinds of cultures they think help them thrive.

1. An e-newsletter that offers fun and irreverent commentary about the agency and the business.

2. A "field trip" to exotic locations like Tokyo that inspire staffers and foster team spirit.

3. "Loyalty rewards" that offer employees with 20+ years of service $10,000 to use on a vacation anywhere in the world. Fellow employees throw a bon voyage party to send the traveler on the way.

4. Good deeds. Some agencies get involved in grass roots charitable efforts to help their communities such as getting out the vote or adopting schools.

5. Job enrichment. Some agencies offer special classes and workshops on topics like technology and innovation to help employee ramp up their skills and prepare for promotions and new challenges.

6. Personal enrichment. Other organizations offer tuition for classes that aren't even linked to advertising or marketing. Rather, employees learn diverse skills like acting or driving.

7. Change of venue. One of the world's biggest agencies, Digitas, offers its 3000 worldwide employees the opportunity to work in one of its 33 international offices. As part of the deal, the employee records her or his experiences to share with others through a video time capsule.

8. No secrets. Some agencies conduct annual meetings that bring all employees up to date on the organization's performance, its outlook for the coming year, and the role of each employee in its success.

9. Talent showcase. New York's Deutsch puts on a talent show for employees to compete for prizes and glory. This kind of thing is typical of the creative competition that advertising professionals enjoy.

10. Creative inspiration. One New York agency brings talent of all kinds into the office during working hours, including forensics experts and Juilliard music professors.

Regardless of the strategy, you can see that different organizations have different styles and cultures and you'll want to land in one that's right for you.

Advertisers

Advertising Age has been tracking the advertising spending of U.S. advertisers since 1956. As noted above, 2009 showed the highest drop in that spending in the last fifty-three years. Of the top ten advertisers (Procter & Gamble, Verizon, AT&T, General Motors, Pfizer, Johnson & Johnson, Walt Disney, Time Warner, L'Oreal, and Kraft), all but Pfizer and Kraft reduced their advertising spending. But the eleventh top advertiser, Walmart, increased its spending by 14 percent—clearly trying to grab market shares during the downturn— and it had a 1.1 percent increase in sales, even though retail sales nationally fell 2.1 percent. So spending more in a downturn paid off for Walmart. It also paid off for Pfizer. In fact, of the twenty-six top advertisers who increased or maintained their spending in 2009, 70 percent increased sales. So it looks as though spending during a downturn IS a good idea (A5; http://adage.com/article?article_id=144555).

Arguably the most precious resource corporations have is their brands. Traditionally, the key individual for a brand in corporations is the brand manager. The challenge for brand managers is in the digital world, where changes occur with lightning speed and where consumers often take over the conversation about brands, even to the point of producing their own brand ads. Recently, Forrester Research, a major analyst of America's consumers, suggested that brand managers become "brand advocates." Along with the name change, brand advocates will no longer stick with yearly budgeting of messages and media for the brand. Instead they will be ready to advertise on the fly in response to changes in consumer buying and social media behavior. Forrester even recommended that much faster switching of agencies needed to be acceptable to the brand advocate. What do giant advertisers such as P&G and Unilever think about this new approach? Is this the harbinger of a real organizational change at America's large advertisers (A6; http://adage.com/cmostrategy/article?article_id=139593)?

Relative Importance of Public Relations and Advertising

Another structural change at advertiser corporations concerns the linkage between public relations (PR) and advertising. Although word of mouth has always been an important communication channel for advertisers, digital word of mouth means that comments by consumers travel much farther much faster. That means that the messages about brands are often in constant flux—and that in turn means that dealing with them needs to be efficiently coordinated between those in charge of communications and those in charge of advertising. As a result, a couple of important changes have occurred in advertiser management structures. One is to put advertising under the communications director. The other is to have one person perform both functions. What are the advantages and disadvantages of each of these approaches? *Ad Age* compares the success of companies where advertising and PR directors are a single person (IBM, Intuit, and American Airlines) with those where the communications function is the boss (BMC Software and United Airlines) (A7; http://adage.com/cmostrategy/article?article_id=139140).

Relationships between Advertising Agencies and Advertisers

As noted at the beginning of this chapter, the relationship between agencies and advertisers runs the gamut between extremely close business partners to one where a "divorce" can come as a complete surprise to the agency. To better understand the complexities of this relationship, we start with the question of what advertisers pay agencies for. A common answer is "great advertising." Before the 1990s advertisers got the greatest proportion of their revenues from commissions on media purchases. For example, if they bought $1 million worth of media to place an ad, they got a percentage of that "spend." Starting in the 1990s the media commission virtually disappeared and advertisers paid their agencies fees depending on the actual amount of work (usually in hours) that they put in. Many have argued that for advertisers and agencies to truly be business partners, payment should be based on "value" of what the agency does. For example, the agency should be paid more for a campaign that creates more sales than for a campaign that produces fewer sales. Today, however, very few advertisers compensate this way, with 75 percent of those polled indicating that they pay fees (A8; http://adage.com/article?article_id=143644).

In an opinion piece, Wayne Arnold suggests that there is little evidence that agencies are playing the role of business partner to advertisers (A9; http://adage.com/article?article_id=138795). He provides the famous examples of how agencies in the past have helped create new products or products sufficiently different to create vast new market shares for advertisers (although one of them involved repainting airplanes!). But recently, Arnold reports, agencies became more focused on producing commercials, and as a result, experts in less profitable specialties were pushed out, with the net result that agencies were good for one thing: producing advertising. Arnold says, "if a pharma client wants to get closer to the medical industry, we . . . give them nurses and a training program which enables a nurse to do 95% of what a doctor can do in half the training time. Now that's delivering real value."

So one reason that agencies might be getting summarily dismissed may be that they no longer play the role of partner and are instead considered by their clients as just a service for acquiring advertising. *Ad Age* suggests some possible solutions (A10; http://adage.com/article?article_id=143508). One problem is that media companies from Google to Condé Nast, which publishes magazines, are offering advertising development that directly competes with agencies. Another is that so many new skills and understandings are needed for handling a brand in the digital environment (from smartphones to Twitter) that agencies aren't able to provide the necessary expertise. What can be done? The experts interviewed have some great ideas. Which ones make the most sense? Consider these possibilities as areas that you can specialize in and provide clear innovation possibilities to the industry.

How to Save the Troubled Agency-Marketer Relationship

Ad Age *Gets to Bottom of the Problem and Helps Point the Way Toward Solution*

In a time of significant change, traditional business relationships are often disrupted and the marketing communication business is a prime example. This article identifies some of the reasons for the fraught relationships between clients and agencies and then gets views from top industry insiders about solutions to improve those relationships.

One key issue is that the lines between different functions and roles are blurred. The author cites the case of Home Depot's efforts to reach out to Hispanic consumers. The home improvement retailer put its business up for review, thus inviting agencies to offer their visions and possible campaigns to promote Home Depot. Some controversy arose between agencies specializing in Hispanic marketing and traditional agencies attempting to increase their multicultural capabilities.

Similarly, media companies that traditionally didn't get involved in creative campaign production have branched out. Some firms created in-house agencies believing they could save money essentially by doing their own advertising.

Here are some of the factors top marketers and agency folks think are important:

- Clients are demanding more for less and production budgets are being slashed. (Production budgets fund the actual creation of ads such as hiring talent, shooting video, photography, and other costs.)
- How to compensate agencies is a continuing problem. In the past, the formulas were quite simple, usually a percentage of the costs of fees charged by television networks, magazines, and newspapers to run the commercials. Today, no one is sure how to charge for a Facebook page promotion or a viral video. Everyone is looking for ways to link "price, performance and value."
- Globalization is putting pressure on firms' marketers and on agencies who are trying to figure out how to appeal to highly diverse cultures in a cost effective way.
- The vast numbers of choices consumers have in selecting media have also vastly complicated the jobs of advertisers. A fragmented media world means that agencies must become specialists in many different types of channels.
- Solid data through research and analysis are increasingly important in showing what worked and why. Creativity and the ability to measure results must go together and it's important that measurement is not seen as the enemy of creativity.

Media

We'll look at the great array of media in detail in succeeding chapters. Here we provide a broad overview. Traditionally, there were four main advertising media: print, television, radio, and direct mail. The digital revolution has led to a much more varied world of channels by which to bring advertising to its target audiences. Once a year *Advertising Age* reviews the top one hundred media companies, with the most recent review in 2009 (A11; http://adage.com/article?article_id=141212). Just as we saw advertisers spending less on advertising, and advertising agencies making less money, revenues sharply declined for media companies in 2009. Eleven of the top one hundred media companies entered bankruptcy, although six of them survived and emerged from bankruptcy court. Newspapers showed the worst drop in revenues, twice that of the second worst, magazines. The winners during this worst year of the downturn were not digital, as we might have expected, but cable. Fronting cable's success was Fox News, up nearly 23 percent; CNN, up 15 percent; Fox Sports Network, up nearly 13 percent; and number-one ranked ESPN, up more than 9 percent. These are media properties that have found their loyal audiences and continue to build audience.

In the media report for 2009, be sure to notice the top twenty social networking sites. How many of these did you visit last week? It is interesting to note that none of them, not even Facebook, have ever made a profit!

As we saw in the analysis of advertising agency problems, many media are attempting to become producers of advertising. Perhaps even more threatening, however, are the large search companies attempting to become media. Columnist Simon Dumenco reviews Google's business efforts aimed at allowing it to obtain greater advertising revenues (A12; http://adage.com/mediaworks/article?article_id=141250). Of course, Google now owns YouTube and certainly has been trying to figure out how to connect advertising with YouTube more effectively, so technically Google already is a media company. But in attempting to buy Yelp, at which it failed, Google indicated a strong desire to create a "news" or directory site that would carry advertising. Google and Yahoo have actually become not only media, but also advertising and marketing companies.

Ag Age considered the question of the future of media companies (A13; http://adage.com/columns/article?article_id=140091). Ironically, Bloom suggests that the successful media company will be more like a marketing company. He suggests that advertisers and agencies want to surround their messages with specific audiences who will welcome those messages. This reflects the new importance of advertising context, programming, or content that greatly increases the likelihood that the advertising makes sense with its presence.

Agencies, Advertisers, and Media

What is clear from the readings in this chapter is that the customization, personalization, interactivity, and targeted delivery that have become possible with the Internet, social networks, smartphone apps, and so on have fundamentally changed the relationships among agencies, advertisers, and media. To operate well in the digital world, the functions of the three industry structures need to be better coordinated, faster on their feet, and willing to innovate at the same rate as new content, new devices, and new features are invented. In the next few years, we will see whether the search companies can actually continue to successfully become media and advertising agencies in and of themselves.

Articles

(A1)   Matthew Creamer. "Creative Exodus in Adland: It's Just Not 'Fun' Anymore." Published September 20, 2010. Available at: http://adage.com/article?article_id=145979

(A2)   Jeremy Mullman. "Cadillac, Chrysler, Mazda Accounts Spin Out at Once." Published June 28, 2010. Available at: http://adage.com/agencynews/article?article_id=144700

(A3)   Bradley Johnson. "Agency Report: Revenue Slumps 7.5%, Jobs at 16-Year Low." Published April 26, 2010. Available at: http://adage.com/agencynews/article?article_id=143467

(A4)   Rupal Parekh. "In Adland, the Best Culture Lures the Best Talent." Published April 26, 2010. Available at: http://adage.com/article?article_id=143477

(A5)   Bradley Johnson. "Top 100 Outlays Plunge 10% But Defying Spend Trend Can Pay Off." Published June 21, 2010. Available at: http://adage.com/article?article_id=144555

(A6)   Jack Neff. "Why It's Time to Do Away with the Brand Manager." Published October 12, 2009. Available at: http://adage.com/cmostrategy/article?article_id=139593

(A7)   Michael Bush. "How PR Chiefs Have Shifted toward Center of Marketing Departments." Published September 21, 2009. Available at: http://adage.com/cmostrategy/article?article_id=139140

(A8)   Jeremy Mullman. "Despite ROI Chatter, Marketers Still Pay Shops Same Old Way." Published May 3, 2010. Available at: http://adage.com/article?article_id=143644

(A9)   Wayne Arnold. "Stop Being an Agency and Start Being an Agent of Change." Published September 7, 2009. Available at: http://adage.com/article?article_id=138795

(A10)   "How to Save the Troubled Agency-Marketer Relationship." Published April 26, 2010. Available at: http://adage.com/article?article_id=143508

(A11)   "2009 Set to Show First Revenue Decline for Nation's Top 100 Media Cos." Published December 28, 2009. Available at: http://adage.com/article?article_id=141212

(A12)   Simon Dumenco. "In Trying to Buy Yelp, Google Is Becoming . . . Yep, a Media Company." Published January 4, 2010. Available at: http://adage.com/mediaworks/article?article_id=141250

(A13)   Jonah Bloom. "What Will a Successful Media Company Look Like in the Future?" Published November 2, 2009. Available at: http://adage.com/columns/article?article_id=140091

3 CHAPTER

Important Times in Advertising History

In the 1984 Super Bowl, the Los Angeles Raiders beat the Washington Redskins 38–9 in Tampa. Although a number of that year's commercials were for computers, the only one anyone remembers was Apple's ad "1984," which introduced the Macintosh computer. Producer Ridley Scott (*Blade Runner* and *Thelma and Louise*) created the $800,000 commercial, which ran in a $1 million time slot during the Super Bowl. In 2004, *USA Today* reporter Kevin Maney, who called the commercial a watershed event, described it in the following way:

> A woman with blond hair and a get-up like Olivia Newton-John might've worn in her Physical video, runs into a sci-fi setting packed with bald human drones who are listening to their leader address them on a giant TV. The aerobics woman, chased by storm trooper types, throws a sledgehammer through the screen. (1)

Although it was only aired once, "1984" was credited with the subsequent enormous sales success of the Macintosh. As we read in the Apple Computer history story from *Advertising Age*, the commercial also won the Grand Prix at the Cannes International Advertising Festival, and the advertising agency responsible for it, Chiat/Day, was named agency of the decade by *Advertising Age* (A1; http://adage.com/article?article_id=98322). But in the more than twenty-five years since the commercial ran, many argue that the commercial not only sold millions of computers, it actually set the stage for Apple's business orientation from then until now. Just as "1984" represented Apple fighting against the Big Brother IBM, subsequent campaigns have continued to represent the company as fighting off big guy evildoers—only the competition has changed. After IBM, Big Brother was Microsoft.

First with the iPod and iTunes, and then with the iPad, the company continues to innovate toward "thinking differently" (and better) than the competition. Most agree that Apple's advertising since then, although good, has never again been able to capture the entire meaning of a product and a company in a single commercial. This fact makes "1984" one of the most revered commercials in advertising history.

Profound Moments in Advertising History and What We Can Learn from Them

This chapter looks at some high and low points in advertising history. These events are stories about advertisements themselves, of products, of advertising leaders, and of companies. The events themselves are interesting, but they also give us insights about today's world of advertising and marketing communication. We begin by looking back at the first decade of this century.

A Wild Decade: 2000–2010

The first ten years of the twenty-first century have brought revolutionary changes. As the old century ended, many of the businesses that dived into Internet ventures found they couldn't make money, and we had the "dot-com bust" where millions were won and lost, often in a matter of weeks. September 11, 2001, changed American life forever. Terrorism had seldom touched Americans, but after the attacks commercial flight became a trial and many events could trigger security alerts. Advertisers had to be alert to present advertising that was sensitive to the new realities of terrorist threats as well as avoiding stereotypical representations of ethnic groups.

As the new century moved forward, the Internet became commercialized; Facebook and MySpace were born, as were YouTube and Twitter as well as all kinds of other social networks. Smartphones became common and started to fill all kinds of mobile information needs—email, text messaging, and geographic-based advertising. E-readers actually gained readers, and in 2010 the iPad revolutionized smart devices with a full-color reader combining many functions of smartphones and laptops. These changes all influenced advertising and meant that whole new categories of advertising were born: text-based advertising, advertising networks for placing advertising in remnant online sites, targeted advertising, and advertising targeted to the behaviors of people online (A2; http://adage.com/article?article_id=141062).

As we'll see throughout this book, the changes that occurred in the last decade have had some of the greatest impacts on advertising—the media in which it's carried, its role compared with other promotional tools, its financial health, and what companies are the big players in the industry itself.

Recessions and Advertising

Toward the end of the decade, we were hit with a worldwide recession. Advertising was particularly damaged. *Ad Age* reported that in the past thirty years, 2009 was first in which advertising revenue from the top media companies fell (A3; http://adage.com/mediaworks/article?article_id=139445). More disturbing, eleven out of the top one hundred media companies entered bankruptcy. Not surprisingly, the hardest hit media were all print: six newspaper companies, two magazine companies, and two Yellow Pages publishers. Even the online companies weren't bright spots—Twitter, Facebook and YouTube had yet to make a profit. In fact, despite Facebook's immense popularity, it's profit picture is unclear since it's a private company (not traded on the stock market) that's not required to report its financial results.

Cable and satellite TV did relatively well in this time period. In fact, as this book goes to press, what can be said about advertising media is that the oldest form—print—is clearly on a rapid descent, but few media companies have figured out how to make a profit on the Internet. Nevertheless, television continues its dominance. Where will advertising media be by 2020? If you guess right, you may stand to make a great deal of money. To remain nimble in advertising today, being on top of media changes is probably job Number One.

The Great Depression and Advertising

Ad Age compared the recession of 2008 with the Great Depression, which began in 1929 (A4; http://adage.com/article?article_id=136262). Unlike the 1930s, this decade's recession has not led to many advertising agency bankruptcies.

> ### After the Boom Time of 1920s, the Game Morphed Into Survival of the Fittest
>
> Like most businesses, advertising booms along with the economy and suffers during downturns. The Great Recession of 2008 and 2009 caused considerable pain for citizens and businesses, including those related to advertising.
>
> But the problems of recent years pale in comparison with the Great Depression of the late 1920s and 1930s that permanently transformed a generation from spenders into savers and brought high-rolling companies and investors to historic lows and losses.
>
> Even through the stock market crash of 1929, many agencies of the time were cocky and bragged they could be part of turning the economy around. But as the crash turned into a depression, agencies were slashing payrolls and salaries. Some went under and others used almost any tactics to poach clients from other firms. Hard-pressed clients insisted on more services for lower fees and agencies desperately looked for ways to cut costs.
>
> The look and feel of creative executions changed, too, and the genteel and elegant ads gave way to hard sell efforts with more graphics, less copy, and more low price appeals that some called the "tabloid aesthetic."
>
> While the recent recession was difficult, it wasn't anywhere near as devastating as the Great Depression. However, today's tough economic times coupled with major changes in the media landscape are transforming the way agencies and marketers do business. As this article points out, the winners will be those *"who can best tap into the messages (and media) that matter now."*

However, many advertising agencies downsized or merged in order to survive. We saw some of that in the current recession. In Chapter 2, we reported that in 2009 there were twenty-nine fewer U.S. advertising agencies than in 2008 (a 3 percent drop). We also saw that, like during the Great Depression, employment in the industry dropped—from 2008 to 2009 there was almost an 8 percent decline. Managing advertising during economic downturns is a crucial challenge to marketers. We'll investigate these challenges further in later chapters.

Birth of Great Products

"Nothing kills a bad product faster than good advertising" is a well-known Madison Avenue slogan. This distills the idea that if a firm develops great campaigns that attract a lot of attention AND generates sales, people will try the product and reject it if it doesn't perform to their satisfaction.

But often what makes advertising fun is the chance to work with a brilliant and groundbreaking product. Our opening example of Apple's Macintosh is a prime example of this linkage. According to *Ad Age*, the great products of the last decade included the iPod, Axe deodorant, the Prius automobile and Activia foods (A5; http://adage.com/article?article_id=141032).

Most experts agree that advertising continues to be an essential tool when introducing new products, and all of the examples in this article reveal how powerful advertising can be. But as we'll see in subsequent chapters, competitors to advertising's role in the introduction of new products are on the horizon.

New Ways to Do Things

Ad Age offered a dictionary of terms that are used routinely by advertising professionals—as well as by others in media and marketing (A6; http://adage.com/article?article_id=141058). As you'll see in the article, these terms reveal big changes for how the media, marketing, and news are structured. In fact, most of these terms are relevant to what Harvard marketing professor Clayton Christensen called "disruptive technologies." (2) Technologies that disrupt marketing and media provide new ways of doing business, targeting customers, and selling brands. They are disruptive in the sense that they threaten the livelihood of traditional marketers and media professionals. The idea of the "marketer as media" is a good example. When companies can create their own websites and draw millions of customers to those sites, they're able to spend less and less on traditional media. They skip the "old" media and go straight to the customer.

Crowdsourcing is another good example. Instead of relying on traditional research to determine what consumers want and need, Procter & Gamble creates sites for mothers to talk about using disposable diapers, for women to talk about coloring their hair, and for other consumers to talk about removing stains. As marketers observe people talking about how they use products, they're able to figure out product changes and better ways to talk with consumers about their brands. As you look through the rest of the great ideas in this article, consider how each of them threatens traditional ways of doing advertising and making money from marketing.

Why Well-Advertised Brands Get Stuck in Your Mind Forever

Another way to look at the history of advertising is by thinking about campaigns that produced unforgettable images and effects. *Ad Age* reviewed the Walk winners from 2004 through 2008 and then offered twenty-six new candidates. (A7) What is the "Walk"? Each one has an iconic brand image, plus powerful and unique selling propositions. It's likely you'll remember many of them. In Chapter 5, when we look at theories of how advertising works and in Chapter 12 about creative executions in advertising, we will look in more detail at what made these advertisements so successful in positioning their brands.

Hitting the Advertising Jackpot

Every once in a while a brand sales concept hits pay dirt and a long-term campaign—and lots and lots of sales—are created. Again, our prime example is Apple's Macintosh. Like "1984," these approaches break the mold of what most advertising looks like. *Ad Age's* review of ten great ideas offers some great examples: a vodka bottle that becomes the communication voice of the brand, a television commercial that runs once and sells millions of computers, a car that makes fun of its small size and funny shape, and a $35 investment that created the logo on one of the world's most successful sports shoe companies (A8; http://adage.com/cmostrategy/article?article_id=142090). Also check out a second list of ten advertising ideas for some more inspiring—and sometimes amusing—stories (A9; http://adage.com/cmostrategy/article?article_id=143873).

Ten Big Marketing Risks That Paid Off for Brands

Liodice Continues His Series by Looking at How Breaking Boundaries Helped These Companies Get Ahead

Advertising and marketing communication are exciting, fun and notably risky businesses and they have been throughout the profession's history. To get consumers' fleeting attention, advertisers try to go beyond what's safe and they often push the margins of accepted practices, good sense and even good taste.

This article provides examples of advertisers who took big risks and reaped big rewards. This doesn't mean that advertisers should take chances just to stand out. Rather, they try to make good decisions based on both the art and science of persuasion. It's important to remember that there's a lot at stake in these decisions: clients can be lost, people can get fired and agencies can even go out of business. Sometimes, as in these examples, they hit the jackpot.

- Eveready powers programming hours.
  Back in the 1920s, most radio advertising used the "interrupt" style to identify sponsors and for station identification—not too different from radio programming today. Eveready hit on the idea of sponsoring a whole show and invented a new type of advertising.

- American Tobacco spends millions to advertise Lucky Strike.
  In 1929, few people knew about the dangers of cigarettes. But Lucky Strike advertising courted controversy anyway by positioning itself as a competitor to candy. They spent more than $12.3 million (equivalent to some $155 million today) to promote "reach for a Lucky instead of a sweet," a campaign aimed at weight conscious women. The National Confectioners Association struck back with anti-smoking messages and finally the Federal Trade Commission investigated and ruled that cigarettes shouldn't be marketed as a weight loss product. Lucky Strike came back with Reach for a Lucky instead.

- Anheuser Busch kicks off stadium sponsorships.
  Few people can remember when private companies didn't sponsor sports venue.
  In 1953, A-B went after naming rights for Sportsman's Park, Home of the St. Louis Cardinals. They wanted to call it "Budweiser Stadium" but finally got the Commissioner of Baseball to approve "Busch Stadium," and pioneered the concept of stadium sponsorships.

- Reese's Pieces picks up where M&Ms left off.
  The producers of a movie about an alien approached M&M candies about using the product in their new film but M&M passed on the opportunity. Hershey foods, maker of Reese's Pieces, said "yes" to the idea and the character of a little boy named "Henry" used the candy to entice the alien into his house. This product placement or integration paid off handsomely when the film "E.T.: The Extra Terrestial" became a hit and Reese's sales went to the stratosphere. Today, product integration is a major tactic for marketers in hundreds of films.

History through Biography

Another way to look at advertising history is by reading about advertising greats. Bill Bernbach, founder of DDB (formerly Doyle, Dane, Bernbach) created and inspired advertising that broke the rules. He created "Think Small" for the Volkswagen Beetle, and "We Try Harder" for Avis car rental.

How did these campaigns break the rules? In those days, car companies made big cars and touted their size, performance and speed. Everyone "just knew" that nobody wanted tiny cars with few options or luxuries. The small, foreign Volkswagen Beetle itself was a rule breaker and Bernbach saw that rather than trying to divert attention from its small size and unusual shape, he'd highlight them in both the ad's design and copy. The Beetle and Bernbach's advertising were smash hits.

Similarly, in "We Try Harder," he made an asset out of Avis's decidedly second place status behind Hertz in the rental business.

The Bernbach biography reviewed in *Ad Age* claims that Bernbach spent too much time polishing his own image, but doesn't argue with the impact he had on how advertising developed during the second half of the twentieth century (A10; http://adage.com/agencynews/article?article_id=136992).

In celebrating its seventieth birthday, *Advertising Age* offered its unique perspective on pivotal events in each decade since the 1930s (A11; http://adage.com/article?article_id=142967). This is a good way to close this chapter: from the Great Depression to the 2008 worldwide recession—ideas, people, products, brands, sales appeals—a fascinating legacy of big moments in advertising changing history.

Notes

1. Maney, K. "Apple's '1984' Super Bowl Commercial Still Stands as Watershed Event," *USA Today*, January 28, 2004.
2. Christensen, C., & Raynor, M. *The Innovator's Solution*. Boston: Harvard Business School Publishing Corporation, 1993.

Articles

(A1) "Apple Computer." Published September 15, 2003. Available at: http://adage.com/article?article_id=98322

(A2) "Book of Tens: Biggest Stories of the Decade." Published December 14, 2009. Available at: http://adage.com/article?article_id=141062

(A3) Bradley Johnson. "In U.S. Media Revenue Set for Historic 2009 Decline." Published October 5, 2009. Available at: http://adage.com/mediaworks/article?article_id=139445

(A4) James B. Arndorfer. "How the Depression Shaped Modern Ad Biz." Published April 27, 2009. Available at: http://adage.com/article?article_id=136262

(A5) "Book of Tens: New Products of the Decade." Published December 14, 2009. Available at: http://adage.com/article?article_id=141032

(A6) Matthew Creamer. "Book of Tens: Ideas of the Decade." Published December 14, 2009. Available at: http://adage.com/article?article_id=141058

(A7) "Advertising Week Walk of Fame." Published September 7, 2009.

(A8) Bob Liodice. "A Look Back at 10 Ideas That Changed the Marketing World." Published February 15, 2010. Available at: http://adage.com/cmostrategy/article?article_id=142090

(A9) Bob Liodice. "Ten Big Marketing Risks That Paid Off for Brands." Published May 17, 2010. Available at: http://adage.com/cmostrategy/article?article_id=143873

(A10) Rupal Parekh. "New Book Paints Bernbach as Much Lemon as Legend." Published June 1, 2009. Available at: http://adage.com/agencynews/article?article_id=136992

(A11) Bradley Johnson. "From the Great Depression through the Great Recession: A Brief History of Marketing." Published March 29, 2010. Available at: http://adage.com/article?article_id=142967

Ethical and Regulatory Contexts of Advertising

"Advertising is only evil when it advertises evil things."

—David Ogilvy

In April 2010, an explosion on the Deepwater Horizon BP oil platform killed eleven people. For the next three months, oil gushed into the Gulf of Mexico. It harmed sea life, ruined the fishing industry in the area, and stemmed the flow of tourists. BP, once considered an exemplary ethical corporation, faced not only an environmental crisis but also a public relations crisis. (1)

Its first set of commercials explaining how it was attempting to stop the flow of oil and clean up the spill featured company CEO Tony Hayward. He promised that taxpayers wouldn't be paying the bill for the damage and apologized on behalf of BP. However, speaking off-the-cuff later to reporters in Louisiana, he also said, "There's no one who wants this over more than I do. I would like my life back."

Many interpreted Hayward's remark as saying he was more concerned about his own life than those affected by the explosion. Later, he was photographed attending a sailing race, adding to public anger. *Ad Age* reported that the comment and the sailing race posed major problems for the company's public relations firm (A1; http://adage.com/article?article_id=144287).

Communicating about as explosive a topic as the BP oil spill raises serious ethical questions. *Ad Age* reported that in an online poll they conducted of public relations professionals, 43 percent of three hundred respondents said they would not attempt an advertising campaign to handle the crisis because of ethical concerns. (A1) Michael Kempner, CEO of Interpublic Group's PR shop, MWW Group, said he would attempt a BP campaign, but "I might consider it only on the condition that they would commit to total transparency and be an agent for change. I would also potentially work with them to provide true solutions to the residents of the Gulf Coast and major funding to repair the damage caused to lives, the environment and the economy. I would not work with them to cover up, 'spin' or justify their past and current behavior."

Advertising and public relations often are used hand in hand when corporations get into trouble. What are the ethics of trying to justify or ameliorate the harm a company has caused? Scholarly and professional literature offers advice about the "right" ways to deal with these occurrences. Truth and transparency have often emerged as the ethical and practical winners.

Ethical Challenges for Advertising

Many have argued that advertising often has negative effects on society. As Hovland and Wolburg point out in their book about advertising ethics, "advertising is inherently controversial." (2) Most advertising historians claim that advertising developed hand in hand with a "consumer culture." Just like any kind of communication message, advertising can contain falsities. In fact, it may contain true statements that are nevertheless misleading. (3) Advertising can promote what some consider the negative trait "materialism" or an excessive focus on buying and consuming material goods at the expense of human relationships, citizenship and other activities. Advertising can lead to the use of dangerous products such as cigarettes or dangerous behaviors such as imitating reckless driving of automobiles as they are shown in commercials. Advertising has been accused of preying on vulnerable audiences such as children or those likely to become addicted to alcohol, gambling, or overeating. Advertising is often accused of stereotyping—women, men, children, family relationships, minorities, really just about anything it depicts.

There are two areas that focus on determining whether advertising does have negative social impacts and if so how to lessen those impacts. One approach is the study of advertising ethics. The other is regulatory—either self-regulation from agencies, such as the Council of Better Business Bureaus or the National Advertising Review Board, or external governmental regulation, such as the Federal Trade Commission (FTC) or local and state regulatory agencies. For example, local government often regulates the size and placement of retail signs. In most states the Attorney General's office deals with such problems as uninvited phone calls from firms selling products or services.

Advertising Age provides a rich picture of news and opinion about advertising's ethical and regulatory problems. In this section we'll look at examples of questionable taste, stereotyping women, the potentially poisonous effects of political advertising, and invasion of privacy. In later sections, we look at advertising regulation and examine examples in which advertising has been lauded for its social impact.

Questionable Taste

Although rap artists and movies commonly make extensive use of profanity, in U.S. television programming, especially by the television networks during the early evening hours when children are likely to be watching, profanity is not allowed. For example, the Federal Communications Commission (FCC) specifically outlaws the use of a four-letter word that begins with F during these hours. But in the future, profanity, sex, and violence may become much more common in network fare. One of the barriers to these topics and language has been advertisers who fear offending the tastes of consumers (A2; http://adage.com/media-works/article?article_id=144159). Irate parents and offended consumers have boycotted brands, but this article suggests that advertisers are now more interested in associating themselves with a large audience than worrying about angering a small group of consumers.

> ### Swearing During Family Hour? Who Gives a $#*!
>
> *CBS Has Little Concern About How Its Hottest New Sitcom Will Be Received,*
> *Despite Airing on Early Side*
>
> Actor and pitchman William Shatner can take a joke—and he can make a lot of money out of it, too. Widely mocked for his decades-old role as Captain Kirk, captain of the Starship Enterprise, he turned his notoriety into roles as an advertising spokesman and the star of a sitcom with an unsayable (on TV) name.

CBS launched the program "$#*! My Dad Says" in 2010 apparently with few worries about unhappy viewers who believe that euphemisms for prohibited words shouldn't be allowed on network television. In fact, the word in question is banned from prime time by the Federal Communications Commission.

Historically, broadcasters have shied away from subjects and words that could create controversy or get the attention of the FCC. According to this article, however, CBS executives said that even at "family hour" (before 9:00 p.m.) the show was expected to be successful and not to garner excessive criticism. At a presentation to advertisers, CBS executives referred to the program as "a place where the Shat hits the fan."

Why were network execs so calm? The article suggests several reasons. First, audiences have been desensitized and programming that once would have shocked people is now routine. Sex, violence and profanity on cable can be seen almost any time of day.

Second, broadcasters and advertisers are less concerned about producing bland programming with content acceptable to large mass audiences. The continuing shrinkage of network viewers means that edgy programming, while not appealing to everyone, can still attract significant numbers of viewers and thus be attractive to advertisers. If they alienate some viewers, so be it.

Third, the potential for outrage, boycotts, and backlash is limited. It's rare that advertisers suffer losses in revenues when targeted by interest groups such as the Parent's Television Council that almost immediately lodged a protest. Mary Price of the Dallas advertising agency The Richards Group commented, "I've not worked with a client whose brand's sales or awareness suffered when they were targeted by outrage or boycotts."

Is this ethical behavior? Do advertisers and networks have a responsibility to the larger society regardless of the profits involved?

It's interesting to compare and contrast instances where advertisers quickly distanced themselves from problematic subjects and individuals such as professional golfer Tiger Woods, who lost most of his sponsorships because of sex scandals while other advertisers stuck with controversial sponsorships or promotional activities.

Stereotyping Women

Teressa Iezzi is annoyed that Dell computers created a special website advertising computers to women (A3; http://adage.com/columns/article?article_id=136825). "Are women too confused and intimidated by the regular Dell site?" she asks. For years, advertising was criticized for stereotyping women consumers as overly focused on beauty and fashion, cleaning their bathrooms, or cooking for their families. You may have noticed commercials that you think stereotyped people by gender, age, or race.

The ethical question here concerns whether such advertising can damage people's belief in what they can do, limits what they expect of themselves, and reduces their life choices. Was Dell stereotyping or actually helping women with less technical interest or experience to buy a computer that would meet their needs?

Does Political Attack Advertising Make People Cynical about Politics?

For decades, researchers, citizens and political observers have debated the role of political advertising, especially attack and negative commercials. Many years of research on how political advertising affects people have provided valuable insights but it's still not clear how attack advertising affects people or may influence voting and democratic processes. Some of the research finds that when candidates attack each other in their ads, it increases the likelihood that citizens will get involved enough to vote. Other research indicates attack ads turn voters off so they don't vote. There's some research that suggests that the more attack advertising in a campaign, the more cynical citizens become about their own government, and certainly more cynical about all politicians. Rance Crain, *Advertising Age* editor, posits another interesting idea—that what Crain calls "raucous" political advertising from both Democrats and Republicans damages citizen responses to *nonpolitical* advertising (A4; http://adage.com/columns/article?article_id=143198). He believes that angry political consumers are the same people who develop attitudes toward brands, and that anger rubs off on the industry as a whole. Crain further suggests that a number of large brand advertisers (e.g., Coke or Budweiser) are failing to provide high-quality advertising support for their brands, and instead are retreating to the Internet where they have less national visibility. In any case, it's critical that researchers and professionals continue to research the potential connection between political advertising abuses and loss of trust in major brands. Even more important, it's crucial that as a society we better understand the relationship between different types of political advertising and promotion and their effects on democratic processes.

In 1993, professors Annie Lang and Betsy Krueger published a study of Americans' beliefs about political and brand advertising. (4) Surprisingly, most people thought that political advertising is regulated by the government. In fact, it's protected by the First Amendment and not regulated at all. People also believed that brand advertising was not regulated when just the opposite is true. We also saw Rance Crain's commentary about political advertising and its potential for fostering negativity toward advertising.

This is important because advertising is only effective when it is considered trustworthy and believable by its audiences. Although the self-regulatory organizations try to encourage a positive reputation for advertising and marketing, questionable behaviors by some marketers and possible misperceptions of some watchdog groups lead consumers, sometimes correctly, to question marketers' objectives and tactics.

In response to this, a group of executives, academics and students united in 2010 to create the Institute for Advertising Ethics (A5; http://adage.com/article?article_id=144288). The Institute conducts research on ethical and regulatory issues and raises awareness about the need for advertisers to regulate and monitor their behaviors and practices. A second activity will be to communicate examples of the extent advertisers will go to making sure they get the story right. Of course, this initiative isn't just about what American consumers think about advertising—this is a worldwide issue. As we'll discuss in an upcoming chapter, marketing and advertising have increasingly gone global. Many of the companies you're familiar with and whose products you may use every day, have far flung operations. You can buy a Big Mac in St. Louis, Sydney and Shanghai and the Coca-Cola logo is said to be the most recognized symbol in the world. Thus any discussion of advertising and communication ethics needs to embrace and acknowledge the national and cultural differences that involve people's values and mores.

Invasion of Consumer Privacy

Ad Age looked at threats to privacy associated with behavioral targeting and what the FTC is considering as remedies (A6; http://adage.com/adnetworkexchangeguide10/article?article_id=143298).

Behavioral targeting uses the tracking of people's website choices to build a profile of what they are most likely to buy, and then on websites that advertise, serve those people with ads for those products. As we'll see in detail in Chapter 6 on segmentation, this is obviously a plus for advertisers who can avoid wasting money delivering advertising to people who would have no interest in their product. It can be argued that it's a good thing for consumers, who instead of getting all kinds of irrelevant ads, get ads for products they are likely to be interested in. But when you think about the pattern of websites you have visited over the last month, it may be easy to see that that information might reflect characteristics you'd rather not have known (of course, so might your Facebook page). Philosophers call privacy a "contested commodity." The advertising industry considers using personal information as a way to provide valuable services to consumers. But that access is contested by ethical considerations of privacy. Regulators and advertisers are trying to figure out how to balance these contested commodity aspects of behavioral targeting.

Perhaps the best way to consider in detail the pros and cons of behavioral targeting is to look in detail at a particular example of what advertisers can find out about a person. Reporter Michael Bush gets the personal treatment, which he reports in "My Life, Seen through the Eyes of Marketers" (A7; http://adage.com/agencynews/article?article_id=143479). After reading about Michael's experience, does your evaluation of the ethical concerns of behavioral targeting change?

My Life, Seen Through the Eyes of Marketers

Ad Age Asks a Database Company to Profile Our Reporter, Revealing a Trove of Personal Information—and Plenty of Difficult Questions

A senior writer for *Ad Age* was shocked by the results when, as an experiment, he asked a major database firm to develop his own demographic and psychographic profile. Demographics, as you may know, is information such as age, income, social class, race and gender. Psychographic segmentation focuses on lifestyle and personality factors.

Even though he is an advertising insider, the writer was very surprised at the profile's accuracy and how much they knew about him, his assets, and his behaviors. The company used readily available information sources such as public records and census data, online shopping activities, catalog and retail purchase history.

He found that they had quickly ascertained his birthday, home phone, marital status, educational level and political party. They found detailed information about the price and current value of his home and the size of his mortgage and accurately estimated his income.

The psychographic profile was surprisingly correct as well, identifying him as health conscious, family-oriented, and an independent decision-maker. It also located his interests in music, running, sports and computers and the types of sports and general information news he prefers.

Several issues related to ethics and convenience emerge from advertisers' abilities to profile and target individuals with persuasive messages tailored just for them. First, many people including government regulators worry about invasion of privacy even if the data are used only for advertising and promotion. Others are concerned that such information could be used for sinister purposes. Second, many people are comfortable with companies knowing this kind of information as long as it is used to target them with messages about product and services they are likely to want. They enjoy the convenience of learning about sales and new items. Third, some people think that this type of profiling is fine, but the subjects of such profiling should be compensated by marketers for using their personal data.

Database companies and other advertisers say they aren't linking information directly to individuals. The article cites an executive at a big agency who says they keep consumer data secure saying their practices include the requirement that they "never store personally identifiable information with customer behavior data. This means don't co-mingle name and address [and e-mail address] with other forms of data." In other words, while they may segment you into certain consumer "buckets" they can't or won't identify you as an individual.

Most in the advertising business are well aware of the potential risks if consumers feel their privacy is being invaded and personal information is used inappropriately. Governmental officials are paying close attention to the matter and already a number of laws and regulations address online privacy issues. In addition, agencies know that if data-gathering practices cross the line where consumers believe they are harmed and not benefited by highly targeted messages, their brands could suffer.

Regulation and Self-Regulation of Advertising

The impact of various regulatory bodies on advertising is difficult to overestimate. *Ad Age* reviews ten important changes in the regulatory environment, starting with the Internal Revenue Service deciding in 1913 to let companies deduct the cost of advertising from their taxes (A8; http://adage.com/cmostrategy/article?article_id=142772). Although Congress has occasionally reconsidered having advertising be tax deductible, industry lobbying has fought that change successfully. Notice that in the 1970s a number of the self-regulation organizations jointly formed the National Advertising Review Council, a move that many think strengthened advertising and probably improved the effectiveness of self-regulation. Advertising for pharmaceuticals and tobacco has proven controversial. The legal movement has been toward more freedom to advertise prescription drugs, but more and more restrictions have been placed on tobacco advertising.

Transparency about Brand Endorsements

Advertising is considered unfair when consumers aren't told that endorsements are paid for by advertisers (A9; http://adage.com/article?article_id=139595). In 2009, the FTC determined that endorsers had to actually use the product, bloggers who are paid to sing the praises of a brand must say that they are compensated, and even those who Twitter for a brand must identify whether they are paid. Most ethics discussions in advertising advocate for as complete transparency as possible. That's also what the FTC will be looking for, as you will see in "Ann Taylor Probe Shows FTC Keeping Close Eye on Blogging" (A10; http://adage.coverleaf.com/advertisingage/20100503?pg=6#pg6).

Protection from Phone Call Harassment

The Do Not Call program is also regulated by the FTC. The legal requirement for being able to directly contact people by phone is whether a company has an "established business relationship" with a consumer. But just what does that mean? If you sign up to receive email from Target, you have an established relationship. But what if you participate in a contest or sweepstakes with Target—is that an established relationship? The answer is "maybe" (A11; http://adage.com/columns/article?article_id=143190).

Facilitating Positive Behavior

Although there is much in advertising to criticize, advertising campaigns have also been credited with saving Americans from catastrophe (A12; http://adage.com/article?article_id=143775). The "See something, say something" slogan of the New York Metropolitan Transit Authority has been running since 2003. It made a significant impact on the street vendor who alerted police to an SUV that turned out to be filled with bomb materials.

Thousands of riders in New York's transit system have called in reports. The lessons learned here are to create a slogan that tells people something simple to do and repeat it over a long campaign. The Ad Council, which helps support scores of public service campaigns, has an impressive history of just such campaigns: "Take a bite out of crime," "Only you can prevent forest fires," and "Friends don't let friends drive drunk," are just a few well-known examples.

Another well-known public service slogan is "Keep America Beautiful," which is also the name of a national organization that since 1953 has focused on reducing litter. It began as an effort to keep the roadsides of America's superhighway system clean. It is also behind local community efforts to have cleanup days when thousands of volunteers show up to pick up. Its most famous ad was of a Native American (Iron Eyes Cody) with a single tear-drop falling down his cheek (http://www.youtube.com/watch?v=j7OHG7tHrNM). This April, *Ad Age* looked into the progress of the environmental movement in the United States (A13; http://adage.com/article?article_id=143364). As you'll see in the story, the news is mixed. With recycling, there has been no net increase in per-capita total municipal solid waste. In contrast, total food waste over the last forty years has more than doubled. Consider the role that advertising has played in America's efforts to control waste and refuse. What are the pluses and minuses?

Advertising: The Good, the Bad, and the Regulated

Social critique of advertising, as can be seen, is extensive. Advertising has also received extensive lauding for its positive social impact. Advertising professionals attempt to regulate themselves, and when that fails, government regulators step in. One thing is clear: It is generally in the best interest of advertisers to tell the truth and be transparent. Without the credibility that quality business ethics builds, advertising quickly loses its power.

Notes

1. Murphy, P., Laczniak, G., Bowie, N., & Klein, T. *Ethical Marketing*. Upper Saddle River, NJ: Prentice Hall, 2005.
2. Hovland, R., & Wolburg, J. *Advertising, Society, and Consumer Culture*. Armonk, NY: Sharpe, 2010.
3. See Preston, I. *The Great American Blow-Up: Puffery in Advertising and Selling*, rev. ed. Madison: University of Wisconsin Press, 1996.
4. Lang, A., & Krueger, E. "Candidates' Commercials and the Law: The Public Perception," *Journal of Broadcast and Electronic Media* 37, no. 2 (1993): 209–218.

Articles

(A1)   Michael Bush. "Brunswick Put to Ultimate Test as BP Grows Increasingly Toxic." Published June 7, 2010. Available at: http://adage.com/article?article_id=144287

(A2)   Brian Steinberg. "Swearing during Family Hour? Who Gives A $#*!" Published May 31, 2010. Available at: http://adage.com/mediaworks/article?article_id=144159

(A3)   Teressa Iezzi. "Dell's Della Debacle an Example of Wrong Way to Target Women." Published May 25, 2009. Available at: http://adage.com/columns/article?article_id=136825

(A4)   Rance Crain. "Consumer Mistrust of Politics Spills Over to Brands." Published April 12, 2010. Available at: http://adage.com/columns/article?article_id=143198

(A5)   Jack Neff. "Ad Industry Battles Back against Bad Rep, Forms Ethics Institute." Published June 7, 2010. Available at: http://adage.com/article?article_id=144288

(A6)   Christopher Weaver. "Does Your Ad Network Know You're Gay?" Published April 19, 2010. Available at: http://adage.com/adnetworkexchangeguide10/article?article_id=143298

(A7)   Michael Bush. "My Life, Seen through the Eyes of Marketers." Published April 26, 2010. Available at: http://adage.com/agencynews/article?article_id=143479

(A8)   Bob Liodice. "10 Legal Moves That Changed Advertising." Published March 15, 2010. Available at: http://adage.com/cmostrategy/article?article_id=142772

(A9)   Abbey Klaassen and Michael Learmonth. "What You Need to Know about the New FTC Rules—and Why." Published October 12, 2009. Available at: http://adage.com/article?article_id=139595

(A10)   Natalie Zmuda. "Ann Taylor Probe Shows FTC Keeping Close Eye on Blogging." Published May 3, 2010. Available at: http://adage.coverleaf.com/advertisingage/20100503?pg=6#pg6

(A11)   Natasha Shabani. "Are You Using Sweepstakes to Skirt the Do-Not-Call List?" Published April 12, 2010. Available at: http://adage.com/columns/article?article_id=143190

(A12)   Rupal Parekh. "Advertising Does Its Part in War on Terror." Published May 10, 2010. Available at: http://adage.com/article?article_id=143775

(A13)   Jack Neff. "Earth Day Is 40 Years Old. What Headway Have We Made?" Published April 19, 2010. Available at: http://adage.com/article?article_id=143364

Theory about How Advertising Works

> *"Nothing is as practical as a good theory."*
>
> —Kurt Lewin, one of the foundational researchers in social psychology

© Rodney Turner/Newscom

Pepsi lost the cola war. That's the lead in a 2011 *Ad Age* article that describes how Pepsi products lost market share in its long-standing rivalry with Coca Cola. Pepsi dropped its traditional advertising approach known in the industry as "generation next." Both Pepsi and Coke compete in the same product categories and they face the same marketing and economic environment. Both are fierce competitors in the cola wars.

What caused Pepsi's slide? Some observers think it's largely related to a significant change in strategy that shifted budget allocations away from advertising including the Super Bowl and toward an innovative program called "Pepsi Refresh."

In what some thought was a brilliant marketing maneuver, Pepsi promoted and distributed some $20 million in grants that consumers could apply for in support of worthy causes. They were supposed to be "refreshing ideas that change the world" tapping into both social media and consumers' social conscience. The connections between Pepsi and community causes were meant to strengthen relationships between consumers and the brand and benefit from significant publicity about the program and its good works.

Problems began to emerge: the Refresh Project received allegations of applicants cheating or gaming the grants. In addition, the amount of exposure the brand received appeared to be insufficient. A former Pepsi executive said, "The key learning for us was that in addition to having a cultural idea that taps into a mass sensibility, you need to make sure your idea is getting enough exposure to be successful."

Pepsi is expected to step up its marketing and likely take it in a somewhat different direction. Stay tuned—the cola wars are still raging (A1: http://adage.com/results? endeca=1&searchprop=AdAgeAll&return=endeca&search_offset=0&search_order_ by=score&search_phrase=how+pepsi+blinked).

What do cola wars have to do with theory? The different strategies for Pepsi's marketing are based on theoretical propositions about what is likely to be successful in marketing their products in a dynamic sales and media environment. The media world is a complicated place—and the question of how advertising influences people is a particularly complicated question. Those who attempt to figure out how to create an advertising campaign need a frame of reference for determining what's important and what isn't and how to design and deliver messages to influence people. The best way to simplify and focus on what's important when you plan an advertising campaign is to have a lens to look through. In the social sciences, this lens is called a theory. It is a description of how things are thought to work—how A affects B, which affects C, and so on. Theory and data help us predict what's likely to happen when we deploy certain strategies. Without research and a solid theory of cause and effect, marketers are stuck with a trial and error approach—one that has much less chance of success and thus is far less practical.

In this chapter, we'll review a range of theories and offer examples of how the theory influenced the planning of the campaign.

Hierarchy Models

In one of the earliest theories about advertising effects, E. St. Elmo Lewis (1887) (1) suggested a theoretical idea that turned out to be fundamentally important to all theories about advertising. "Attention to a message led to Interest in the focus of the message, which led to Desire for the idea/object, which led to Action to comply with what the advertising advocated." The AIDA model was the first of what have come to be called "hierarchy" models of how advertising works. What hierarchy models have in common is that they identify an ordered set of responses that people can have to advertising. Then, based on the consumer's response, the theories attempt to predict whether they eventually "act" or respond in some measureable way to what the advertising promotes.

Researchers have introduced a number of important and useful hierarchy models of advertising. Here we'll look at a blend of their features, but you can check individual approaches if you're interested. (2) A main advantage of hierarchy models is that that they are general, so they can incorporate many other helpful theories of advertising, as well as serve as a checklist of information processing aspects that the advertising manager needs to track.

Think of consumers traveling through four information processing responses between being exposed to the commercial and making a purchase. First, they have to attend to the message. Second, they must understand it. Third, they must desire the brand; that is, they must want it. And fourth, they must remember that desire until they have a chance to buy the product. For example, a person who is exposed to a commercial for L'Oreal hair color has to register some of that message's content, (i.e., pay attention to it). She has to understand that the product will cover gray hair, she has to want to cover her own gray hair, and she has to then remember the brand name so she can buy it the next time she is at the store. From a management point of view, commercials must be considered in terms of where they come from (L'Oreal), what's in the commercial, the fact that it appears on network television (channel), in a television program popular with women aged 45 to 60 (receivers).

We can then combine the management variables with the information processing stages in a persuasion matrix:

Processing Variables	Communication Management Components			
	Source	Message	Channel	Receiver
Message presentation				
Attention				
Comprehension				
Desire				
Retention				
Behavior				

Each of the processing and management components needs to be evaluated when designing an advertising campaign. For example, sources need to be credible, attractive, and perceived as powerful or high status. Messages, the ads themselves, can appeal to someone's appetite or desire for status. It can offer sex appeal or a range of other emotions. Ads can be short (15 seconds) or long (30 minutes). They can be for brands or public health promotions. The communication channel can be any mode of delivering the ad, including network television, banner ads on a website, and ads delivered to a mobile phone. Desire is often defined as an emotional response, such as liking something or feeling good.

As advertising professionals developed planning models, the hierarchy theory consistently contributed the basic idea of a matrix relating communication components to people's responses. An early and still influential model made one of its first appearances in *Advertising Age*. Richard Vaughn of Foote, Cone & Belding (FCB) introduced the FCB grid. He suggested that products that require time and thought before the purchase are high involvement. He also suggested that whether people tend to decide on those products predominantly rationally or emotionally should drive advertising planning. High-involvement rational products (cars) involve a "thinking" approach. High-involvement emotional products (designer watches) involve a "feeling" approach. Low-involvement rational products (detergent) involve "habitual" processing, and low-involvement emotional products (lipstick) are reactive or impulsive purchases. Vaughn developed elaborate theories about what kinds of messages and channels should be used for each of the four types of products. (3)

Additional Persuasion Theories

Many academic theories have appeared in the last forty years. A good overview of the most important of these theories can be found in "Persuasion Theory" (A2; http://adage.com/article?article_id=98959). Carl Hovland and his associates at Yale were concerned with how source characteristics such as credibility and expertise influenced people. Albert Bandura theorized it was important that media messages provide examples for people to imitate (for example, showing a woman who earns the attention of a handsome man by using a particular brand of shampoo). Classical conditioning from the early days of experimental psychology was employed to try to explain how people came to connect brands with reflexive responses (e.g., stimulating a hunger response when you watch a pizza commercial). In case you've forgotten your psychology course, classical conditioning is exemplified by Pavlov's dog hearing a bell, getting meat powder injected into his mouth, followed by reflexive salivating. After a number of trials, the sound of the bell make the dog salivate even without the meat powder. The reflex is said to be conditioned to the bell. This is essentially a simple form of learning.

The Elaboration Likelihood Model (ELM) identified attention to advertising messages as being centrally processed (lots of attention paid to the verbal part of the ads) and peripherally processed (liking the looks of the model or the sounds of the music in the background). All of these theories have been applied extensively in trying to understand how advertising works and to plan an effective strategy for an advertising campaign.

The hierarchical theories of advertising and many of those described in "Persuasion Theory" emphasized the thinking or rational consumer who carefully considered attributes of brands and then made a decision. For the rational consumer an advertisement is informative. But with Vaughn's model, conditioning theories, and the ELM, it became clear that emotion was often a more important marker for the success of an ad than any measure of rational processing. Academic researchers found that liking an advertisement itself (rather than just the brand) was the strongest predictor of how well the ad would sell product. *Advertising Age* reviewed the history of the use of recall—the measurement of how many people remembered the ad the day after it ran (A3; http://adage.com/article?article_id=98847). *Advertising Age* also told the story of yet another advertising agency that found that how much people liked ads is a better predictor of sales than how well they were recalled (A4; http://adage.com/article?article_id=49312).

Ad Age importantly offered explanations for why emotional advertising is so effective (A5; http://adage.com/article?article_id=120017).

The danger in ad recall tests

One of the most persistent research streams in advertising has been "unaided recall" or how well a viewer or reader remembers the brand and message in an advertising message. This was thought to be a reasonably good predictor of the likelihood a consumer would make a purchase. But a team of advertising researchers shared a mistrust in the effectiveness of recall measure and hypothesized that the role of emotion in ads was a powerful predictor of purchase. They further suggested that a strong linkage between liking and emotion were crucial motivators of consumers and the recall missed the emotional elements in ads.

Their research found that advertising that triggered "episodic memory" or stories that featured the consumer and the brand were emotion driven and thus were able to forge powerful relationships between the consumer and the product.

The researchers argued that their findings showed that advertising research could help advertising strategists and creative teams to develop more effective advertising. Acknowledging that decoding the emotional impact of advertising on purchases is difficult and complex, they advocate continuing efforts to understand how we process persuasive messages and where emotions rule.

The article also develops another kind of persuasion matrix that suggests the kinds of responses people have to combinations of emotions. If an ad creates both happiness and sadness, the results are feelings of yearning and nostalgia. In fact, scholarly research has shown that the combinations of feelings, specifically nostalgia, have particularly high impact on consumers. (2)

Another particularly powerful emotion is humor. Whether it's Spuds MacKenzie or Real Men of Genius, Bud Light commercials for years have successfully used humor to sell the beer. Eventually, they cornered an amazing 20 percent of the American beer market. In 2008, however, the company abandoned humor and focused instead on "drinkability." *Advertising Age* reported that when the brand abandoned humor, it lost a good chunk of its sales (A6; http://adage.com/article?article_id=138371). *Advertising Age* also took a more theoretical look at how humor operates in consumer information processing. It drives attention to advertising, makes it more enjoyable over many repetitions, and when ads integrate the brand with the humor, solidifies brand image (A7; http://adage.com/article?article_id=56992).

> ### BOOK EXCERPT: Make 'Em Laugh, Make 'Em Buy
>
> Surprisingly, humor in advertising is a problem. Authors Max Sutherland and Alice K. Sylvester in *Advertising & the Mind of the Consumer*, offer a brief history of advertising and point out that historically, humor has often been seen as brutal, derisive, and crude.
>
> While our attitudes toward humor have changed a lot, advertisers know that while it can be effective, it can also be a two-edged sword that can damage brands more than enhance them.
>
> Humor often emerges from the unexpected or incongruity. Think of your favorite jokes: they usually take you in one direction and then surprise you with a change. We don't expect babies to talk about investments, but when the E-trade baby talks about his stock trading schemes, the incongruity makes us laugh and gets our attention.
>
> Is humor in ads persuasive? Well, that depends. Sometimes humor distracts us and we don't remember the brand commercial that made us laugh. On the plus side, humor often results in less "counter-arguing." We engage with the funny message and don't try to rationally counter it as we might with a more serious ad. In addition, people like funny ads and there seems to be a linking between liking brands and buying the brand's products. Importantly, people notice humorous ads, gaining more attention than serious spots.
>
> The authors argue that for humorous ads to be effective, they must be integrated into the brand message and "woven into the story line" else the product is likely to be forgotten.
>
> Of course, advertisers also need to be aware that their attempts at humor can backfire—that which I find funny and quirky, you may find offensive and crude. The punch line? We still don't know enough about effects of humor in advertising, but theoretically driven research studies are getting us closer to understanding how it may work in the purchase process.

Fiber One

As we now better understand the theory of how humor works, let's think about another product. How might we build an effective advertising campaign for Fiber One, a cereal that is supposed to be good for you, but which many people think tastes like cardboard.

Can we make humor work for us? Fiber cereal doesn't seem like a naturally funny topic, but given the power of emotion to guide attention to a low-involvement product, a humorous ad could help break through the clutter. The humor should not be built on any stereotypes. Check out *Ad Age*'s report to see if you agree that the brand's use of humor works (A8; http://adage.com/bigtent/post?article_id=144809). The grocery store manager is an Asian American actor Ajay Mehta. In his conversation with a young woman who is sampling Fiber One, he responds to each of her comments before she makes them. She starts to say "it can't have half a day's fiber," but he beats her to it. Mehta tells her he "doesn't have ESP." She says, "OK, I'll take a box" and then stops momentarily and then "you probably already knew that." The humor and surprise of this store manager's predicting everything the woman says is pleasant but still drives home the selling point: Even though Fiber One has half the fiber you need every day, it doesn't taste like cardboard—it's delicious. This is a textbook example of combining emotion with a selling proposition.

The debate over rational versus emotional processing continues. "Why Emotional Messages Beat Rational Ones" summarizes the book *Brand Immortality*, about how to keep brand equity alive and healthy (A9; http://adage.com/cmostrategy/article?article_id=134920). The authors explain that emotional advertising in their case studies was twice as effective in generating profit gains as rational advertising.

Theories for the Digital Age

Do we need new theories to understand and plan advertising that uses the Internet, mobile marketing, and iPads? It is certainly clear that consumer behavior is changing rapidly as a result of that digital environment. *Ad Age* looked closely at a lot of those important changes (A10; http://adage.com/article?article_id=137795).

Do these changes require new advertising theories? We doubt it. The theories we've looked at in this chapter handle "channel" changes without a problem. Maybe there are differences in watching a commercial on your iPad or watching it on network television, but whether the commercial adopts a rational or emotional appeal will probably lead to the same differences we see in the television ads. *Ad Age* reported that advertising campaigns on iPads are getting more attention than in other channels (A11; http://adage.com/article?article_id=144440). Let's think about what the hierarchy model would suggest about an iPad-delivered Ford ad campaign. Receivers are clearly a different group from those only watching network television and would be expected to show higher attention to everything on their iPads—even the ads. And that is just what this article reports. We would also theorize that iPad owners are focused on efficient accomplishment of their communication goals—so we would predict that over time, unwanted intrusions from commercials would become much more unwelcome unless they can be integrated into the desired content in a way relevant to these demanding consumers. So we see again the utility of thinking about advertising with a theory guiding us. And as the digital environment makes all communication more complex, theory can be expected to become an even more important tool for the advertising professional.

Notes

1. It appears that St. Elmo introduced the AIDA concept when discussing sales techniques. *Autorenkollektiv, Handbuch der Werbung,* Berlin, 1968., p. 24.
   1. Examples of hierarchy models
   A. Lavidge, R. J., & Steiner, G. A. "A Model for Predictive Measurement of Advertising Effectiveness," *Journal of Marketing* 25 (1961): 59–65.
   B. McGuire, W. J. "Directive Theorizing: The Communication/Persuasion Matrix," in *Handbook of Social Psychology*, Vol. 2, ed. Gardner Lindzey and Elliot Aronson (New York: Random House, 1985), 258–262.
   C. Preston, I. "The Association Model of the Advertising Communication Process," *Journal of Advertising* 11 (1982): 3–15.
2. Friestad, M., & Thorson, E. "Remembering Ads: The Effects of Encoding Strategies, Retrieval Cues, and Emotional Response," *Journal of Consumer Psychology* 2, no. 1 (1993): 1–24.
3. Vaughn, R. "How Advertising Works: A Planning Model", *Journal of Advertising Research* 20, no. 5 (1980): 27–33.

Articles

(A1) Natalie Zmuda. "How Pepsi Blinked, Fell Behind Diet Coke." Published March 21, 2011. Available at http://adage.com/article/news/pepsi-blinked-fell-diet-coke/149496/

(A2) "Persuasion Theory." Published September 15, 2003. Available at: http://adage.com/article?article_id=98959

(A3) "Recall." Published September 15, 2003. Available at: http://adage.com/article?article_id=98847

(A4) John Kastenholz and Charles Young. "The Danger in Ad Recall Tests." Published June 9, 2003. Available at: http://adage.com/article?article_id=49312

(A5) Dan Hill. "CMOs, Win Big by Letting Emotions Drive Advertising." Published August 27, 2007. Available at: http://adage.com/article?article_id=120017

(A6) Jeremy Mullman. "How Bud Light Lost Its Sense of Humor—and, Subsequently, Sales." Published August 10, 2009. Available at: http://adage.com/article?article_id=138371

(A7) "Make 'Em Laugh, Make 'Em Buy." Published September 11, 2000. Available at: http://adage.com/article?article_id=56992

(A8) Bill Imada. "Fiber One Spots Serve Humor Without the Stereotypes." Published July 6, 2010. Available at: http://adage.com/bigtent/post?article_id=144809

(A9) Hamish Pringle and Peter Field. "Why Emotional Messages Beat Rational Ones." Published March 2, 2009. Available at: http://adage.com/cmostrategy/article?article_id=134920

(A10) Michael Bush. "Retailers Must Embrace Emerging Media Like Consumers Have." Published July 8, 2009. Available at: http://adage.com/article?article_id=137795

(A11) Michael Learmonth. "iPad's Early Adopters Are Gazing at the Ads—For Now." Published June 15, 2010. Available at: http://adage.com/article?article_id=144440

6 CHAPTER

Segmentation, Brand Positioning, and Defining the Brand Value Proposition

> *"When a customer enters my store, forget me. He is king."*
>
> —John Wanamaker

Lots of people shop at Macy's, but during the recession of 2008 and 2009, Macy's sales fell drastically. With less profit, there was less money for advertising. So given the fewer advertising dollars, but a major need to attract more people into the store, what should Macy's do? As is the case for many brands, a small percentage of Macy's shoppers spend most of the dollars. So Macy's decided to focus advertising and marketing programs on its loyal buyers. Who were these people? Why did they spend so much more at Macy's than others? What was the value of the Macy's shopping experience to them? These questions are the focus of this chapter. We will return to Macy's solution shortly and see how it led to rapid buying recovery for the department store.

Why Segmentation Is So Critical

Of course, advertising is supposed to have an effect on people's attitudes, beliefs, and behaviors. "Wasted advertising" has no effect. It doesn't increase interest or motivation toward the brand, doesn't bring attention to the message itself or, even worse, may cause some negative feelings such as annoyance about being exposed to an advertisement of no relevance.

Paying to deliver pantyhose ads to males is likely to result in wasted advertising. Today it's probably also a waste to deliver that message to women aged 18 to 35. To prevent advertising waste and the attendant loss of marketing dollars, it's critical to deliver the right message at the right time to the right person—someone to whom that ad will make a difference. Being successful at this depends on being able to combine the three functions shown in the Figure 6-1. (1) The first task is to research how consumers can be divided into segments. If this is done right, each segment will have shared characteristics that help marketers craft messages and appeal to those people. There are all kinds of dimensions to use as the basis for the segments: demographics, geography, psychographics, behavior, and product benefits, among many others.

The second task is to determine what the brand can mean or does already mean to these segments. For some people, Macy's is a place to purchase a special gift—get it wrapped and be ensured that the recipient can return it. For others, it's the place to go to purchase most of their wardrobe. For still others, it's a place to sample makeup and fragrances. The

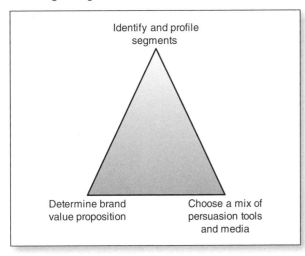

Figure 6-1   Thorson and Moore's Strategic Planning Triangle

"value proposition" of Macy's is quite different for these various segments.

This brand value proposition serves as a guide for designing the content of the advertising. The final job is to figure out how to use advertising, public relations, and promotional activities such as coupons or special shopping days as part of the strategic mix. For the advertising, the agency has to decide what media channels to use, such as television, print, Internet, or mobile devices, to reach the target audience.

As we will see in *Advertising Age*'s coverage of segmentation, the challenges of defining brand value propositions and determining the blend of persuasion tools have become *harder* in some respects and easier in others. It's now harder because there are so many more ways to segment and to reach segments. It's also *easier* because many of the ways of reaching people allow for much tighter, more specific targeting than was the case prior to the Internet and digital devices.

Demographics: The Simplest Segmentation Approach

One of the most common demographics used to segment audiences is age. *Advertising Age* makes the point that appeals to youth work well with those 25 and under, but often also work well with older segments (A1; http://adage.com/article?article_id=98305). It's fun to "think young," as Pepsi proved with its iconic "Pepsi Generation." But being elderly is not glamorous, as witnessed by Depends, long-term care insurance, hemorrhoid remedies, and false teeth adhesives. Of course, it's important to avoid negative stereotypes when appealing to any generation. As mentioned in a previous chapter, demographics also include gender, education, income, family size, and social class.

Psychographic Segmenting

Of course, demographic segmentation has its limitations. People of the same age and income, for example, may have much different attitudes and lifestyles that drive their purchase behaviors. "Psychographics" is a concise summary of how this segmentation procedure works—clustering people by their activities, interests, and opinions (A2; http://adage.com/article?article_id=98836). William Wells created the DDB Life Styles Survey in the 1970s. It was a mail-based questionnaire that helped DDB segment consumers for their clients' brands. The company shared much of the research with scholars, and now Google lists scores of studies of consumer lifestyles based on it.

Another important marketing research tool is the VALS™ Framework. Strategic Business Insights (SBI) is a consulting firm that offers VALS which stands for "values and lifestyles." The service began in 1978 to help advertisers and marketers understand and segment customers based on certain psychological variables. The VALS methodology uses surveys and focus groups to identify those traits and attitudes.

As mentioned above, marketers believe that demographics alone don't give a complete picture of a consumer, but combined with psychological insights, marketers can much more closely tailor and target their messages and predict buying behavior. The VALS typology segments consumers into eight categories described as Innovators, Thinkers, Believers, Achievers, Strivers, Experiencers, Makers and Survivors. The characteristics of consumers in these segments, SBI claims, reveal their interest, ability and desire to buy certain products and services. If you're interested, you can take a trial version of the survey to see if you think your VALS category seems to fit you. (2)

Rance Crain, publisher of *Ad Age*, provides a good introductory example of lifestyle segmenting: the Dunkin' tribe (A3; http://adage.com/columns/article?article_id=140728). As Crain points out, if you are a Dunkin' Donuts consumer, "You're busy, you don't like pretense, you love routine, you're proud to have things to do." This is a clearly defined and simple segment—but now also a segment challenged by the recession. So the company turned to a Dunkin' Donuts Facebook page, where fans can vote for their favorite Coolatta flavor, post photos of themselves enjoying a donut, or share stories about their relationship with the brand.

Much of the lifestyle data today is collected from people's use of the Internet. *Ad Age* explained how important lifestyle and demographic information can be harvested by companies that place markers on people's Internet address so they can track and classify their behavior. *Ad Age* reported that from a segmentation point of view, this is an important tool for advertisers to use in reaching the right person with the right message at the right time (A4; http://adage.com/adnetworkexchangeguide09/article?article_id=136003).

Will Using Behavioral Data Lead to Smarter Ad Buys?

Aggregators and Exchanges Aim to Create 'Liquid Market' Based on Users' Activities, Not Their Locations—but Can They Get Past Privacy Concerns?

As you've seen in Chapter 6, marketers are constantly researching ways to better understand and segment audiences. One of the best ways to predict future behavior is to know about people's previous behavior. This is known as behavioral segmentation. It's valuable because what people say they're going to do (such as in survey research) is often much different from what they actually do.

Tracking behaviors has become easier for marketers who can track and analyze point-of-sale data from electronic cash registers and by observing people's Internet activity. Data companies watch which sites people visit, how long they stay, and what they buy. They analyze, aggregate and segment the data for sale to publishers, marketers and advertisers.

The article discusses a rather complex concept called "data exchanges." How these exchanges work will give you some insights into the challenges and opportunities marketers have today.

Researchers gather behavioral data from websites or from collecting demographic data like census information from offline sources. The researchers sell the information to a data exchange which then resells it to advertisers. Here's the example offered in the article:

> Data exchanges collect information from [the] travel site Kayak about users who are booking flights to Orlando, then sell that cookie-based data to a buyer in the exchange. That buyer then uses that data to go to another party to buy and serve ads (say, for a hotel stay) to those users when they are surfing another site.

Marketers are doing the same thing on social media sites like Facebook, often watching "influencers" and their sharing and uploading behaviors. The article reports that more than 65% of marketers are using or plan to use behavioral targeting and most of them believe this targeting is effective. Also keep in mind that the companies gathering these data are charging advertisers and thus those costs need to be factored into budget planning.

Once again, privacy concerns continue to arise regarding these practices and it's a given that the Federal Communications Commission will be keeping an eye on data exchanges and behavioral targeting both offline and online.

The way this tracking occurs is with cookies and beacons, both of which are basically tracking programs placed on people's computers when they visit a website. A recent *Wall Street Journal* investigative report reported that the fifty most popular U.S. websites (which account for 40 percent of web pages viewed) placed 3,180 tracking files on a test computer. (3) The data that these files collect on people include such things as their favorite sites, favorite movies, name, address, marital status, and number of children. These data are then sold to advertisers (or anyone who wants information on people) for targeting and segmentation. Because the information is so detailed, it is more valuable to advertisers than any of the other kinds of segmentation information they have traditionally used.

Unfortunately, as we discussed in Chapter 4 on ethics, this kind of detailed information gathered from people who know nothing about the observations is a privacy concern. On one side of the argument, the data allow advertisers to segment people accurately with digital messages, which reduces wasted advertising and promotion. On the other hand, just how much personal information do you want marketers to know?

Lifestyle marketing of beer is no joke (A5; http://adage.com/article?article_id=140106). The American beer industry is a 6.9 billion dollar business, and getting the brand value proposition wrong when creating an advertising campaign can lead to the loss of millions of dollars. Those of you who drink beer should check to see if the lifestyle descriptions of your favorite brand matches your profile.

As the American economy tanked in 2008, segmenting changed for advertisers. Many Americans had no jobs, less money, and certainly less security about their economic future. When a sea change like this occurs, segmentation researchers go to work to see what consumers are doing differently. *Ad Age* reported that Campbell Soup studied thousands of consumers to see how their shopping habits changed as their finances were threatened (A6; http://adage.com/article?article_id=138823). Because people started eating out less, this provided a clear opportunity to help often-hurried cooks create interesting meals at home. At the same time, however, store brands became much greater competition to brands like Campbell's, so changes had to be taken into account as the company changed how it communicated with consumers. As the economy recovers, there will have to be more research, because as Melissa Goida, the recessionary consumer in the article, says, "What's happened in the last 18 months is going to leave us permanently scarred. Perhaps it's a good scar, but behaviors have changed; there is ruthless value assessment."

Segmenting by Generation

For some products, generations are an important way of identifying customers. *Ad Age* tackled the central question for many media trying to keep their heads above water: Just what online content will upcoming generations be willing to pay for (A7; http://adage.com/digital/article?article_id=143220)? Newspapers and magazines generally give away all or most of their content for free, so many Americans, regardless of generation, are used to not paying for news. *Ad Age* has written an extensive white paper that looks in detail into what people of various generations are willing to pay for. Youth and young adults aged 12 to 24 (the On-Demand Generation) are the focus of this study. These folks are heavy media consumers—7.5 hours per day—and they have become used to getting the media content that they want—whether by downloading songs, recording television programs on DVRs and playing it back when they want to watch, or getting movies on Hulu. So the question is whether this demand for personal convenience will lead them to be willing to pay for media content. Generational responses to media are then crucially important to the future of these media.

On-Demand Generation Will Pay to Play

White Paper: Though Portrayed as Freeloaders, They Will Shell Out for Right Content

Many people assume that "digital natives" or younger consumers will be very difficult to turn into paying customers for media. However, as this *Ad Age* article reveals, they will pay for certain kinds of highly desirable content. The success of iTunes is an example of a company identifying the right price and the right product to change that "everything-on-the-Internet-is-free" behavior.

That said, the article and a related *Ad Age* white paper report that media companies, advertisers and brands need to understand what kinds media people are willing to pay for and why.

The amount of media time this segment spends is remarkable: almost eight hours a day and continuing to rise. Indeed, almost all segments and age groups are spending increased time with media, offering opportunities to advertisers who understand the interests and expectations of consumers.

Here are some highlights of the *Ad Age* research:

- The youthful segment wants instant gratification. If advertising accompanies other content, it has to download fast and not interfere with consumption of that content. Downloading songs is better and faster that buying in a store.

- The younger groups like free stuff, but they'll pay either in time or money for content they really want. The "price" could be watching advertising as in the Hulu video model or it might be in micropayments such as in the iTunes example.

- Digital natives have little tolerance for low-tech. Most have spent their lives with well-designed technology products that offer good user experiences.

The need for continuing and in-depth research on consumer preferences will be a priority for advertisers as those preferences evolve and change.

Back to Macy's

As noted at the beginning of this chapter, Macy's decided to focus on its frequent buyers. These people use their Macy's credit card so they could be contacted directly. The easier the company made it for this segment to buy, the more they bought. So one important program was their free iPhone app. Credit card holders can use the app to make a purchase, search for products, find a store, find bargains and promotions, and post reviews of products. They can also access Macy's Facebook and Twitter sites directly. So Macy's solved its segmentation problem by combining credit card holders with iPhone users—clearly a group that will have higher income and be more technologically savvy, which turned out to be a powerful segmentation strategy. Macy's reports that for every dollar a customer spends online, he or she spends another $5.70 in the store within the following ten days. In spite of the economic downturn, Macy's has shown one of the best sales strength by this kind of segmentation approach.

Getting Segmentation Right

Segmentation is a powerful tool for advertisers, but it can be used incorrectly (A8; http://adage.com/cmostrategy/article?article_id=135961). Sometimes segmentation efforts can lead advertisers astray. Often, consumer behavior that defines segments changes faster than the advertiser knows, meaning that advertising is being aimed at people who no longer behave in ways they used to. This probably happens most quickly with teen clothing preferences. Recent loss of market share by Gap, Abercrombie, and Aéropostale are good examples. Perhaps more fundamental is the fact that many consumers seek their own information through search. This means they are often much less influenced even by the best segmentation targeting because they know exactly what they want and also know how to get it—at the right time and at the best price. This doesn't mean that segmentation is less useful, but just that the advertiser must track changes in consumer behavior constantly and closely.

Segmentation and the Problems of Privacy and Vulnerable Audiences

In Chapter 4 on ethics and regulation, we saw that how marketers get segmentation information from consumers can threaten people's privacy. We also discussed how marketers who "spy" on consumers and don't tell them they are collecting personal information upset many consumers. In Chapter 4 we also discussed that ads that segment the elderly and children are often accused of negative stereotyping. These issues are also important considerations to segmenting. For example, *Ad Age* reported that advertisers need to keep a close eye on the fairness and behavioral impact of targeting kids (A9; http://adage.com/columns/article?article_id=127144). Since the 1980s when the FTC considered, then declined, to regulate children's advertising, there have been many skirmishes over whether advertising that targets children is appropriate market segmentation. The article reports that advertisers are spending $17 billion a year to advertise to children.

There are many arguments about why this tsunami of messages to kids is damaging. The fast food industry is accused of making kids overweight or obese. Television advertising is accused of creating materialistic orientations in the young, encouraging them to prefer processed foods over fruits and vegetables, and making them couch potatoes, unwilling to entertain themselves and get exercise. This commentary suggests that there are many efforts afoot to try again for government intervention.

Advertisers pay close attention to these problems because so much money is at stake. Although segmentation is a powerful and positive force for getting the right messages to the right people, it is unclear just how segmenting and targeting children should be handled. The current conflict focuses predominantly on fast food and soft drink advertising to children especially when, in the U. S., a record number of children are overweight. Market segmentation can be expected to continue to be a flashpoint of conflict.

Positioning and Brand Value Propositions

Jack Trout and Al Ries introduced the concept of positioning in the 1970s. They suggested that every brand has a meaning or "position" in people's minds, and that the stronger, clearer, and more positive that positioning is, the more the brand will sell. Positioning is closely related to brand value propositions. Trout explains the intimate link between positioning and brands (A10; http://adage.com/article?article_id=102513). The position of a brand in people's minds is the fundamental meaning of a brand. Brand extensions, a changing competitive marketplace, and changing consumer habits all can threaten brand market share. Often the result is the dissolution of formerly strong brand positions. Trout's point is that regardless of how you segment audiences for your brand, the positioning (or value proposition) must remain simple and clear, even though it may have to be modified over time. He says MacDonald's successfully modified its positioning from "fast burgers" to the "world's favorite place to eat." This article helps you understand the critical link in the strategic planning triangle between brand value proposition and segmentation.

Trout's co-author, Al Ries, talks about all the criticisms of the idea that brands must be singularly positioned rather than having different meanings for different segments (A11; http://adage.com/article?article_id=102700). When you first think about it, it seems obvious that a brand will mean different things to different groups of consumers—such as Macy's meaning different things to different types of shoppers. But what Ries and Trout argue is that advertisers must discipline themselves to using the same basic positioning with all segments. They offer the example of BMW—the ultimate driving experience—and point out that whether you drive an SUV, a sedan, or a BMW sports model, the focus is always that the driving experience of all these different kinds of vehicle is the ultimate—and that's why you pay more for BMW.

Ad Age provided a cutting-edge case of how positioning remains a central concept for advertisers (A12; http://adage.com/article?article_id=142848). As GM headed toward bankruptcy, reducing the number of brands and refocusing efforts on those it kept became crucial. Cadillac remained in the line-up but changed its positioning and the advertising agency that created it. The brand returned to a long-ago position "art and science." Check the Cadillac website to see how this positioning integrates the site.

Brand positioning with iPhone applications is an example of where a forty-year-old concept gets connected to a new advertising channel, in this case smartphone apps. Apps associated with brands can be crucial, especially if they match the brand positioning. *Ad Age* offers the twelve best practices to employ when figuring out how to design a brand-focused app (A13; http://adage.com/article?article_id=139233). If you look at how fast iPhone apps developed from the time they were introduced in 2008, it's clear that apps can provide a powerful message-based approach to building brands. Apple opened its app store in July 2008. It was projected that consumers would spend $6.2 billion on mobile apps in 2010, downloading 4.5 billion times from app stores.

Notes

1. Moore, J., & Thorson, E. "Strategic Planning for Integrated Marketing Communications Programs: An Approach to Moving from Chaotic toward Systematic," in *Integrated Communication: Synergy of Persuasive Voices*, ed. Esther Thorson and Jeri Moore (New Jersey: Lawrence Erlbaum, 1996), 135–152.
2. Available at: http://www.strategicbusinessinsights.com/vals/presurvey.shtml.
3. Angwin, J. "The Web's New Gold Mine: Your Secrets," *Wall Street Journal, Weekend Journal*, July 31, 2010, 1–3.

Articles

(A1)   "Age: Representations in Advertising." Published September 15, 2003. Available at: http://adage.com/article?article_id=98305

(A2)   "Psychographics." Published September 15, 2003. Available at: http://adage.com/article?article_id=98836

(A3)   Rance Crain. "Welcome to the 21st Century. Now, Let's Fix the Mess." Published November 30, 2009. Available at: http://adage.com/columns/article?article_id=140728

(A4)   Rich Karpinski. "Will Using Behavioral Data Lead to Smarter Ad Buys?" Published April 20, 2009. Available at: http://adage.com/adnetworkexchangeguide09/article?article_id=136003

(A5)   Beth Snyder Bulik. "What Your Taste in Beer Says about You." Published November 2, 2009. Available at: http://adage.com/article?article_id=140106

(A6)   Emily Bryson York. "Meet Melissa, Your Recessionary Consumer." Published September 7, 2009. Available at: http://adage.com/article?article_id=138823

(A7)   Beth Snyder Bulik. "On-Demand Generation Will Pay to Play." Published April 12, 2010. Available at: http://adage.com/digital/article?article_id=143220

(A8)   Michael Fassnacht. "The Death of Consumer Segmentation." Published April 13, 2009. Available at: http://adage.com/cmostrategy/article?article_id=135961

(A9)   Lenore Skenazy. "Keep Targeting Kids and the Parents Will Start Targeting You." Published May 19, 2008. Available at: http://adage.com/columns/article?article_id=127144

(A10) Jack Trout. "Branding Can't Exist Without Positioning." Published March 14, 2005. Available at: http://adage.com/article?article_id=102513

(A11) Al Ries. "The Battle Over Positioning Still Rages to This Day." Published March 28, 2005. Available at: http://adage.com/article?article_id=102700

(A12) Laura Clark Geist. "Cadillac to Return to 'Art and Science' Brand Positioning." Published March 22, 2010. Available at: http://adage.com/article?article_id=142848

(A13) Kunur Patel. "How Brands Can Build a Successful App Strategy." Published September 23, 2009. Available at: http://adage.com/article?article_id=139233

CHAPTER

Research: The Magic Ingredient in Effective Advertising

"Half the money I spend on advertising is wasted; the trouble is, I don't know which half."

—John Wanamaker, pioneer of the department store concept

John Wanamaker (1838–1922), famed developer of department stores, used advertising to lure customers into his stores. Today he is best remembered for his quote about not knowing which half of his advertising was wasted. Is there a modern research approach that could determine exactly what advertising works and what doesn't?

There have been many attempts, although some advertising experts still consider systematic advertising research a waste of time. [Albert Lasker, who in the beginning of the twentieth century built advertising agency Lord & Thomas, said that when he developed advertising for Kotex, "we didn't have to make investigations among millions of women. Just a few of us talked to our wives." (1)]

Because the digital revolution allows us a much closer look at people's exposure to advertising and what they do as a result, efforts to determine which advertising sells product and which does not are getting more sophisticated.

What do advertisers most want? They want to know if their advertising worked and how much it drove sales or other desired behavior. This chapter is about what research can tell us about advertising effectiveness. With the coming of the digital landscape, research linking advertising directly to effectiveness measures is becoming better and better. We look in detail at some new ways to do this advertising.

So How Much Advertising *Is* Wasted?

Because digital media allow a much closer look at people's exposure to advertising and what they do as a result, the efforts to determine which advertising sells product and which does not are getting more sophisticated. In 2006, Rex Briggs and Greg Stuart published a broad attempt to determine the effectiveness of advertising (A1; http://adage.com/article?article_id=110937). In *What Sticks*, the authors examined thirty-six case studies of advertising from major U.S. advertisers. To their surprise they found that most of the advertisers did not have clear criteria for advertising success, much less a clear idea of whether it was successful. In general they concluded that about 37 percent of advertising worked.

The earlier work of professor John Philip Jones was perhaps more convincing (A2; http://adage.com/article?article_id=84265). Jones collected data showing that there were measureable effects of advertising after just one exposure, thus challenging a long-held belief that to work, an advertisement had to be seen three times. In his book *When Ads Work*, Jones went beyond what is reported in this *Ad Age* article.

> ### One-Hit Or Miss: Is a Frequency of One Frequently Wrong?
>
> One of the biggest and potentially costliest questions that advertisers must answer is how often to run their ads. Traditionally, it's been an article of faith that more exposures to an advertising message are important and that repetition sells.
>
> Surprisingly, Professor John Philip Jones argues that his research demonstrates that "all you need is a frequency of one" for effectiveness. This sounds enticing because, of course, advertisers would love to reduce their media expenditures by scaling way back on placements and your textbook outlines his reasoning.
>
> But as the *Ad Age* article reveals, those decisions are complicated by a number of factors that show the complexity of using and applying research. Here are some of the main points the author makes:
>
> - The product category is important. Jones's research focused on "package goods brands" that include items that are consumable like beverages, food, shoes and other things that you use relatively quickly and must replace. Other products are durable or hard goods like cars, appliances, electronics and furniture that are used over time. Most people don't need to be motivated to buy breakfast cereal, but advertising can nudge them into buying a certain kind of cereal. As the article points out, that's different from attempting to persuade someone that she needs a smart phone to replace her mobile AND she needs a Verizon iPhone. That would likely be a tougher sell and may require more ad exposures.
> - The product's price is a factor. You'll likely mull over a purchase that's costly or riskier in some other way. For example, in buying a new sofa, you may be concerned about the cost and whether your purchase is fashionable or appropriate. Again, more and different kinds of advertising may be necessary.
> - The product's complexity and/or the complexity of the advertising message is another element to take under consideration. Do the product's features and benefits require a lot of explanation?
> - How memorable and effective are your ads? As you know from your own experience, some commercials are compelling and easy to remember. Others, not so much.
> - What are your competitors up to? If you were to reduce your ad schedule, you'd need to keep an eye on how much they're advertising. As you know, promotion doesn't take place in a vacuum and it's possible your messages could be lost among your competitors' more frequent spots.

Based on two thousand U.S. households, Jones calculated that there was a difference in the purchase of seventy-eight brands between those people exposed to an ad and those not exposed to an ad. On average there were 24 percent more purchases of those brands when the household had likely been exposed to the ad. But when Jones broke the data into quintiles from the lowest differences to the highest differences, he truly shined light on the question of "waste." For those brands in the highest quintile, there was a 90 percent increase from ad-exposed to non-ad-exposed households. In the fourth quintile there was a 30 percent increase. In the third quintile there was a 12 percent increase. But in the second quintile there was no difference; and in the first quintile, there was an 18 percent loss. So Jones concluded that 40 percent of advertising is wasted. It is interesting to see how closely this mirrors the *What Sticks* estimate.

This is one of many examples of the power of research. In this instance, we're looking at the question of how much advertising seems to be successful. But what about individual campaigns? It's often suggested that research is most useful for three kinds of insights about individual campaigns:

1. The nature of the target market—what they want and expect, what the brand can do for them, or what need it can fulfill.
2. The effectiveness of the advertisements created (an enterprise called copy testing).
3. Tracking how well sales and market shares are influenced by the ad campaign.

As we've noted, digital media have changed much about advertising research, although some aspects of it remain fundamental. Searching for information on potential audiences for a brand has become much simpler and faster with search engines. Testing what are called convenience samples of audience members (those who choose to respond, in contrast to a random sample, which is far more representative of the audience) has become easy, quick, and inexpensive by inviting people to participate in online surveys. But the Internet has also created many new ways to do research, and *Ad Age* covers these innovations and trends. We take a look at some of them here.

New Research Methods

Shopper Data

In the 1990s research companies introduced "single-source" data in which computers allowed researchers to connect what television ads went into homes (although not whether anyone was watching them) with what those households bought within the subsequent seven days (A3; http://adage.com/upfront2010/article?article_id=143867). Today, significant research dollars flow into tracking (usually with loyalty card programs) what people buy, and then sending them a variety of messages about the brands they buy. These messages can be email, direct mail, or even sales receipt coupons. Shopper buying behavior provides an important component to research that identifies brand targets.

Text Mining

Text mining refers to programs that search through billions of blog or social media messages, searching for comments about products or brands (A4; http://adage.com/digital/article?article_id=138110). Consumers talk online about almost any kind of product. They talk about brands in social networks and provide brand reviews on all kinds of sites. What they say is not influenced by knowing that someone is watching, as they would be in focus groups or interviews. What consumers say provides information about why they buy brands, how they influence each other to make purchases, and even why certain brands are being shunned.

Buzz Tracking

One of the most dangerous things that can happen to a brand is having negative word-of-mouth and social media messages go viral. In April 2009, two Dominos employees posted a YouTube video that featured their spitting on and otherwise insulting pizzas. Millions viewed the video, which was even featured on the network news (A5; http://adage.coverleaf.com/advertisingage/20100111/?pg=3#pg3). Clearly it was critical for Dominos to respond. Listening to what consumers are saying about your brand has become so critical that the Advertising Research Foundation has a published a guide to how to track "buzz."

In-Store Behavior Monitoring

Millions of dollars are devoted to in-store advertising. Walmart, for instance, constantly runs mini-television ads throughout the store. Computer monitoring of mini-video cameras now allow companies to watch consumers as they decide to put a brand in their shopping cart. *Ad Age* reported that one analyst predicts that in-store consumer research will eventually be able to tell us how to increase the likelihood that consumers will buy a brand and then respond to a second personalized suggestion about another brand offered by the same company (A6; http://adage.coverleaf.com/advertisingage/20100315). Such a tactic may help consumers discover a brand, and it may be a perfect fit for their needs. But as noted in Chapter 4, these kinds of practices can easily bump up against privacy issues, particularly if people are not aware they are being watched. Would you want every store purchase you make known to researchers?

They Learned it by Watching You

Shopping aisles now the cutting edge of consumer research and tech

The article warns that this *Ad Age* story will make you feel like a lab rat during your next visit to the grocery store. The reason? Retailers are placing cameras at strategic locations and observing what you put in your shopping cart and how long it takes you to browse and make decisions.

Bringing together several technology capabilities, Kraft Foods is one of the pioneers of conducting real time research in your supermarket aisles.

The company uses what they refer to as "mom cues" that offer emotional in-store motivations to pick up its product. In addition, researchers have found ways to overlay your shopping behaviors with your use of mobile apps and mathematical modeling to figure out what percentage of the product category Kraft is winning.

While this article is several years old, the practices described in efforts to understand your purchase behaviors and motivators are still in use and marketers are constantly looking for new methods to understand shoppers.

Many marketers now use psychophysiological research to gauge consumers' attitudes toward packaging and media formats. Researchers measure heart rate, skin galvanization (perspiration), breathing and eye tracking as well as traditional interviews to evaluate subjects' emotional responses. Campbell's Soups conducted this type of research in redesigning its packaging.

As firms develop new and sophisticated ways to learn about their customers and prospective customers to hone their persuasive techniques, once again, privacy concerns are likely to emerge. This will be a continuing balancing act.

Wiki Sites

Wikipedia-like sites have cropped up on many topics—and advertising researchers can harvest much of the information on these sites (A7; http://adage.com/article?article_id=143636). Wikia.com, owned by Jimmy Wales, who created Wikipedia, hosts wiki sites for television programs, games, and music groups. If you want to see what people have to say about breakfast cereals, relevant comments can be found in scores of wiki sites. Again, these comments are not in response to researcher questions but express what consumers think about brands and thus may be truer reflections of their preferences than advertising researchers have been able to observe in traditional research environments.

On-the-Fly Research

Advertising research takes time. Whether it's research prior to developing the campaign or copy testing or impact tracking, there's constant pressure to get on with things rather than wait around for research results. *Ad Age* reported that the kinds of new research that Internet and computer technology are encouraging let marketers make course corrections immediately during ongoing campaigns (A8; http://adage.com/article?article_id=143887). Often just a small correction can make a big difference to the success of a campaign. Now advertising campaigns can change with the weather or even with what team wins a big game. Where once advertising plans were made for an entire year, now these plans include contingencies for change and how they will be decided. Of course, if an employee claims to be contaminating your pizzas, you have to respond instantly, but on-the-fly campaign planning uses immediate change not just for damage control, but also for positive purposes.

New Metrics of Advertising Impact

How to measure the impact of advertising is a continually changing and controversial discussion (see earlier discussion in Chapter 5). For years, there was disagreement about whether recall or recognition of ads was the more important measurement. Recently, affective responses such as attitude toward the ad and attitude toward the brand have become dominant research indicators. There is also hot conversation about consumer engagement—in the media they consume, in commercials, and even in the brands they buy.

When we move to the Internet, not only does the look and feel of advertising change, but what we measure to see if the advertising works also changes. If the advertising is sent by email, then research is relatively straightforward. How many people respond to the email to get more information or to make a purchase?

Banners, pop-up or pop–under ads, and display ads are generally evaluated by the number of clicks that open them. *Ad Age* has noted that this percentage is small and getting even smaller (A9; http://adage.com/article/digital/online-measurement-16-web-clicking-display-ads/139367). On the other hand, an ad can have an impact, even if the consumer doesn't bother to click on it.

A further complication is that most online advertising is part of a multimedia campaign. How does the advertiser isolate the comparative impact of television ads, magazine ads, and Internet ads in that campaign? *Ad Age* reported that the industry has some new ideas for measurement that sorts out the effects of multiple voices in the same campaign (A10; http://adage.com/mediaworks/article?article_id=138982). The key is to be able to determine how many people are using television and online or online and mobile delivery of ads, or any other combination. Right now Nielsen uses in-home computing to look at audience exposure to television, and does track clicks, but measuring the combination effects of multiple messages is critically important. So far, neither Nielsen nor any of the big U.S advertisers have figured out how to best accomplish that measurement.

Why are people clicking less frequently on online display and banner ads? As you'll see in the article, online research company ComScore suggests that online advertising is associated with more searches on the advertising's brand names, so "search encouragement" might be a reasonable measure to use instead of the number of clicks on ads. (A10) The ads may also lead people to the brand's website, so immediate website traffic can serve as a measure of the impact of display and banner ads.

Many local advertisers are finding that print advertising is more effective at getting people into the store than online advertising, so the loss of clicks on banners and display ads may simply show that in spite of its lower price, online advertising just isn't as effective as advertising in the traditional media. That wouldn't mean that online advertising is, in general, less worthwhile, but it might mean that targeted delivery of messages is more effective than just shooting banner and display ads to everyone.

Ag Age collected suggestions about how online video advertising programs might be evaluated (A11; http://adage.com/upfront2010/article?article_id=143867). These approaches were employed during the World Cup games in 2010. ESPN used one form of this evaluation strategy to tell advertisers whether consumers were following Cup games on ESPN TV, websites, radio, print, and mobile. Another innovation was to look beyond Nielsen in-home television monitoring and gather more data from people who get their television through phone companies or satellite. As has been the case for many years, some advertising companies continue to use psychophysiological measures of brain activity or pupil dilation to try to get at the details of such questions as which spot in the commercial break is the best one for maximum audience attention.

Research in a Strapped Economy

The recession that started in 2007 hit advertising hard. Given the sometimes controversial value of advertising research, spending on research was cut. But what do you do without advertising research? And what advertising research do you cut first? *Ad Age* suggests focusing on most-loyal customers because these consumers buy the greatest proportion of the brand and are therefore more profitable than those who buy less—or simply may ignore the brand (A12; http://adage.com/cmostrategy/article?article_id=136527). It's much easier to get people who eat cheese to buy Kraft Singles than it is to get people who never eat cheese to buy them. And it's easier to get beer drinkers to drink more Budweiser than to recruit those who either don't consume alcohol at all or don't drink beer. The authors also argue that the most important research is copy testing—which is aimed at getting the ad messages right in the first place. They also suggest that although doing survey research with convenience samples online is cheap and fast, the quality of the data might be such that it just isn't worth doing—and it might be wrong.

Are There General Research Truths from Advertising Research?

Ad Age explored what findings from research might apply generally and therefore be a fundamental part of our toolbox for knowing and understanding advertising (A13; http://adage.com/article?article_id=136993). One such finding is that word of mouth (WOM) is effective. Happily for advertisers, the biggest influencer of WOM is advertising. In fact, television advertising, in spite of many challenges (such as prerecording with DVRs and fast forwarding through ads) or the general loss of viewers, especially from network television channels, has not meant that television advertising has become any less effective. Thirty percent of online buzz conversations can be traced to paid television advertising.

Most advertising agencies no longer have their own in-house research departments. They farm their research out to a variety of research providers. Most of these companies have their own specialty measures, which are based on proprietary norms. This means that a significant portion of advertising research never sees the light of day beyond the supplier and the advertiser's use of it. We would know a lot more about advertising research if more of this research were accessible to scholars and analysts. *Ad Age* plays a particularly important role in alerting the field about this proprietary research.

Note

1. Cruikshank, J. L., & Schultz, A. W. *The Man Who Sold America*. Boston: Harvard Business School Publishing, 2010.

Articles

(A1) Jack Neff. "New Book Reports 37% of All Advertising Is Wasted." Published August 8, 2006. Available at: http://adage.com/article?article_id=110937

(A2) Jim Surmanek. "One-Hit or Miss: Is a Frequency of One Frequently Wrong?" November 27, 1995. Available at: http://adage.com/article?article_id=84265

(A3) Andrew Hampp. "The New Ad-Buying Measures That May Be on Tap This Fall." Published May 17, 2010. Available at: http://adage.com/upfront2010/article?article_id=143867

(A4) Michael Bush. "Text Mining Provides Marketers with the 'Why' Behind Demand." Published July 27, 2009. Available at: http://adage.com/digital/article?article_id=138110

(A5) Jack Neff. "Listen Up: You'd Be Foolish to Treat Unsolicited Consumer Opinions as Curse Rather Than a Blessing." Published January 11, 2010. Available at: http://adage.coverleaf.com/advertisingage/20100111/?pg=3#pg3

(A6) Emily Bryson York. "They Learned It By Watching You." Published May 15, 2010. Available at: http://adage.coverleaf.com/advertisingage/20100315

(A7) Edmund Lee. "Wikia's Self-Policing Social-Media Model Lures Big Marketers." Published May 3, 2010. Available at: http://adage.com/article?article_id=143636

(A8) Jack Neff. "On-the-Fly Advertising Swiftly Becoming More Commonplace." Published May 17, 2010. Available at: http://adage.com/article?article_id=143887

(A9) Kunur Patel. "What to Measure? Only 16% of the Web Is Clicking Display Ads But ComScore, Starcom Study Shows Banners Are Still Effective—Especially When Paired With Paid Search." Published September 30, 2009. Available at: http://adage.com/article/digital/online-measurement-16-web-clicking-display-ads/139367

(A10) Andrew Hampp. "Nielsen on Notice: Industry Demands a Meatier Metric." Published September 14, 2009. Available at: http://adage.com/mediaworks/article?article_id=138982

(A11) Andrew Hampp. "The New Ad-Buying Measures That May Be on Tap This Fall." Published May 17, 2010. Available at: http://adage.com/upfront2010/article?article_id=143867

(A12) John A. Quelch and Katherine Jocz. "Research May Be Costly, But It's Critical." Published May 11, 2009. Available at: http://adage.com/cmostrategy/article?article_id=136527

(A13) Jack Neff. "Future of Advertising? Print, TV, Online Ads." Published June 1, 2009. Available at: http://adage.com/article?article_id=136993

8 CHAPTER

Advertising and Promotion Management and Planning

Peter Krivkovich, CEO of the Cramer-Krasselt (CK) agency, was furious following the 2007 Super Bowl. According to Krivkovich, the online job search firm CareerBuilder put the account up for review based only on a *USA Today* poll of the public on the day after the game spots—and CK didn't finish in the top ten. When an account is "up for review" it's an ominous sign for an agency that it's likely to lose the business. Krivkovich quit the CareerBuilder account, using some very salty language, before his agency could be fired. As *Ad Age* reported from Krivkovich's in-house memo:

"They wanted us to make them famous; we did that in spades (brand awareness up by 64% . . .). But the TV ads did not make the top 10 in the *USA Today* poll—a poll that everyone knows doesn't mirror results (see the continuing Bud sales decline for one!)—they just told us they will do a creative review."

"'Wait a minute,' we said, 'what about the incredible growth that is going on, the shares, the revenue, the awareness, the two best internet sites ever, the massive buzz, etc, etc.? What about all of that? That's huge.'"

"'Yes,' they responded, 'but you [C-K] didn't get the top 10 in the *USA Today* poll.' 'Hold on . . . we crushed every possible business metrics/barometer for success. Out of all the metrics and polls, it's all about this one? You have to be F'ing kidding, right!?'" (A1; http://adage.com/agencynews/article?article_id=115130).

CareerBuilder fired the agency that replaced Cramer-Krasselt and took all the business in-house, meaning that a department within the company was assigned to handle the company's advertising.

In this incident you can see the drama and complexity of the persuasion business. For most of us, the Super Bowl is a fun event, as much for the entertaining ads as the game. But for companies and agencies, this game is deadly serious and the stakes are huge. One 30-second spot costs millions of dollars just for the media time during the game—and that doesn't include the millions it usually costs to produce many commercials. And there are no guarantees of success.

A myriad of management decisions led to this event. We can't predict whether CareerBuilder did the right thing or come up with a definitive view of whether Krivkovich was justified in his testy reaction. But the incident throws the complexities of advertising and promotion into sharp relief.

Imagine that you could persuade anyone to do anything. That would be powerful stuff. But the fact is, persuasion is difficult. People usually know when somebody is trying to persuade them and they're wary, watchful, and resistant. Contrary to what many people think, advertising can't magically persuade anyone—and ads usually don't result in a customer purchase. All kinds of intervening factors can get in the way, including consumers' economic situations, time resources, competitive products, the overall economy, and changing cultural and technological trends. In addition, products and services must fill people's needs and desires. No matter how brilliant advertising and promotion might be, no one can sell you parakeet food if you don't own a pet bird or have a need for parakeet food.

Advertisers and marketers are constantly seeking ways to persuade audiences that their product, service, idea, or candidate will fill a need better than the competition, and to overcome consumers' indifference and defenses to advertising. In this chapter, we'll discuss different perspectives on planning, advertising, promotion, and manager's choices in organizing their employees, appeals, and objectives.

Planners generally have three main goals: to bring about awareness, usually of a new product or new product features; to effect attitude change, such as encouraging a positive attitude or belief about a product or brand; or to encourage desired behaviors—usually a purchase. The easiest goal to achieve is a gain in awareness and the most difficult involves actually moving someone to action. And of course, having the customer take action is what marketers most want.

At the macro level, managers need to set marketing objectives that will yield the biggest revenues and profits. In "Setting the Right Business Goals for Ultimate Success." Pringle and Field argue that "soft" objectives such as audience awareness don't result in optimal returns as opposed to "hard" objectives such as quantified profit levels or share growth (A2; http://adage.com/cmostrategy/article?article_id=136405).

Let's briefly explore this. At first blush, increasing the numbers of products sold by a certain amount would seem to be a good, quantifiable business goal. But sales alone aren't enough. If costs of a campaign promotion are too high or if aggressive price discounting drives the increased sales, then both profits and the brand's reputation can suffer. "Share growth" in this article refers to the brand's percentage of all products in its product category—it's a measure of how the brand is doing against the competition. "Value-share gain" as described in the article is a measure that shows how much a marketing plan or campaign improved the product's performance vis-à-vis the competition.

According to Pringle and Field, achieving improved value share hinges on two factors: first, lowering consumers' price sensitivity, the point where they will no longer buy because the cost is perceived as too high. The second and related factor is the goal of increasing consumers' liking for the brand based on perceptions of its quality as compared with other products in the category.

Media fragmentation and an explosion of media choices are among the factors making strategic planning more complex. Traditional mass media news and entertainment programming don't deliver the big audiences of the past, and consumers are able to select from an increasingly rich array of choices. Digital content, search marketing, mobile information and ads, and social media are among the huge disruptors of media and advertising. Traditional business models for media such as broadcast television, newspapers, and even advertising agencies are under tremendous financial and structural stress.

The good news? The planning, research, and analytical tools available offer the opportunity to home in on customers with greater precision, helping them solve problems and take advantage of opportunities. We're able to tailor our offerings and our messages much more closely to narrower segments and even individual customers.

Our optimal goal in most situations would be to foster a relationship that is as close as we can get to a one-on-one interpersonal conversation, rather than a one-to-many message that may or may not connect with the target's needs and interests. Lindsay refers to this as a "conversation economy" and "a message strategy that connects brand meaning with search habits and accommodates ongoing contributions that can range from casual conversations to consumer-generated content." "How to Develop the Right Communications Strategy for a Conversation Economy" offers insights into the advertiser–customer relationship and how managers think about their planning processes. (A3) This article focuses on a particular strategy that many marketers are putting in their planning mix. It describes the increased use of bloggers and social media by marketers (influencer program) (A3; http://adage.com/cmostrategy/article?article_id=139989).

How to Develop the Right Communications Strategy for a Conversation Economy

Begin With the End in Mind: What Message Can Drive Sufficient Revenue to Support a Business Model?

Sometimes a new term or label can capture the essence of a change. In this case, the author uses the words "conversation economy" to capture how marketers are changing in response to cultural and economic pressures.

In your textbook, we refer to the "interruption" model of advertising that was prevalent in the past—you'd be watching or listening to a program and an advertising message would force you to take a break from whatever you were doing. While the interruption model is certainly not over and indeed, is often very effective, some new approaches are proposed.

The author of this article thinks marketers' new requirement is to market and foster conversations—conversations among consumers and those who are selling products.

But what's the best conversation strategy? Clearly it's not simply through having a web or social media presence. You need to be worthy of others' time and interest to engage in the conversation.

The writer argues that in order to enable a productive marketing conversation, it's important to use all of the available tools: search optimization, media, message and consumer contributions. She points out that it's important to start with a clear idea about what message and action you're looking for, how it might be deployed across many platforms, and if it's "scalable," meaning can it be effective with many more consumers and geographic areas. And it's important to remember that traditional media like TV can be very important components in spurring the conversation.

As the article suggests, your marketing conversation will always be in an environment with many other commercial and personal conversations. As with conversations with other individuals, you'll enjoy those that involve your interests, attitudes, passions and ideas.

Similarly, Gustav Martner, the owner of the Swedish agency Daddy (recently acquired by mega-agency Crispin Porter), commented, "The philosophy we share is that everything is interactive. It should all be a dialogue between brands and consumers." (A4; http://adage.com/article/agency-news/crispin-porter-buy-digital-ad-agency-daddy/137228/).

"We call it social influencer relationship management," said John Bell, managing director 360 Digital Influence at Ogilvy PR. "We provide them with new content and values they can pass along to their readers to get them involved in the program."

The strategy described in "How Marketers Use Web Influencers to Boost Branding Efforts" describes an evolution of a long-used approach in locating cool and influential consumers that others are likely to look toward as leaders and trendsetters (A5; http://adage.com/article/digital/marketers-web-influencers-boost-branding-efforts/141147/). Influentials don't just include fashionistas or style leaders. For particular segments they can include moms, music aficionados, sports fans, or even social media commentators such as http://mashable.com/ and Diva Marketing on Bloomberg at http://bloombergmarketing.blogs.com/.

You can probably see the evolution in thinking about how to connect with customers and you're probably thinking that advertising and marketing as professions sound pretty daunting. And they can be. But they can also be enormously rewarding when your team creates and executes a great strategy that gets results and leaves customers satisfied.

And that's just the beginning. The planners need to pull together budgets, work with the creative team to develop compelling messages, work with media buyers to develop an effective media schedule, and so on. The planners also need to pay attention to potential problems. For instance, what if some individuals or groups see a potential health or social problem with a product? What risks are we taking and what rewards can we realistically expect?

Ad Age continues to report on the evolution of the business and explore how agencies and firms are always testing and refining their strategies of persuasion. You'll hear more about this later—but let's start by thinking about how you as a marketing executive might try to promote a new high-caffeine drink—let's call it Zoopp—to a youthful audience. Research has told you that the best target market for this new brand is young men aged 15 to 30. What kinds of decisions are you going to have to make? Here are a few:

- What's the marketing environment? What kinds of historical factors do you need to take into consideration?
- Who should be on the marketing team and what skills and capabilities do they need?
- What's my budget for the campaign?
- What's the overall economic climate?
- What's the competition for Zoopp?
- How big is the audience?
- What persuasion tools do I have at my disposal?
- What media do my audience use a lot and prefer? Games? Facebook? Mobile? All?
- What messages are likely to be effective?
- Would events, music, or other channels be good vehicles for the brand?
- Is my brand traditional and conservative or edgy and out there?
- How will I measure success?

Putting Together a Plan

Executives and planners try to systematize dealing with these questions through a management process. Three important foundational items should be at the heart of your planning.

First, put the consumer or prospect first. Who are you trying to reach and what does she care about? In "Why Customer Centricity Is More Than a Marketing Trend," Michael Radigan points out that "'customer centricity' means focusing on the customer you're talking to rather than on the product you're trying to push" (A6; http://adage.com/article?article_id=140761).

This is important because one of the most difficult challenges for professional persuaders is getting out of their own way. This is a particular problem for managers who tend not to interact with customers on a day-to-day basis. Most people tend to think about what they want or like instead of what the customer wants. The customer wants advertising to show him how to be wealthier, cooler, safer, happier, healthier, more popular, and more attractive. The persuader's job is to show how the benefits of the product or service will solve problems and make things better for her. No one buys anything without being able to envision a benefit.

Second, use evidence-based decision making in pulling your plan together. Gather the best intelligence you can afford in terms of time and resources. We talked about this in the chapter on research. Research helps you establish realistic expectations and allows you to establish measureable objectives. Even the best research can't give you every answer, but good information vastly increases your chances of succeeding. The most successful firms and marketers foster an environment that rewards evidence-based decision making.

This doesn't mean that researching and planning should be slow and bureaucratic or that objectives are set in stone. The best plans are flexible and can make midcourse corrections as needed. In "On-the-Fly Advertising," Jack Neff highlights how marketers are using new tools to make midcourse corrections or additions (A7; http://adage.com/article?article_id=143887). If you watched the 2010 Super Bowl, you might have noticed that only a few hours after the game, the New Orleans Saints' Drew Brees was on television in Dove's "victory shower" commercial.

Of course, Unilever, Dove's manufacturer, didn't know which team would win the Super Bowl. So behind that quick turnaround lay months of planning, including arrangements with four different players and shooting commercials featuring both Brees and the opposing quarterback.

Agencies and marketers are seeing the need for contingency plans and organizing for agile and adaptive responses. Social media feedback and other analytics can tell a marketer how audiences are responding and which spots or campaigns appear to be most effective in a kind of real-time research.

Neff also points to Scotts Miracle-Gro, the fertilizer, pesticide, and feed company that used local weather reports to trigger changes in ad messages for radio spots and other media. As an example, in 2009, the Scotts Company knew which localities were experiencing flooding and it was able to deploy ads in Birmingham, Alabama, and Atlanta, Georgia. Company researchers knew that flooding increases problems with fire ants and so were able to promote their products at exactly the right time for optimum sales.

A Scotts manager who had been at Campbell's soups brought the weather-driven strategy with him: spots for soup are likely to be more effective on cold winter days. Similarly, mild spring days are a great time for fertilizer companies to reach garden-conscious consumers. (1)

Third, understand the difference between strategies and tactics. Too many media managers, marketers, and firms become transfixed by the latest technology, innovation, or media trend. Marketers and their clients race headlong into social media marketing, advergaming, mobile ads, iPad apps, blogs, or other tactics without thinking clearly about what their target audience prefers and uses. Certainly, these approaches will often be exactly right for selected consumers and brands. But it's the planner's job to figure out if and when these tactics are likely to be effective.

We define *strategy* as the logic behind one's approach to consumers in a campaign or promotion. O'Guinn and colleagues refer to strategy as "the mechanism by which something is to be done. It is the expression of a means to an end." (2) For example, let's go back to Zoopp. Assume that our research tells us that the most promising Zoopp segments are dedicated gamers, especially those who play massively multiplayer online games (MMOGs).

With this insight into their desire for games and their associated entertainment and social benefits, we can develop a strategy that builds on that affiliation using a variety of tactics: social media fan pages, sponsorships, contests, and sweepstakes might be some of the specifics we'd choose. Going straight for tactics, whatever they may be, is shooting in the dark. You may end up with a lucky hit, but the odds are against you. Planning, backed up by research and thoughtful analysis, can help you win.

Here's a brief outline of the step-by-step process real marketers and account planners use to increase their chances for success:

1. Overview or statement of the marketing/advertising problem or opportunity
2. Situation analysis including competitive analysis and research findings

3. Statement of goals (the overall direction of the effort or campaign)

   For example: *Launch Zoopp in three geographic areas, positioning it as a delicious energy drink.*

4. Statement of objectives (specific, time-bound, measureable)

   Improve market share of Zoopp in three targeted geographic location by x percentage within six months of launch.

5. Statement of strategy. As mentioned above, the research showed that a strategy of linking Zoopp to the target audience's obsession with MMOGs would be successful. Here's a potential strategy statement:

   Use game-based experiential and competitive strategies to create awareness among the target demographic and link to the gamers' lifestyle.

6. Tactics. Tactics are the activities you undertake to execute the strategy. They'll include the media choices, integrated promotional plans, creative messaging, and the like. You'll likely have several to many tactics in order to execute each strategy. Tactics that might follow from this strategy statement above:

   • *Sponsor an MMOG special event.*

   • *Create additional publicity through sweepstakes and celebrity promotions.*

   • *Create a game-based website built around Zoopp.*

   • *Create a viral video featuring Zoopp as a crucial component to a gamer's success.*

   Many other potential tactics might be used in support of the game-based strategy.

7. Assessment and evaluation. In this phase, we return to our measurements and identify whether we are achieving the objectives specified in the plan. (3)

Both agencies and clients need to become more agile and adaptive according to Malbon and Andersen in "How Marketers Might Change to Deliver 'Adaptive Branding'" (A8; http://adage.com/article?article_id=139789). The authors suggest that the era of bureaucratic and often slow, top-down communication is over, and executives will need to organize their companies differently in order to move as fast as they need to in a technology-fueled and interactive marketing world. This will often require networked and team-based work that can be reconfigured quickly depending on the marketing opportunity.

How Marketers Might Change to Deliver 'Adaptive Branding'
Seven Ways Clients' Structure, Skills and Approaches Must Shift to Succeed in an Accelerated Environment

The authors highlight the issues of successful branding in a fast-moving digital age. Of course, agencies are talking about how to be more agile and adaptive, but unless clients move in that direction nobody will accomplish their marketing goals. Maintaining relevance is more and more challenging in a fragmented media world and with audiences whose attention spans are short.

Traditionally, marketers attempted to plan every detail of campaign and product launches looking to create polished and perfect executions. Today, marketers must stay abreast of cultural and consumer trends while keeping a close eye on competitors' moves.

As you probably know, software companies often release early or "beta" versions of new programs that may still have gaps or flaws. The authors of this article suggest that agencies must adopt a "continuous beta" mentality, ready to jettison underperformers and quickly reinforce support for winners. While the advertising business has always been fast-moving, the new media world is calling for even greater acceleration using constant testing, real-time feedback, and technology-fueled learning.

As the business environment changes, leadership must change as well. Hierarchical (top down) decision-making as is common in many firms is likely not going to be agile enough to meet the challenges.

The authors offer seven recommendations for empowering more agile and adapting branding:

1. Consumer intelligence (research) at the center.

   Knowing your customer has always been crucial and today's technology gives us access to many different types of data. However, marketers need to adopt "agile measurement" that identifies the most important information for a campaign's purposes and is able to avoid information overload with data that may be interesting but not truly applicable to the problem or opportunity at hand.

2. Marketing as a catalyst for change within the broader company.

   The article suggests that companies should reorient themselves around the marketing organization and function. Marketers often lead in developing knowledge and expertise of new technologies and cultural practices. Their insights can benefit the whole company in innovating products and services.

3. The networked organization.

   The "networked organization" is one that is flexible, fosters teamwork, and fosters an atmosphere of collaboration. This type of cultural change encourages working across traditional functional areas to bring the best talent and outcomes to every project.

4. Brand leaders as curators.

   A curator is someone who supervises and selects content for certain needs. This article suggests that not only do marketers need to adapt and coordinate, they need to be curators of existing content and campaigns. Translated, this means that it's okay to borrow and learn from materials created for different activities, though of course, you wouldn't steal ideas from other people or organizations.

5. Reframing investment timelines.

   Budgets are realities in any environment and the new agile/adaptive world marketers inhabit now is no exception. What's different is that the traditional planning periods, fiscal years and deadlines will need to become more fluid and opportunistic.

6. To fail is to learn.

   Many of the world's best companies insist that they not only tolerate failure, they expect it sometimes as part of encouraging risk-taking. When marketers are bringing campaigns out faster and often with lower expenses, they'll also have to be ready to make course corrections and changes on the fly. As mentioned above, this will likely involve ongoing research efforts, not just research before launching communication programs.

7. The time is now.

   The "Great Recession" of 2008/2009, like other times of great economic stress, didn't simply reduce revenues for companies and agencies. Instead, the article argues, this has led to "a complete reset for the industry." This means that the smartest players are streamlining and making their work more efficient, upgrading their skills and hiring for a different kind of advertising future.

Developing a marketing and advertising plan requires a combination of evidence, data-driven decision making, and imagination. Although good advertising planning and budgeting relies on solid research and a hard-eyed approach to numbers, planning also needs the creative leaps that are often referred to as artistic rather than scientific.

The best planning and execution results in advertising and marketing that delights, surprises, and sells. It helps brands connect with people and shows them how your product and service is meaningful to them. Bob Garfield writes that most people don't think of advertising as art, but he believes great advertising is just that. He writes: "Add to the brief list one more [campaign]: the "True" campaign from Budweiser, which from the beginning has been a shrewd and trenchant observer of human behavior" (A9; http://adage.com/article?article_id=49835).

You may recall that the True campaign most famously featured beer-drinking men saying "Whassup?," a line that almost immediately became a pop culture phenomenon. Garfield writes, "The object here is to connect Budweiser's allegedly "true" beer to all that is true in the preoccupations of its target audience."

Although this is a brilliant creative execution by the agency's writers and designers, it's also something more. It's grounded on a powerful understanding of what engages the target segment. These understandings are based on research and emerge from a thoughtful and insightful strategy. In short, great campaigns and ads come out of great management, planning, and creativity.

Notes

1. Mahoney, S. "Scott's Miracle-Gro Amps Up Local Marketing," *MediaPost*, March 19, 2010.
2. O'Guinn, T. C., Allen, C. T., & Semenik, R. J. *Advertising and Integrated Brand Promotion.* Mason, OH: South-Western Cengage Learning, 2009.
3. Inspired by Pfeffer J., & Sutton, R. I. *Hard Facts, Dangerous Half-Truths, and Total Nonsense: Profiting from Evidence-Based Management.* Boston: Harvard Business School Publishing, 2006; Cutlip, S. M., Center, A. H., & Broom, G. M. *Effective Public Relations.* Upper Saddle River, NJ: Pearson, 2006; Shimp, T. A. *Advertising Promotion and Other Aspects of Integrated Marketing Communication.* Mason, OH: South-Western Cengage Learning; and O'Guinn, T. C., Allen, C. T., & Semenik, R. J. *Advertising and Integrated Brand Promotion.* Mason, OH: South-Western Cengage Learning, 2009.

Articles

(A1) Jeremy Mullman. "Cramer-Krasselt Resigns as CareerBuilder's Agency." Published February 23, 2007. Available at: http://adage.com/agencynews/article?article_id=115130

(A2) Hamish Pringle and Peter Field. "Setting the Right Business Goals for Ultimate Success." Published May 4, 2009. Available at: http://adage.com/cmostrategy/article?article_id=136405

(A3) Marsha Lindsay. "How to Develop the Right Communications Strategy for a Conversation Economy." Published October 27, 2009. Available at: http://adage.com/cmostrategy/article?article_id=139989

(A4) Emma Hall. "Who is Daddy and Why Did Crispin Want it?" Published June 11, 2009. Available at: http://adage.com/article/agency-news/crispin-porter-buy-digital-ad-agency-daddy/137228/

(A5) Michael Bush. "How Marketers Use Online Influencers to Boost Branding EffortsBrands Like Kodak Are Taking a Targeted Social-Media Approach." Published: December 21, 2009 Available at: http://adage.com/article/digital/marketers-web-influencers-boost-branding-efforts/141147/

(A6) Michael Radigan. "Why Customer Centricity Is More Than a Marketing Trend." Published November 30, 2009. Available at: http://adage.com/article?article_id=140761

(A7) Jack Neff. "On-the-Fly Advertising Swiftly Becoming More Commonplace." Published May 17, 2010. Available at: http://adage.com/article?article_id=143887

(A8) Ben Malbon and Greg Andersen. "How Marketers Might Change to Deliver 'Adaptive Branding.'" Published October 20, 2009. Available at: http://adage.com/article?article_id=139789

(A9) Bob Garfield. "Garfield's AdReview: Budweiser's Latest 'True' Spot Proves Advertising Can Be Art." Published April 7, 2003. Available at: http://adage.com/article?article_id=49835

9
CHAPTER

Advertising Planning—An International Perspective

In the 1960s, American companies were hungrily eyeing the Japanese market. Based on the company's market analysis, General Mills wanted to introduce its American-style cake mixes to the Japanese. That analysis showed that the Japanese were open to Western products, had the money to spend, and liked American-style sponge cakes. In addition, General Mills partnered with a big Japanese food company. What could go wrong?

It turns out, a lot could go wrong.

The first glitch was that most Japanese homes at the time didn't have ovens—they mostly used rice cookers. Undeterred, General Mills created a cake mix that baked up nicely in the rice cookers found in almost every Japanese home. Initially, sales were good but soon fell flat. The reason was a powerful cultural fact revealed in focus groups. For most Japanese at the time, rice itself had meanings beyond mere food. It was a food that had spiritual implications and connoted purity and national pride. Many Japanese felt that baking cakes in their rice cookers sullied the purity of rice in both taste and tradition. Today, as in the past, rice for the Japanese is part of their national identity. (1)

Despite globalization and the increasing internationalization of trade and media, cultural differences among nations and even in different regions of the same countries are significant. Advertising and brand promotion are rooted in culture and values.

By culture, we aren't referring to high culture references such as opera, symphonies, or Shakespeare. Rather, we're looking at how things are done in our social worlds. For example, Valentine's Day in the United States is freighted with expectations about romance. In U.S. culture, men usually give gifts to loved ones in their lives and are obliged to live up to certain romantic standards. In some other cultures, women are the gift givers. In this chapter, we'll discuss the challenges of international marketing and advertising and the cultural and social factors that can make or break campaigns.

Break Me Off a Piece of That Soy-Sauce Bar

The Nestlé company carefully considered cultural differences when it introduced a snack bar in Japan. Kohzoh Takaoka, Nestlé's executive vice president for Japanese operations, realized that the Japanese would need their own flavors of the Kit Kat bar (A1; http://adage.com/globalnews/article?article_id=144397).

Nestlé determined that limited editions of the snack in Japanese-friendly flavors, including green tea, wasabi, and miso, would be highly appealing in part because of their scarcity value. Those flavors likely would not appeal to most Western audiences, but Nestlé's experience in Japan highlights how well researched and localized products and appeal can be keys to success.

A crucial element of marketing and promotion success is a deep understanding of how and why consumers buy. We don't buy things simply because we have functional needs to fulfill, though that certainly is part our motivation. We buy things to express ourselves, to communicate with others, to make ourselves more appealing, sexier, popular, safer, and wealthier. As Grant McCracken writes, "the consumer is an individual in a cultural context engaged in a cultural product." (2) In other words, we buy to demonstrate our place in society, our values, our spirituality, and our belief systems.

When you're buying a new pair of flip-flops or a soft drink, you're assigning cultural meanings and imagining how using the product will make you feel or how it will make you appear to others. "Consumer goods, charged with cultural significance, serve as dramatic props and meaning sources," according to McCracken and many other social observers. Many advertised and promoted products are commodities, which means that the products are not significantly different from their competitors. Even where some differences exist they may not be compelling enough to encourage a consumer to buy one brand over another. Advertising is an effort to attach story and meaning to a product and to invite consumers to be a part of that story.

Does that notion sound too extreme? Consider how cultures conceive of gender roles. Following is dialogue from a "Seinfeld" episode in which the character George mistakenly picks out a pair of women's glasses:

JERRY: They're ladies' glasses! All you need is that little chain around your neck so you can wear 'em while you're playing Canasta . . . .

KRAMER: May I have one of those, *Madam*?

GEORGE: Madam? What are you calling me madam for?

KRAMER: They're ladies' glasses. Now look here, see it's right here: Gloria Vanderbilt Collection.

GEORGE: He sold me ladies' glasses!

George is clearly outraged and humiliated that he bought women's glasses even though the differences in the frames are likely indistinguishable from frames labeled as "for men." Gender roles are just one of the ways products are connected to cultural connotations.

Clearly, different cultural contexts will lead to much different meaning-making for consumers, particularly in global marketing efforts. The ways we clean ourselves and our clothing are brimming with cultural meaning. You probably haven't given a lot of thought to laundry and laundry products—but they comprise a $41 billion dollar business. Those kinds of numbers get marketers' attention. As *Ad Age* reports, in "The Dirt on Laundry Detergents around the World," "Every half hour 7 million people in the world wash their clothes with Unilever products, and 6 million do so by hand" (A2; http://adage.com/globalnews/article?article_id=144398).

Unilever's research showed that even when we compare Westernized countries like the United States to European countries, we find that washing habits, technologies, and preferences are very different and very resistant to change. Laundry, it seems, is powerfully influenced by culture, and beliefs about appropriate cleaning products and procedures are passed down from generation to generation.

Go Global or Go Local? Research and Local Knowledge Matter

Some consumer brands such as Coke or Ben & Jerry's are so powerful that a broader and less locally focused strategy can work. Could it work for a brand like Sprite? Sprite, one of Coca-Cola's brands, launched its first global campaign called "The Spark" in the summer of 2010. The product launch featured new packaging, a digital-first media plan, and numerous musical and mobile tactics (A3; http://adage.com/article?article_id=142073). Its target was teens in several international markets. "Spritea" is a new product created to appeal to many Chinese. Although at the time of this writing it was only offered in China, the Coca-Cola Company thinks Spritea has a bright global future. Firms not only need to adapt their advertising strategies, but also often need to modify their own products or create new ones.

It may be useful to think of international marketing along a continuum of strategies and creative executions. At one end of the continuum, *globalized campaigns* send very similar messages to all of the international target audiences they're seeking. Ads they use will have similar strategic approaches, similar taglines, and similar creative executions. At the other end of the continuum are *localized campaigns* that try to narrowly target consumers and customize the strategy and messaging for a country, region, or city. (3)

The decision to choose a globalized or more localized approach is complex. On the one hand, a global strategy with less customization and tailoring for each market can be cost effective. On the other hand, some product categories just don't seem to benefit from this strategy. As shown in the Neff article (A2), people's distinctive tastes and lifestyles are particularly important when marketers are selling such personal care products.

Despite the difficulties, many companies attempt to use campaigns that can be rolled out in multiple countries and regions. The contrasting strategies of Nike, Anheuser-Busch, and McDonald's for the 2010 World Cup reveal how each company positioned its efforts on the continuum between global and local in "World Cup Kicks Off Marketing Games on Epic Scale" (A4; http://adage.com/article/news/world-cup-kicks-marketing-games-epic-scale/143889/).

Nike's "Write the Future" campaign was an effort to use different types of media developed and deployed so they were understandable and persuasive on a global scale (A5; http://adage.com/mediaworks/article?article_id=144640). The campaign included a three-minute video of famous international soccer stars and a huge interactive billboard on a South African skyscraper. Taking a cue from the worldwide popularity of social media sites, fans were invited to post a headline that "writes the future" of their favorites on Facebook or other sites.

As we discussed in Chapter 8, marketers seek ways to engage consumers with a message as opposed to simply showing a message to passive viewers as in traditional television commercials. Nike sought to get engagement by selecting some of the social media messages sent in by fans and displaying them on the massive interactive billboard's LED screen. Fans whose messages were chosen received a personal notification that included a picture of their headline on the billboard along with an animation of their favorite player.

Similarly, Anheuser-Busch moved toward the global side of the continuum with "Budweiser United" emphasizing its traditional long-term support for sports of all kinds. One of its tactics was highly global in that it created a digital reality program showing fans from thirty-two countries living together.

McDonald's World Cup sponsorship approach was far more localized and experiential with a sweepstakes that connected kids and players using various digital programs. McDonald's developed different strategies and tactics for each market. Dean Barrett, McDonald's senior vice president for global marketing, said that the company believed the focus on local stores was critical: "There are always some things that we can do globally, and digital is something that can be global. But the reality is that the World Cup is team-driven and local-market driven." (A4)

Management Matters

Even the world's savviest international marketers don't create winners every time, but the best have learned from their own missteps. As Jack Neff points out, Walmart, Procter & Gamble, and Unilever have stumbled in some international efforts but have adjusted their strategies (A6; http://adage.com/article?article_id=137296). Walmart has shifted its global marketing from a clear division between domestic and international efforts by establishing a unit within its international division that "looks to cross-fertilize ideas between the U.S. and the 14 other countries" in which it operates. P&G has generally been quite centralized but is emphasizing local markets giving employees experience in local markets and global units.

The article makes it clear that management's approach to international marketing is a key to success. For example, some managers opt for a top-down approach in which decision making resides at a central office. From there, they hope to create and control strategies that will be successful in multiple countries with minor adjustments. Many others, such as the companies mentioned above, divide their business efforts into "global category units" that handle positioning and branding, and have other units develop the execution of strategies, often within the local country. The differences among these very successful international companies are instructive in showing that a single strategic approach won't work in every situation or for every product. Neff cites Paul Polman, who's worked in three major consumer product companies. Polman says that no single model will be successful in international marketing.

The potential pitfalls we find in domestic campaigns are even more challenging in global efforts. Among these challenges are so-called best practices that can lead to one-size-fits-all "solutions," the pursuit of fads and the media flavor of the week, an inward focus and lack of engagement with social and technological changes, complacency based on current profitability, and measurement fallacies where companies do not have reliable metrics to evaluate their success. Managers are often tempted to go into markets that are currently thought to be exciting and offer a lot of potential while ignoring international opportunities that may offer lower growth but fewer problems in executing campaigns.

It's Not about You

All of us tend to be more comfortable with our own ways of doing things, and we tend to like people who are more like us. This is called ethnocentrism. Everyone involved in product development and campaigns must constantly remind themselves that they are not the target audience and what they prefer or think is interesting, dramatic, or funny may not appeal to those in different countries.

An example from the Middle East emphasizes this. In "U.S. Military Goes Native in Afghanistan Ad Push," *Ad Age* reported that the U.S. military decided that an important part of its Afghanistan strategy should be communicating the benefits of building a more peaceful nation (A7; http://adage.com/globalnews/article?article_id=143223). Lt. Col. Allen McCormick, a former P&G marketing expert, needed to find themes that resonated with Afghan culture and didn't offend citizens' sensibilities. He also needed to identify effective media in a country where few media vehicles exist. McCormick's research-based strategy involved using a local agency and a combination of posters, radio, and television ads. The campaign featured themes drawing on the Afghan tribal culture and love for children—boy children, that is. He found that in advertising in the male-dominated Afghan culture, the babies all had to be boys, and the ad copy focused on males. This strategy would likely offend many Westerners, but it proved to be popular among many Afghans.

All of the advertising executions were in the Dari or Pashtu languages.

On the other hand, some elements of Western popular culture can be successful even in regions with profound cultural differences. Afghan media entrepreneurs created a hit television program called "Afghan Star," a show inspired by "American Idol." Though it may be inspired by "Idol," "Star" had to make some significant changes to be acceptable to its audience. For example, producers needed to emphasize that if someone's favorite singer lost, it was not good to seek revenge.

A Global Consumer in Our Future?

Ad Age asked Nike's vice president of global brand and category management what he, as a global marketer, spends the most time worrying about. This is what Trevor Edwards said:

> Making sure we're staying ahead of where we think the consumer is going. Are we making sure our teams are enabled to do creative in the best way they possibly can? At Nike, the value of what the marketing organization brings to the company is embedded in everything. We spend much of our time thinking about how the landscape is changing and how we have to change our brand in the context of that landscape (A8; http:// adage.com/article/cmo-strategy/global-cmo-interview-trevor-edwards-nike/144359/).

The Global CMO Interview: Trevor Edwards, Nike

'Ideas Rule. Ideas Are in Charge'

Ad Age regularly consults leaders in corporate marketing, agencies and research companies. Nike Corporation is famous for it's 360° marketing—a concept that captures the idea that the best marketing touches customers and prospects at many different points in their media and "real life" activities.

Their successes are driven by innovation and a focus on ROI, or Return on Investment. Return on investment is defined in different ways, but for our purposes here it means how much money your company gets back from its investments in marketing and promotion. This is a crucial concept whether you're working in local or international venues. If you pay $5 million for a campaign, you clearly want to get more than $5 million in attention, sales or whatever metric you're using.

Nike has pioneered success with innovative products like the Nike Plus that's integrated with customizable real-time iPod tracking capabilities for average or premier athletes. It's also renowned for its ability to develop and distribute content that online viewers want, thus avoiding much of the high priced media placements typical of television. By the way, Nike's global marketing budget is measured in billions, not millions of dollars.

In the article, Nike's Trevor Edwards doesn't call Nike's approach a strategy, but it's unquestionably strategic as we define it in this book. According to Edwards, the team "starts with a story to tell consumers and then decides which media or technological tools will be best suited for it."

Importantly, the company doesn't start with a tactic like "let's use social media to tell the story" or even "let's use a global versus local strategy." Rather, they have a company process that allows for input from their employees around the world to help develop better strategies and thus better tactics.

Edwards also points out that some of their ideas and campaigns don't work so well and that those are learning processes as well. But he emphasizes that rather than having strict corporate control of messages and the flow of campaigns, "ideas are in charge." Nike also emphasizes that the many agencies they employ around the world are team members whose ideas are taken seriously: "Our model focuses really on getting the best message to that consumer in the most holistic way."

Changing consumers, culture, technology, and media have always been part of the marketer's world. Today, the pace of change is accelerating. As we've seen technology permeate even the most remote areas of the planet, geographic distinctions have become less important. The Advertising Research Foundation reported many similarities among the world's young people with regard to their social lives and media use and with the role of technology in their lives. (4)

Can we anticipate the emergence of a global consumer? And what will it mean to global marketing? Consider the phenomena of social networking, communication, shifting cultural values, and digital technologies. Facebook founder Mark Zuckerberg had the attention of hundreds of international marketing executives at the Cannes Lions International Advertising Festival when he said that the firm was halfway to its goal of one billion users. Social networking site Orkut.com has more than 20 million users and Japan's mixi.jp has 28.6 million users. Millions of social networkers are sharing similar motivations for going online (A9; http://adage.com/cannes2010/article?article_id=144628).

Even language is part of the picture. *Globish* is a term coined by a former IBM executive, Jean-Paul Nerrière, who observed that in many countries non-native English speakers developed a small but useful store of English words. Using globish, they could communicate not only with English speakers, but also with others who speak different languages. (5)

Marketing researchers once believed that an inclination toward collectivism or putting the needs of the larger group ahead of individual needs and benefits was a hallmark of many Asian societies. Western societies were more individualistic and focused on a person's personal success and preferences. Advertising was seen to reflect these differences in its appeals. (6) However, more recent research, such as that by Li and Li in 2009 (7) and

Zhang and Shavitt in 2003, (8) shows that advertising appeals by both Eastern and Western multinational companies were mainly individualistic, perhaps blurring the differences between cultures.

In the same vein, *New York Times* columnist Thomas Friedman wrote that the world is becoming flat. (9) By that, he means that globalization has lowered barriers for individuals and companies to connect with each other. Through communication and connections, organizations of all sizes can conduct business all over the world. As "A World of Inspirational Problem-Solving, Savvy Brands and Smart Marketing" shows, from the consumer standpoint, people are able to see and experience products and services from distant places. They are also able to envision themselves leading different lives (A10; http://adage.com/globalnews/article?article_id=144404).

A World of Inspirational Problem-Solving, Savvy Brands and Smart Marketing

Sure, the Global Economy Is Challenging Right Now, but These Companies Have Found Ways to Make Their Brand Messages Work Harder to Reach Consumers

You've probably heard of some of the World's Hottest Brands reported in an *Ad Age* white paper about 30 brands that are successful at every level—local, regional, national and global.

Nando's is a chicken restaurant in the "fast casual" category, Azul is a Brazilian airline, and H&M is the Swedish high fashion/low price retailer that some refer to as offering aspirational luxury goods. Each offers brand positions that differentiate them from their competitors: Nando's focuses on local markets and a cheeky sensibility, Azul on excellent customer service and H&M on sticking to its trendy image in every market it enters.

The goal of the white paper wasn't to identify the biggest or highest market value brands, but rather to identify those that offer "great marketing lessons [that] can happen in your backyard . . . or halfway around the world."

Even in tough economic times, some companies continue winning ways.

In the car category, BMW exploited the Chinese consumers' interest in upscale transportation with its' "Joy" campaign. You may have heard of Zipcar's model of car sharing, a kind of easy short-term rental plan within a city for those who don't own their own cars or don't want to use them. Their technology-enabled model lets people reserve and check out cars on their smart phones.

India's Tata Nano isn't an iPhone application but a tiny urban car with a tiny price tag ($2000) and a tiny footprint (10 feet from front to back.) Some say it's the car of the future.

Computer maker Lenovo has used creative promotional ideas in China's "smaller" markets, third-, fourth- and fifth-tier cities that still have millions of people but are much smaller than the huge urban centers of Guangzhou, Shanghai and Beijing. The company often used free movie screenings to attract potential customers.

We mentioned H&M, but other retailers made the list by offering trendy quality at great prices. Others have a different approach—charging premium prices for high fashion footwear like Havaianas flip-flops.

Other brands that *Ad Age* highlighted were noted for their smart or lucky timing—Nintendo's Wii using technology to make gaming more like "real" gaming.

All of these brands are very different from each other in their features and consumer benefits as well as the widely different strategies they use. The similarities? Here's how *Ad Age* described it: "Despite economic downturns and increased competition, the power of a well-managed brand endures."

For instance, PC maker Lenovo identified the huge potential markets in rural China by targeting smaller cities that offered a market of some 700 million customers who were likely ready to buy their first computers. Lenovo's strategy was to show free movies with Lenovo ads and to use the venue as a way to demonstrate its interactive PC.

In many parts of Africa, mobile devices have gone mainstream. In the Democratic Republic of the Congo, cell subscribers numbered 9.3 million in 2008 or fifteen users per one hundred citizens. By 2010, numbers of subscribers had grown to fifty users per one hundred citizens.

These marketing campaigns certainly sell PCs and mobile services. But they also introduce new "world-flattening" elements into the lives of millions. New PC owners will begin to have similar experiences to those living in more developed and technology rich areas. Of course, some people don't think these changes are necessarily good. Critics point out that consumerism and technology have mixed benefits and may damage traditional cultures, family cohesiveness, and fragile natural environments.

Regardless of one's attitude about the juggernaut of multinational marketing and globalization, these trends are crucial elements in many firms' success. If the trends are creating a new global consumer and marketing environment, the winning companies will be those who are agile and adaptive.

Notes

1. Knight, G. "Marketing Blunders by American Firms in Japan," *7th Marketing History Proceedings*, Vol. VII (1995). Available at: http://faculty.quinnipiac.edu/charm/CHARM%20proceedings/CHARM%20article%20archive%20pdf%20format/Volume%207%201995/175%20knight.pdf

2. McCracken, G. "Advertising: Meaning or Information," *in Advances in Consumer Research Vol. 14*, ed. Melanie Wallendorf and Paul Anderson (Ann Arbor: Association for Consumer Research), 121–124.

3. O'Guinn, T. C., Allen, C. T., & Semenik, R. J. *Advertising and Integrated Brand Promotion*. Mason, OH: South-Western Cengage Learning, 2009.

4. Uyenco, B. "Circuits of Cool," presentation to the ARF Emerging Media & Youth Councils. January 31, 2008. Available at: http://s3.amazonaws.com/thearf-org-aux-assets/downloads/cnc/emerging-media/2008-01-31_ARF_EM_YM_BUyenco.pdf

5. Chotiner, I. "Globish for Beginners," *The New Yorker*, May 31, 2010.

6. Han, S.-P., & Shavitt, S. "Persuasion and Culture: Advertising Appeals in Individualistic and Collective Societies," *Journal of Experimental Social Psychology* 30 (1994): 326–350.

7. Li, H., & Li, A. "Internet Advertising Strategy of Multinationals in China: A Cross Cultural Analysis," *International Journal of Advertising* 28, no. 1 (2009): 125–146.

8. Zhang, J., & Shavitt, S. "Cultural Values in Advertisements to the Chinese X-Generation: Promoting Modernity and Individualism," *Journal of Advertising* 32, no. 1 (2003): 23–33.

9. Friedman, T. (2007). *The World is Flat*. New York: Farrar, Straus and Giroux.

Articles

(A1) Normandy Madden. "Break Me Off a Piece of That Soy-Sauce Bar." Published June 14, 2010. Available at: http://adage.com/globalnews/article?article_id=144397

(A2) Jack Neff. "The Dirt on Laundry Trends around the World." Published June 14, 2010. Available at: http://adage.com/globalnews/article?article_id=144398

(A3) Natalie Zmuda. "Sprite Launches 'The Spark,' Its First Global Ad Campaign." Published February 11, 2010. Available at: http://adage.com/article?article_id=142073

(A4) Jeremy Mullman. "World Cup Kicks Off Marketing Games on Epic Scale." Published May 17, 2010. Available at: http://adage.com/article?article_id=143889

(A5)   "'Write the Future' Writ Large." Published June 23, 2010. Available at: http://adage.com/mediaworks/article?article_id=144640

(A6)   Jack Neff. "Walmart, P&G, Unilever Learn from Their Mistakes." Published June 15, 2009. Available at: http://adage.com/article?article_id=137296

(A7)   Laurel Wentz. "U.S. Military Goes Native in Afghanistan Ad Push." Published April 12, 2010. Available at: http://adage.com/globalnews/article?article_id=143223

(A8)   Jeremy Mullman. "The Global CMO Interview: Trevor Edwards, Nike 'Ideas Rule. Ideas Are in Charge.'" Published June 14, 2010. Available at: http://adage.com/globalnews/article?article_id=143223

(A9)   Rupal Parekh. "How Facebook Plans to Get to 1 Billion Global Users." Published June 23, 2010. Available at: http://adage.com/cannes2010/article?article_id=144628

(A10) Ann Marie Kerwin. "A World of Inspirational Problem-Solving, Savvy Brands and Smart Marketing." Published June 23, 2010. Available at: http://adage.com/globalnews/article?article_id=144404

The Creative Strategy of Advertising Messages

> *"Creative without strategy is called 'art.' Creative with strategy is called 'advertising.'"*
>
> —Jef Richards, Advertising Professor,
> University of Texas-Austin

Since 2007 Pepsi has been attempting to sell Pepsi Max, a full-flavored, zero-calorie soda designed for men (A1; http://adage.com/article?article_id=145505). The first creative strategy was "Wake Up, People!," which positioned the soda as an energy drink without calories. The strategy was changed to "I'm good!" in a 2009 Super Bowl commercial, along with the name change to Pepsi Max and dropping the word *diet* from the can. Unfortunately, by late 2009 the brand had achieved only a .4 percent market share. In 2010, a third strategy was born.

The idea is that for real men, Pepsi Max has a better full-bodied taste than Coke Zero. In other words, it's a direct comparison of Pepsi Max with Coke Zero. In the newest commercial (http://www.youtube.com/watch?v=EX0fmBHiZy40) a Coke Zero driver is shown sampling a Pepsi Max and then realizing that the Pepsi Max driver is videoing him for YouTube. There's great parody use of 1974's "Why can't we be friends?" by 1970s rock group War.

Pepsi Max's search for a successful creative strategy shows just how costly failing to get it right can be. In fact, it's estimated that the company spent $55 million in 2007 alone attempting to launch the first creative strategy.

In this chapter we connect everything you've learned so far with the crucial step of figuring out what a commercial is going to say: that is, the creative strategy. In Chapter 11, we connect what your ad is going to say with how you're going to say it—your creative execution. As Texas advertising professor Jef Richards points out, creative has to be linked with strategy or you're an artist, not an advertising professional.

Do Real Men Drink Diet Soda?

Creative Strategy

In previous chapters we've looked at how advertising works, the value of research in understanding consumer behavior, the impact of different kinds of ads, and how people think about, develop attitudes toward, and decide whether to purchase products. We also looked at the value of segmenting audiences so that the cost of advertising isn't wasted. In this chapter, we'll link these understandings with the concept of creative strategy. The first step toward a creative strategy is to write a creative brief (or "creative platform").

The brief varies somewhat for different agencies, but this is always the starting point. To keep things simple, we'll assume that there are six components to the brief: product specification, target audience, brand positioning, objectives, creative strategy, and creative execution.

Product specification is everything you know about the product. Let's say it's cranberry juice. Where are cranberries grown? How do they taste? Are there health benefits? What is the cost of cranberry juice relative to other juices? Many advertising greats have talked about how important it is to learn everything you can about a product in general and in the brand specifically.

You've already read about targeting audiences. You can't sell to everyone so you have to decide who your best prospective customers might be and talk specifically to them.

We've also talked about brand positioning. What's unique about your brand? In what ways is it better than competitors? What benefits does it offer your target consumer?

Objectives are what you want the consumer to do in response to the ad. If you think back to the theories of advertising (Chapter 5), you'll remember that there are lots of possible responses you might want. Getting the customer to run out and buy the product would be an excellent response. But you also might want the consumer to remember the brand name or something about the brand. You might want the consumer to feel good when she thinks about the brand. You might want her to recognize it when she sees it at the drug store. You might want her to pay attention to the commercial when it comes on television.

These first four stages of the brief have now set you up to figure out what you want the advertisement to say about the brand. This should be as specific as possible. In our Pepsi Max example, there are two benefits: taste and zero calories. Focusing on features like these is called a "benefit" or "promise." The unique selling proposition for men is: "Pepsi Max has powerful taste that men like and they don't have to worry about the calories."

Taste and calorie benefits are physical. The brand also has emotional benefits—it's intended to be special for men. A product can make you feel special because it's just for people like you; it can reduce fear, create good feelings, make you laugh, or make you feel nostalgic. The advertisement can promise you social outcomes, such as increased status, connectedness with others, or general social approval. It can appeal to your desire to be sexually attractive or look younger. It can appeal to your senses of taste or touch or smell. Other examples of benefits are guarantees that may lower your risk in making a purchase or higher quality construction that might mean better performance or a longer life for the product. There's just about no end to the kinds of benefits that a brand can provide to a target market. The key is that your research leads you to choose the best benefit as the centerpiece of your creative strategy.

One of the most interesting things about advertising is following how advertisers come up with creative strategies and seeing how effective these strategies turn out to be in our highly competitive marketplace. New positioning also brings new creative challenges. You've probably seen many ads for Corona beer and you may automatically associate that brand with good times at the beach—the major creative setting for its fun in the sun approach. As *Ad Age* put it, Corona tried to be "an ocean vacation in a bottle" (A2; http://adage.com/article/news/corona-light-ditches-beach-commercial/226928/). But in 2011, the company's marketing executives conducted research that seemed to indicate a change of location would benefit the brand. The new approach? Corona Extra will continue to be beach-related but Corona Light will go for a new more urban vibe and a stand-alone creative campaign.

CHAPTER 11

Telling a Story That Showcases the Creative Strategy: Creative Advertising Executions

Budweiser is an iconic American beer, second in U.S. sales only to Bud Lite. InBev NV, a Belgium-based beer company, bought Anheuser-Busch (A-B) in 2008 with an eye to economize by increasing brewery efficiency and reducing Anheuser-Busch's historically large investment in advertising. The company decided to use the 2010 World Cup games to introduce Budweiser worldwide (A1; http://adage.com/globalnews/article?article_id=142987). Although Bud has a large market share in the United States, Canada, and Europe, it is much less a player in South America and Africa.

A-B increased its sales and marketing costs 10 percent in the second quarter of 2010, probably most of which was invested in the World Cup effort. First, Budweiser bought exclusive rights to beer sales and signs in the soccer stadiums. Then it created an online reality show in which a representative from each of the thirty-two countries in the Cup competition lived together. When their team was eliminated, they got knocked off the "island." And finally, there was an extensive television advertising campaign "Budweiser United" in which the creative concept was that Budweiser represents an aspirational, can-do spirit worldwide.

The *Wall Street Journal* reported details of the success of this program. (1) In contrast to downward sales trends by most of the other major beer brands, the company's volume was up 2.1 percent compared with the previous year. And in Brazil, volume was up nearly 14 percent. It was a massive marketing/advertising investment, but these initial results show that the creative executions worked as they were strategically designed to do.

From Creative Brief to Commercials

This chapter examines how the content of advertisements themselves is created to tell the brand story for which research, advertising theory, and target research have provided a foundation. The creative strategy (Chapter 10) integrates that background and completes the creative brief. The step from creative brief to advertisements is where some magic steps in.

Many students choose advertising because they want to be involved in this magic step: execution of great creative advertising. But as we've seen, most advertising wizards emphasize that making creative ads has to be connected with deep understanding of how advertising works, the consumers you want to target, and results from smart research—interwoven into a clear, well-founded creative strategy. This chapter examines how, after research and theory show the way and the creative brief maps the terrain, the content of advertising is created.

As media choices have multiplied with the invention of many new media and electronic devices, the opportunities for creative messages that link intimately with these new media have vastly expanded. Advertising professionals are creating new kinds of ads delivered through many different devices and media, including smart phones, websites and e-readers. Strategists combine ads in these new media with ads in traditional media to create comprehensive campaigns that aim to reach consumers wherever they might be.

Old Navy's 2011 campaign replaced the Supermodelquins, taking the retailer in a new creative direction with a music focused approach and the tagline "real music, real people." It includes original music under the Old Navy label and is linked to the song-identifying app Shazam. Shoppers can open Shazam while browsing Old Navy's commercials. The app identifies the sign and redirects the shopper to a mobile e-commerce site featuring outfits from the video. (A2; http://adage.com/article/special-report-digital-conference/traction-navy-s-music-shazam-ad-campaign/226882/).

Traction for Music-and-Shazam Ads That Replaced Old Navy's Supermodelquins

How Some Mobile Apps Are Creating the Real Interactive TV

Old Navy was pleased to see early reaction to its new and mostly social media-based campaign that creatively connects original music with a mobile app, coupons and an e-commerce website, all created by the agency CP&B.

The company knew that its primary customers were young women who watched popular television programs such as "American Idol," "Glee," and "Grey's Anatomy," but also multitasked on their computers or other devices. Research showed that these audience members also used mobile devices to take pictures, email, and text with their kids. Music and entertainment were shown to be important to them. A related study revealed that at the time, 86% of viewers used mobile devices while watching television. Again, you can see the relationship between knowledge about the consumer, media platforms and creative executions.

Let's look at each element in turn. Old Navy produced four original songs and when a user watching an Old Navy online commercial opened the Shazam mobile app, the app recognized the tune and opened an e-commerce site showcasing the fashions in the commercials. Another element involved sales promotion with coupons for the first 1000 people opening the app with an offer for free jeans.

Shazam, a song recognition app, benefited from the significant increase in downloads resulting from the campaign. The Old Navy song featured on the first commercial was so popular that it became number one on the Shazam site over the very popular Lady Gaga.

Old Navy and CP&G reported that they were happy with the increases in commentary about the campaign on Twitter and Facebook. Partner television programs also showed increases to their websites.

"We struggle with social return-on-investment, like everyone," according to Old Navy's top marketing officer. Amy Curtis-McIntyre said "I'm not declaring it a transactional phenomena [sic], but from a brand standpoint, our customer is on Facebook and Twitter and, in terms of brand health, seeing those spikes is only good for us."

Message Creativity or Creativity in the Selection of the Medium?

In the Budweiser campaign described above, you can see that the effects of the choice of media (e.g., online reality show versus the Budweiser United television commercials) and creative execution are both important to sales success. It's difficult, as we've seen, to separate creative message impact from creative selection of media to carry those messages. Many advertising experts have argued that to reach targeted consumers effectively, the medium and the creativity of how that medium is used are most important. Megan Mcilroy suggests, based on research from the Starch Research company, that for magazines, loyalty to the magazine itself has little impact on responses to the ads (A3; http://adage.com/article?article_id=121728). It seems to be the creative power of the ads themselves that leads them to be remembered and successful in encouraging a purchase. It helps if people already feel positive toward the brand being advertised. This same research shows that greater engagement with a website means embedded ads get a less positive response. This suggests that, at least for magazines, the impact of medium of choice is less than the impact of the creativity of the messages themselves.

It's the Message, Not the Medium

GfK Starch Study: Print, Web Ads Have to Work Harder to Persuade

The debate continues: what's most important in a persuasive message, the medium or the message? The research reported in this article uses thousands of readership studies in an effort to understand the effectiveness of print and online advertising.

When you're reviewing research reports of any kind, it's important to look at the criteria the researchers used to develop their findings.

This Starch study based its findings on users' reports on these elements: 1) how much the ads were remembered; 2) how much readers were involved with them; and 3) whether the ad directly influenced consumers to buy something.

The findings were somewhat surprising regarding print magazines. Fans of the magazine weren't found to be necessarily engaged with its ads. So even though a reader might enjoy the articles and even be a subscriber, that didn't seem to translate to advertising engagement. The main motivators to get readers to notice and read an ad in a print magazine appeared to be their interests in the product category and the brand.

How does an advertiser use this information? The report offered the suggestion that advertisers should try to locate publications whose readers already like the brand or product category and who are known as product category "influentials" or thought leaders.

That may sound like an obvious conclusion. But many people might assume that loyalty or liking for a publication would translate to greater affinity to most of its advertising. That didn't appear to be the case.

The study also found that the creative copywriting aspect was crucial for getting readers to buy. It concluded that if advertisers are looking for people who don't already like the product or product category and if they can encourage readers to actually read the copy, those readers are far more likely to take action.

In the online environment, Starch made other rather counter-intuitive findings. The research showed that when people have a high level of engagement with a website and when an Internet ad is highly stimulating, it's more likely that they'll have a negative reaction to the ad. Starch suggests that online advertisers have only a brief window of opportunity to get users' attention and offer relevant information and product benefits. As Phil Sawyer, senior VP of Starch said, "The most important thing is to get their [visitors'] attention quickly and to tell them the benefit immediately. There is no greater violation [on the part of] Internet advertisers than to assume that the Internet visitor has plenty of time on his or her hands."

There's significant evidence that online advertising, whether banners, pop-ups, or display ads, often is not effective. Millward Brown, a well-known advertising research company, provides some likely explanation for this relative ineffectiveness. The company studied 170,000 online ads (A4; http://adage.com/digital/article?article_id=139795). It found that creative visual features, plus clear links with creative strategies, were better predictors of people's attention to and memory for online ads than were media variables such as being on pages carefully targeted to particular kinds of consumers. Dynamic Logic, an online advertising research company, pointed out that when advertisers approach the web, they may be so focused on behavioral targeting that they fail to make sure that good creative has gone into those ads. It seems clear that even the best-targeted web pages won't overcome poor creative and strategic features of the advertising on those pages.

Does the Creative in an Ad Have to Be *about* the Product?

Another creative controversy is whether an advertisement has to be about the product (A5; http://adage.com/article?article_id=58817).

Most of you have seen the Benetton "Colors of Benetton" ads (http://www.hyphen magazine.com/blog/2008/05/asian-baby-united-colorbenetton-ad), which are not about clothing at all but about human issues. Ten years ago, the company created a controversial campaign about capital punishment. As *Ad Age* publisher Rance Crain points out, famed advertising guru Jerry Della Femina called the campaign tasteless and ineffective. Italian adman Oliviero Toscani, who created the campaign for Benetton, retorted that all clothing is the same, and therefore attempting to "sell" it to consumers is hopeless. Instead, his approach was to gain attention for the brand by talking about salient human rights issues.

Although Toscani would disagree, our knowledge of advertising theory suggests that if Benetton ads worked at all, it is because consumers associated the brand positively with the human rights issues. In other words, the advertising works through an emotional appeal. Although Benetton's "Colors of Benetton" has not been in the news lately, the company continues both its issues advertising and its clothing sales with six thousand stores worldwide.

Advertising Appeals: A Potpourri

We now turn to the nuts and bolts of creative executions. We can caterize the type of appeal that advertising uses as its central creative element in a number of ways. Table 11-1 shows some of the most common examples of advertising appeals, although it's important to note that great creativity in advertising messages will often blend these types. As we discovered in Chapter 5 about advertising theories, strong evidence exists that emotion is a uniquely effective appeal. But great creative can employ any of the approaches in Table 11-1. The website Creativity-Online.com offers hundreds of examples of advertising, often accompanied by information about how successfully the ads changed behavior. We can't look at examples of every single one of the creativity appeals, but let's look at a handful of particularly effectives ones. [Creativity-online is another *Ad Age* property but is different from *Ad Age* on campus.]

Nike's Greatest Ad Ever

Nike modestly described its three-minute ad that ran during the 2010 World Cup as its "greatest ad ever" (A6; http://adage.com/article?article_id=144010). The article describes the interesting, arousing, feel-good ad "Write the Future," which included shots of plays that changed outcomes in historical ways (watch the ad at http://adage.com/article?article_id=144010). The photography is good, there are some fun surprises, and the ad is three times longer than the typical television commercial. Recall tests in the United States and Britain showed that indeed Nike had the highest mind share of any World Cup advertising (A7; http://adage.com/mediaworks/article?article_id=144611). (Mind share is measured by asking people what ads they remember from the World Cup games they watched.) Emotion is a powerful appeal, and it's clear that this groundbreaking ad produced a powerful response among soccer fans.

Old Spice Humor

Ad Age spotlights creative work each week. In May 2009, one selection was the Terry Crews Old Spice 15-second commercials (watch three of them at http://adweek.blogs.com/adfreak/2010/04/old-spice-blows-up-more-terry-crews-spots.html). What emotions do

Table 11-1	Common Advertising Creative Appeals

Lectures	Social appeals
Demonstrations	Status
Transformations	Affiliation
Comparisons	Social approval
Problem solution	Sex appeals
Slice of life	Youth appeals
Spokesperson/Endorser	
Testimonials	
Emotional appeals	
Humor	
Fear	
Poignancy	
Feel good	

these ads this stimulate in you? A lot of the buzz about these commercials indicated that lots of consumers found them funny. Others found them just plain vulgar—but notice how closely each commercial links the humor component with the main selling feature of the deodorant—that is, how long it stops odor.

Sex for All Kinds of Products

Ad Age provided some examples of the long tradition of using sex to sell products (A8; http://adage.com/article?article_id=78473). Underwear seems to be a natural to use sex appeal while shampoo seems somewhat more a stretch. Much has been written about the cultural meanings of the representations of women in these ads (see Chapter 4). And ads have to use sexuality carefully, both to avoid the wrath of regulators and to avoid insulting consumers.

Smoking, Fear, and Disgust

A common appeal in anti-smoking ads is the use of fear, or as in the ad "Artery," a strong dose of disgust. Watch the ad at http://www.youtube.com/watch?v=lEc-Rsv9pMc and read about it in "Graphic Anti-smoking Ad Registers High Impact in U.K." (A9; http://adage.com/article?article_id=39796). You've been warned—the disgust factor is strong.

Does Prize-Winning Advertising Sell Effectively?

You're now equipped to explore online advertising, watch television, and read magazines and newspapers to identify and analyze creative executions. It's not always easy to guess the creative strategy behind these ads, but if you're exposed to an ad, it's likely targeted to your age group and perhaps also your gender. One last question we need to consider in this chapter is whether award-winning ads also sell product. The effectiveness of award-winning creativity has been controversial throughout the history of advertising. You've probably noticed that American advertising tends to be more tightly focused on strategy and sales, whereas a lot of international advertising, particularly from Europe, is much more creative in the sense of messages as art rather than as advertising. Will the ads that are creative enough to win awards actually sell products? In case studies of more than two hundred campaigns, those ads that won awards were far more likely to show higher effectiveness in terms of such significant indicators of success as market-share growth, sales, profits, and return on investment (A10; http://adage.com/article?article_id=144942).

> ### IPA Report: Ads that Win Awards Are 11 Times More Effective
>
> *British Advertising Group Says Study of VW, Budweiser, Cadbury and Others Argues for Quality Over Cost*
>
> Agencies and marketing executives are always under pressure to deliver more for less money and, as this article argues, this cost-cutting pressure may jeopardize the quality and results clients receive. This can include both short and long term campaign success.
>
> In addition, agencies' quests for advertising awards have always been somewhat controversial as it's unclear whether awards for brilliant creativity are related to campaigns that are successful from the standpoint of increased sales or other metrics.
>
> The United Kingdom's Institute of Practitioners in Advertising (IPA) conducted a study that sought to link measures of advertising awards for creativity to business success,

essentially arguing that clients shouldn't sacrifice quality for cost. Of course, this professional organization has a vested interest in greater client spending, but the study is interesting nonetheless.

The IPA analyzed 213 case studies from firms such as Cadbury, Volkswagen, Budweiser, Honda, Audi and Orange. It found that the award-winning campaigns were "11 times more effective than campaigns that do not win creative awards."

The director general of the IPA further claimed that cuts in procurement or what clients allow agencies to spend to produce campaigns will ultimately have negative impacts on effectiveness. (Often firms' procurement employees receive extra compensation for cost containment or reductions, including what's paid for marketing and advertising efforts.)

According to the marketing consultant who conducted the research, the study examined various measures to judge effectiveness such as growth in market share, sales, profits, return on investment, and emotional appeals.

The report concludes that the campaigns garnering awards are a good investment and that "the link between creativity and effectiveness is driven by two important factors: the emotional communication model favored by the most creative campaigns, and the much greater 'buzz' effect that creativity engenders."

You should also notice that many of the prize winners in the case studies use emotional appeals, further verification of just how compelling emotional appeals can be.

Note

1. Miller, J. W. "Anheuser Gets Boost from World Cup," *Wall Street Journal*, August 13, 2010, p. B4.

Articles

(A1) Jeremy Mullman. "A-B's Digital Reality Show Showcases World Cup." Published March 25, 2010. Available at: http://adage.com/globalnews/article?article_id=142987

(A2) Kunur Patel. "Traction for Music-and-Shazam Ads That Replaced Old Navy's Supermodelquins." Published April 7, 2011. Available at: http://adage.com/article/special-report-digital-conference/traction-navy-s-music-shazam-ad-campaign/226882/http://adage.com/digital/article?article_id=139795

(A3) Megan Mcilroy. "It's the Message, Not the Medium." Published November 2, 2007. Available at: http://adage.com/article?article_id=121728

(A4) Kunur Patel. "Online Ads Not Working for You? Blame the Creative." Published October 20, 2009. Available at: http://adage.com/digital/article?article_id=139795

(A5) Rance Crain. "Jerry and Oliviero Duke It Out Over What's Vital in Advertising." Published April 10, 2000. Available at: http://adage.com/article?article_id=58817

(A6) Jeremy Mullman. "See the Soccer Spot Nike Says Might Be Its Best Ad Ever." Published May 20, 2010. Available at: http://adage.com/article?article_id=144010

(A7) Jeremy Mullman. "Nike's Not a World Cup Sponsor, but It's Stealing the Show." Published June 22, 2010. Available at: http://adage.com/mediaworks/article?article_id=144611

(A8) Pat Sloan. "Underwear Ads Caught in Bind Over Sex Appeal." Published July 8, 1996. Available at: http://adage.com/article?article_id=78473

(A9) Hoag Levins. "Graphic Anti-Smoking Ad Registers High Impact in U.K." Published April 12, 2004. Available at: http://adage.com/article?article_id=39796

(A10) Emma Hall. "IPA Report: Ads that Win Awards Are 11 Times More Effective." Published July 14, 2010. Available at: http://adage.com/article?article_id=144942

12
CHAPTER

Creative Copywriting

> *"Good ads sell stuff."*
>
> —Steve Kopcha

In big-time marketing, there are few things on earth as powerful as the right strategy at the right time, brilliantly executed. "This Bud's for You" was a campaign with the perfect theme line embedded within perfect executions of a perfect strategy. It is a classic example of not just countering, but actually one-upping the excellent battle plan of a tough competitor.

Miller Brewing had been eating into Budweiser's market share with its brilliant "Miller Time" advertising strategy, helped along by tons of Philip Morris money (Morris was Miller's parent company at the time). This new campaign was a reversal of its previous "Champagne of Bottled Beer" strategy. It repositioned Miller High Life as the gritty, workingman's beer of choice when the day is done. It was hugely successful.

Then Budweiser switched dramatically from its long-standing white-collar beer approach to an overt blue-collar strategy. This new strategy was not just historically different; it was a reversal of its previously successful approach. And it was superior to Miller's work because it went *beyond* positioning the brand as one to enjoy after work; it actually paid tribute to the daily, honest toil of American working people, and it did so with outstanding components: sparkling words, cinematography, and music. The fact that the tagline "For All You Do, This Bud's for You" was also catchy, memorable, and ice-pick sharp was the final nail in Miller's coffin.

Sometimes, a successful strategy takes an opposite tack from the competition. But in this case, Budweiser hammered Miller soundly at its own blue-collar game, and in the process, managed to retain its previous customers, too. This was not a case of the right strategy outperforming the wrong one; it was a maintain-and-gain strategy for the marketing history books, in which "superb" defeated "excellent." (1)

Ad Age calls "This Bud's for You" campaign "iconic" in "Budweiser Gets Emotional, Tells DDB to Study D'Arcy" (A1; http://adage.com/article?article_id=136547). *Ad Age* reported that Anheuser-Busch suggested that its current agency (DDB) analyze thirty-year-old commercials from an agency that's no longer in business. "This Bud's for You" is what agency pros call A Big Idea. Big creative ideas are simple—but as we'll see, generating them is hard.

One of advertising's most brilliant creative people was the late David Ogilvy. (2) He wrote that you can recognize a big idea if you ask yourself five questions:

1. Did it make me gasp when I first saw it?
2. Do I wish I had thought of it myself?
3. Is it unique?
4. Does it fit the strategy to perfection?
5. Could it be used for thirty years?

This chapter is about creative copywriting in advertising and promotion. The pages of *Ad Age* are laced with intense discussions and critiques of what is smart, creative, and most importantly, *effective*. Copywriters try to create prose and poetry that sells. That is, copy that not only is engaging, but also gets cash registers ringing.

Throughout this book, we've talked about strategy, and in the previous chapter you saw different persuasive appeals and routes to persuasion. Creative strategy involves making hard choices, both big and small: What will appeal to the target audience? What persuasive messages should I use? Is my idea edgy and appealing or tasteless and crude? Can I cut through the clutter with my big idea or will people be so distracted (or even entertained) that they won't know what they're supposed to buy? Like most aspects of marketing promotion, there are many ways to make great ads. In the next few pages, we'll discuss the backstory behind ads and campaigns starting with how big ideas begin with fact finding and research.

Next, we'll examine the strategic thinking that underpins a promotion, usually summarized in a document called the creative brief. The creative brief recaps what we know about the product, the competition, the target customers, customers' motivations, and key insights that can inspire the creative copywriter. It may include information about media preferences and habits and possibly surprising routines and patterns of prospective customers.

And last, we'll look at different perspectives on persuasion and creativity as they relate to advertising. We'll look at the processes creative people use in working the magic of distilling all of this information into compelling copy that captures attention and sells a product.

Research versus Creativity

At its most basic level, research is learning everything you can about your audience, your product, and your product's functions and benefits. As we saw in Chapter 7, it's crucial to know what motivates people to buy a product—not only the functional benefits they expect to receive, but also the intangible cultural, social, and emotional benefits they seek. Luke Sullivan, author of *Hey, Whipple, Squeeze This: A Guide to Creating Great Ads*, suggests that it's important not only to read the findings of researchers, but also to immerse yourself in the world of the customer. He writes, "Take a deep breath and sink slowly into the world of the person you're writing to. . . . How does it *feel* to be them?" (3)

Consider persuasion in your everyday life. When you and your friends are planning to go out for a meal, you may try to persuade them to go to your favorite place. The better you know what your friends like and don't like, the better your odds of finding the best messages to help them see things your way. You also probably have identified the most influential people in the group and shape your messages mostly for them. This is the heart of successful persuasion: knowledge of the other person and what's important to him or her.

When many people hear the word *research* in connection with advertising and promotion, they imagine the two are incompatible—one is science and one is art. Many creative professionals complain that data and metrics discourage agencies and clients from taking risks, and some creative directors say that market research about consumer preferences inhibits their creativity. Others dislike valuation and measurement of campaign results. Still others hark back to what they believe was the golden age of advertising where creative stars "just knew" what was right and disdained efforts to quantify outcomes.

"Why Metrics Are Killing Creativity in Advertising" represents some of those beliefs (A2; http://adage.com/columns/article?article_id=142600). The author, a creative director, writes, "in ever-increasing fashion, our clients' (and our own) rote dependence on the dusty world of metrics is exactly why creativity is going to hell." He's no doubt correct that you can't truly quantify creativity, but it's worth noting that in the Comments section of the article the author backtracks somewhat. He says he really "believes in metrics" but thinks the dependence on them has become lopsided.

"R-E-S-P-E-C-T: Why Market Research Just Doesn't Get It" further explores the research–creativity tension (A3; http://adage.com/article?article_id=120634). Greg Stuart, author of *What Sticks?*, says in the article that the anti-research attitude is out of date and argues that gut instinct and "tribal custom" are unworkable given the complexities of contemporary marketing. However, in the same article, practitioners point out that for research to be useful, it has to be rigorously conducted and that findings must be translated into insights creatives can use.

The research–creativity tension has always existed, but resolving that tension is even more important today. We're much better equipped to gather and analyze data than ever before. We're able to narrowly focus and tailor our messages to audiences that are most likely to be receptive. Digital media make it even easier with tools such as Omniture and Google Analytics. In *What Sticks*, Briggs and Stuart write:

> The Internet promised to be the "most measurable media ever"—and it delivered on that promise. We're not talking about the fact that marketers get a count of how many people clicked on an advertisement (that's just a tiny piece of the measurement); instead, we're talking about the ability to quantify the attitude and purchase behavior shift caused by advertising. (4)

Companies, especially in difficult economic conditions, aggressively seek accountability for their expenditures on all of their operating activities, including advertising and promotion.

This doesn't mean that agencies and creative folks are unjustified in the mistrust of some research. As Briggs and Stuart point out, often data are used incorrectly or to push an agenda and sometimes marketers "use research the way a drunkard uses a lamppost: more for support than illumination." (4)

In our view, creativity for the sake of creativity doesn't work in today's advertising and promotion world. Organizations use creativity to solve a problem or take advantage of an opportunity, not as a goal in itself. The best creative people understand research, because it helps them get into the heads of the people they want to influence. Without research and fact finding, you're just guessing. Research may not be effective or predictive in every situation, but it helps your odds of success. You may not be able to quantify creativity, but you can quantify results whether in brand awareness, attitude change, or most importantly, sales.

Strategy

The word *strategy* comes from the Greek word *strategos*, meaning "to plan the destruction of one's enemies through effective use of resources." Although that may sound belligerent, remember that your goal as a researcher, strategist, and creative copywriter is to win in the marketplace—to outthink and outcompete the other guys. The strategic plan is critical because it crystallizes the direction the creative team should take.

A strategy can't simply be a list of facts about the product or the customer. It has to offer fact-based insights. Walmart, for example, has long based its marketing on offering the lowest prices. Consider two very different creative executions that drew on at least one shared fact: shopping at Walmart, according to two different studies, could save an average family over $2,000 annually. The *Ad Age* article "Walmart Looks to Refurbish Image with Political-Style Ads" describes a campaign called "Sam's Dream" (A4; http://adage.com/article?article_id=114179). This campaign had the look and feel of political advertising. It touted founder Sam Walton's legacy and emphasized that Walmart is a good corporate citizen and saves money for families. The two-ad campaign was controversial and widely panned by several interest groups.

In September 2007, Walmart's new agency, the Martin Company, came up with a much different and, many said, much better strategy, direction, and execution. "Long-Awaited Walmart Ads Are Obvious . . . Yet Brilliant" demonstrates how strategic and research-based insights can lead to riveting creative work (A5; http://adage.com/adreview/post?article_id=120476). *Ad Age* columnist Bob Garfield points out that the campaign takes the "save money" mantra and makes it concrete for viewers. For example, if you save $2,500 over a year by shopping at Walmart, the benefit promised in the ad is that you can take the family to Disney World or even buy your teenager a used car. The slogan: Save money. Live Better. It's a big idea because it's simple and powerful. As Garfield writes: "You wouldn't think anybody would have to spell out the benefit of having more money, yet it's an unexpectedly potent brand promise."

Some might think that a specific strategy would be too constricting to creative copywriters. Another legend of the business, Norman Berry, said this: "Many strategies . . . are too vague, too open to interpretation. 'The strategy for this product is taste,' they'll say. But that is not a strategy." Berry goes on to say that only precise strategies offer creative freedom: "Vague strategies inhibit. Precise strategies liberate." (5)

Drewniany and Jewler explain it this way: "Strategy is the way you plan to sell the product, not the words and images you use to do so. But mere facts do not a strategy make. To the facts you must add your insight—you must see connections that no one else has noticed." (6) A well-researched and sharply honed strategy can lead to an infinite number of different executions.

Features and Benefits

The selling idea should be rooted in the benefits of what the product or service can offer. Imagine the many ways you could dramatize the compelling benefit of "accrued savings," as Garfield calls it, by shopping at Walmart. As legendary copywriter Steve Kopcha says, "Ads don't work without benefits; they're the heart of any proposition." (1)

Consider "red rubber boots." (2) What are the attributes or features of red rubber boots? Well, they're constructed of rubber material, they're footwear, and they are, of course, red in color. They may have corrugated soles, a high gloss finish, cushioned sponge insole, and a buckle on the top. But what are the benefits or potential benefits of the boots?

Dry feet. Safety. Comfort. Durability. We call these functional benefits, and they are the more obvious outcomes of using a product with those characteristics. A watch tells you the time. A car provides transportation. Boots protect your feet.

But few products appeal to people only for the practical or functional benefits they offer. Most products also offer emotional benefits that aren't necessarily obvious elements of construction or design. Those glossy red rubber boots may be a fashion statement, may offer the pride of wearing a designer product, or the pleasure of imitating a celebrity. The advertiser's job is to help the consumer make the connection between the product's features and the benefits he or she is likely to get. As Drewniany and Jewler put it, "To be creative, an ad must make a relevant connection with its audience and present a selling idea in an unexpected way." (6)

This doesn't discount the fundamental importance of creative insights and execution. In fact, with thoughtful audience research and a well done strategic brief providing clear direction, creatives are able to focus their efforts and avoid approaches that miss the mark for customers.

Creativity in 140 Characters?

Twitter, Foursquare, Facebook, product placement in games, and a host of other applications and technologies offer new opportunities and creative challenges for marketers. How can your brand benefit from or be threatened by social networks and other innovations? The *Ad Age* article "On Twitter, Justin Bieber Is More Popular Than Jesus," Simon Dumenco tracks Twitter trends that are often mischievous and sometimes downright offensive (A6; http://adage.com/mediaworks/article?article_id=143881).

Nevertheless, these media platforms are becoming increasingly important aspects of marketing plans and offer their own creative challenges in strategy, copy, and design. The article "Once Skeptics, Brands Drink the Facebook Kool-Aid" outlines the investment big marketers are making in social ads, channels, tagging, and networking (A7; http://adage.com/digitalalist10/article?article_id=142223). Axe, the men's personal care brand, is using its vanity URL Facebook.com/Axe to post viral videos related to brand launches and to offer contests, merchandise, and other engagement devices.

Once Skeptics, Brands Drink the Facebook Kool-Aid

"Drinking the Kool-Aid" refers to people's tendency to go along with what everyone else is doing or saying with potentially fatal results.

Procter & Gamble is the world's biggest marketer and offers scores of brands from Hugo Boss fragrances to Charmin bathroom tissue to Pepto-Bismol. What all of P&G's brands have in common is a relentless focus on their consumers and their preferences. This article describes how P&G's chief digital executive changed his mind and the company's plans by attempting to create stronger customer connections through Facebook pages.

Marketers and advertisers need to both resist conventional thinking and yet be open to changing their minds when they get new evidence. P&G thus decided that their overall promotional strategies needed a big dose of Facebook to supplement their existing digital approaches.

As we'll discuss in a later chapter, strategies and creative executions for one medium may not be so hot for another. Does this mean that the roadmap to effective persuasion described above is out of date?

Not at all. Using research to understand audiences, to develop smart strategies, and to develop simple, elegant communication has never been more important. People with the skills to understand how and why people use these media will be winners in tomorrow's marketing world.

What's Creative?

Innovation and great ideas are at the heart of advertising and promotion. They can be brilliant merchandising ideas such as the 1970s L'Eggs distinctive plastic eggs for pantyhose or Absolut vodka's unusual bottle shape that sparked extraordinarily successful ads celebrating the shape in unusual and often artistic ways. "A Look Back at 10 Ideas That Changed the Marketing World" is a snapshot of innovations that meet the standard of Big Ideas (A8; http://adage.com/cmostrategy/article?article_id=142090).

> ### A Look Back at 10 Ideas That Changed the Marketing World
>
> Innovation and creative insights have always been at the heart of great advertising and Bob Liodice's article celebrates some of the most inspired thinking in our field.
>
> His top 10 list includes design brilliance as well as daring and controversial messages. In the '70s, L'Eggs brand packaged pantyhose in distinctive plastic egg sand pulled off one of the most best product launches in marketing lore. Another design triumph was Absolut vodkas apothecary-styled bottle that became the centerpiece of its advertising.
>
> Inspired by Burger King's promise that diners could "have it your way," a website with a viewer-controlled "subservient chicken" helped generate millions of website hits and almost a 10% increase in the restaurant chains' sales.
>
> In the '60s, Avis car rentals shocked everyone admitting that they were number two, far behind its hugely successful rival, Hertz. The slogan: "We Try Harder" boosted profitability and market share and has now become integral to the brand.
>
> The takeaway? No matter how many new technology tools and trends are out there, great marketing requires brave and ingenious people to buck conformity, challenge what "everybody knows," and take creative risks.

"Skin you love to touch" was Woodbury Soap's introduction of sex appeal as a persuasive element. It was a Big Idea of 1911 written by one of the first women in advertising agencies. Apple's famous "1984" Super Bowl ad ran only once with the strategy that its computer would save the world from Orwellian conformity. Each of the innovations in the article makes most of us think, "Wow—I wish I'd thought of that." (A8)

On Advertising and Promotional Creativity

You can find thousands of books and articles about creativity and innovation. Many offer good advice about how to ignite the creative spark. Of course, we all have different strengths and paths to creativity. Here are some of the key takeaways from some of the most brilliant copywriters in the business:

- Burt Manning: "Copy should sell by an understanding of the people it seeks to reach."
- Mary Moore: "Great advertising . . . is rarely comfortable . . . it's probably risky."

- Jim Johnston: "Good creative people don't mind rules—you can't write a sonnet unless you know the rules."
- Gene Federico: "Elegant advertising is distinguished by simplicity—and that simplicity makes it effective."
- Cheryl Berman: "Human insight is the most powerful tool you have in affecting how consumers behave and how they view your brand."
- Steve Kopcha: "Cleverness alone doesn't sell. You have to say the right thing and you have to say it brilliantly." (5)

Copywriters must be creative on demand. They can't wait for inspiration to strike. As the *Ad Age* articles and the insights above show, great advertising is built on deep understandings of people's needs and motivations. It's based on unconventional thinking, artistic leaps, and the discipline to keep the clients' goals firmly in mind.

Don Draper, a fictional creative genius in AMC's "Mad Men" series about advertising in the 1960s, is certainly not a perfect role model for today's advertising. But this line of dialogue does capture something of the magic of the business:

> Advertising is based on one thing: Happiness. And you know what happiness is? Happiness is the smell of a new car . . . It's freedom from fear. It's a billboard on the side of the road that screams with reassurance that whatever you're doing is okay. You are okay.

> Don Draper, "Mad Men"
> From Season1, Episode 1/ Pilot

Notes

1. This vignette is courtesy of Steve Kopcha, brilliant advertising creative copywriter who wrote advertising for Anheuser-Busch and General Motors, among many other top clients. He is professor emeritus at the Missouri School of Journalism. He emphasizes that although he admired the "This Bud's for You" strategy and creative execution, he was not involved in the project.
2. Ogilvy, D. *Ogilvy on Advertising.* New York: Vintage Books, 1965.
3. Sullivan, L. *Hey, Whipple, Squeeze This: A Guide to Creating Great Ads.* New York: John Wiley & Sons, 1998.
4. Briggs R., & Stuart, G. *What Sticks.* Chicago: Kaplan Publishing, 2006.
5. These quotes are drawn from excellent profiles courtesy of the Advertising Educational Foundation. Available at: http://www.aef.com/images/creative_leaders/.
6. Drewniany, B. L., & Jewler, J. *Creative Strategy in Advertising.* Boston: Thomson Learning, 2008.

Articles

(A1) Jeremy Mullman. "Budweiser Gets Emotional, Tells DDB to Study D'Arcy." Published May 11, 2009. Available at: http://adage.com/article?article_id=136547

(A2) Patrick Sarkissian. "Why Metrics Are Killing Creativity in Advertising." Published March 4, 2010. Available at: http://adage.com/columns/article?article_id=142600

(A3) Jack Neff. "R-E-S-P-E-C-T: Why Market Research Just Doesn't Get It." Published September 24, 2007. Available at: http://adage.com/article?article_id=120634

(A4)   Mya Frazier. "Walmart Looks to Refurbish Image with Political-Style Ads." Published January 8, 2007. Available at: http://adage.com/article?article_id=114179

(A5)   Bob Garfield. "Long-Awaited Walmart Ads Are Obvious . . . Yet Brilliant." Published September 17, 2007. Available at: http://adage.com/adreview/post?article_id=120476

(A6)   Simon Dumenco. "On Twitter, Justin Bieber Is More Popular Than Jesus (but Jesus Is More Popular Than Betty White)." Published May 14, 2010. Available at: http://adage.com/mediaworks/article?article_id=143881

(A7)   Jack Neff. "Once Skeptics, Brands Drink the Facebook Kool-Aid." Published February 22, 2010. Available at: http://adage.com/digitalalist10/article?article_id=142223

(A8)   Bob Liodice. "A Look Back at 10 Ideas That Changed the Marketing World." Published February 15, 2010. Available at: http://adage.com/cmostrategy/article?article_id=142090

Creative Design and Visuals

13 CHAPTER

Courtesy of THE PROCTOR & GAMBLE COMPANY

SMELL LIKE A MAN, MAN.
Old Spice

Old Spice. It sounds, well, *old*. It was a brand that had lapsed into relative obscurity until Wieden+Kennedy (W+K) pulled together a campaign that transformed Grandpa's aftershave into a social media hit. The campaign launched with a TV spot "The Man Your Man Could Smell Like," and won a Grand Prix award at the Cannes Lions International Advertising Festival.

Handsome campaign star Isaiah Mustafa showed us that for an Old Spice man, nothing's impossible. With smart dialogue, clever digital design, brilliant production, and a sophisticated media plan, the whole campaign had the sweet smell of success (A1; **http://adage.com/article?article_id=144688**).

The interactive piece of the integrated strategy, which also included print and television, exploded across the social media world with the Old Spice "Questions" campaign. Mustafa answered questions posted on social media sites from such celebrities as Ellen DeGeneres, Alyssa Milano, and George Stephanopoulos as well as from regular folks. Twitter, Digg, Reddit, and of course, YouTube, all were media tools. The interactive creative team scripted Mustafa's responses that, consistent with his character, were funny, ironic, and full of swagger. The production team and designers set up shots on the fly and posted over 150 videos. Within three days, Old Spice had attracted thirty-six million YouTube viewers. Ultimately, the "Questions" video far outstripped the original commercials in page views.

How did W+K do it? Creative talent, of course, but close collaboration among the agency's staff was critical for success. An interview with Creative Director Jason Bagley of W+K Portland shows the high levels of collaboration and precision teamwork involved.

Bagley: We had a kind of NASA control center about 15 feet away from Isaiah at two different tables. At one table were Josh Millrod, Dean McBeth and Cody Corona, interactive community managers and digital strategists who were going through all the comments and monitoring all web activity. They were selecting the comments to respond to. Baldwin, Eric Kallman, Craig Allen and I sat at

> another table furiously writing the responses. We would pass our computers back and forth to one another checking one another's work and adding jokes to one another's copy. The four of us took turns directing. In another room was a team of editors cranking out everything we shot. Not to mention the entire production crew of camera, lighting, teleprompter worker person, etc. (1)

Although this chapter is mostly about creative design and visual persuasion, the Old Spice vignette makes it clear that today's marketing organization can't be rigidly structured around functional activities. The stars and innovators in advertising and promotion today are crashing through walls, tearing down silos, and generally wreaking havoc with the way we used to do things. Although we've organized this book into sections that cover various aspects of the promotional process, the advertising world is becoming increasingly nonlinear and team driven.

Once upon a time, copywriting and art direction were very different animals. Media planning and placement were almost different species. Of course, both copywriters and art directors needed to work together at various points to create ads and campaigns. But the experts in writing wrote, and the experts in design designed. Media people planned budgets and bought time and/or space on television networks or radio stations, in newspapers, and in magazines.

Today those lines are blurring. Larry Powell, vice president and account director at Sanders\Wingo Advertising in Austin, began his career as an art director. He finds the best creative work from agencies and marketers that have a culture of collaboration. "I see two really important factors," Powell says. "First, we have so many more avenues for creativity and design, especially online. Second, great people are testing the limits of creativity and media. Today almost anything from subway steps to a bottle cap can be a medium, and the creative copywriters and designers are working together to imagine what's next." He cited the Burger King "Subservient Chicken" as an example of creativity going in new and difficult-to-define directions (A2; http://adage.com/article?article_id=110370).

Persuasion and Visuals

We understand the world in large part through our visual experience. Messaris suggests that visual images in ads can play powerful roles: First, they can conjure strong emotions by "simulating the appearance of a real person or object." (2) Second, visuals can offer evidence for product or service claims. Third, visuals can show a connection or correlation between the images and activities presented and the products offered. Messaris argues that these advertising functions underpin a whole range of strategies including celebrity endorsements and politicians who make sure the dais at the convention is draped in the Stars and Stripes.

Visual persuasion was the heart of a campaign in which the Huggies Diapers brand introduced faux denim diapers printed to look just like a pair of Levi's. The *Ad Age* article "Are Those Designer Diapers You're Wearing?" identifies the key consumer insight from research: Moms love seeing their babies in jeans, and 60 percent of them buy denim clothing for their babies before the kids are six months old (A3; http://adage.com/article?article_id=144989). Moms, of course, know the functional role of diapers, but for the ad to be effective it was crucial to show a charming toddler in his denim-look diapers strutting like a runway model and baby-about-town. The verbal and the visual came together to create a funny ad that conveys the key benefit of functional fashion for kids.

Each medium offers different creative challenges in art direction, and copywriting and strategy need to drive decision making. For many print ads, for instance, we assume that readers are too busy to read a lot of words and the visuals have to communicate powerfully and quickly to be effective.

Art directors and copywriters often spar over the length of copy. Clients often want more explanation of their products' features and benefits than the creatives think appropriate. In general, if the buying decision is fairly complex or risky, longer copy may make sense. Read "Is Copy Dead or Just Evolving?" for a sense of the debate (A4; http://adage. com/smallagency/post?article_id=119664). In "The Visual Hammer and the Verbal Nail," Ries uses the analogy of hammer and nail when analyzing the creative process of advertising and brand creation: What's more important?

> It's like asking what's more important in building a house, a hammer or a nail? Both have to work together. The best hammer in the world is useless if the hammer misses the nail. And the best nail in the world is useless unless there's a hammer to hammer the nail in.
>
> The visual is the hammer. It's difficult to build a strong, powerful worldwide brand without a strong, shocking, dynamic visual. (A5; http://adage.com/columns/ article?article_id=128160)

Again, we see the need for the creative team to work together to make sure that their positioning can be translated into powerful persuasion. The article "Verizon vs. AT&T: Blistering Battle Raging Over Map" uses the example of the campaign that compares Verizon's mobile coverage with rival AT&T's (A6; http://adage.com/article?article_id=140748). The Verizon map shows a U.S. map almost covered in Verizon red, whereas the AT&T map shows only sparse blue blotches.

Verizon staked out network reliability for its mobile strategy, an approach that offered consumers a significant desired benefit, and the ads were able to illustrate the difference in a visually arresting way. Michael Newman, creative director for Saatchi & Saatchi-Australia, writes, "great art direction is about leading the viewer's eye through your communication." He goes on to say that the take-away lesson is "to write visual ideas. Ambiguity and surprise are what force our interest." (3)

Television and other mass media advertising once dominated the advertising landscape when three networks ruled the airwaves and digital competitors hadn't decimated print publications. Advertising became an art form as some of the most talented writers, directors, still photographers, and special effects experts created imaginative and beautiful print and television advertisements. Their work transformed both the advertising business and the American pop culture landscape (A7; http://adage.com/article?article_id=62917).

Imagemakers Impart Advertising with Style, Special Effects and "Shaky Cam"

The exciting and imaginative advertising and promotions you see on television, in magazines, online, and even on your cell phone grew out of a creative revolution that began in the 1960s. Artists, photographers, and film directors became part of the creative process elevating advertising to what some call a true art form. The "shaky cam," a film style that became popular in the '80s is probably familiar to you. It doesn't use stable shots, but purposely uses a technique that looks like video taken with a hand-held camera. The goal is to give the film the feel of a documentary or "real life" production and is used today by many movie-makers and advertisers. For examples, check out "Black Swan," "The Fighter," or any of the "Bourne" films. Domino's "Pizza Turnaround" campaign uses this technique as well: http://www.youtube.com/watch?v=AH5R56jILag.

The combination of artists and renaissance people transformed advertising forever and, as this article notes, offered the ability to "capture human emotions in deft, subtle performances."

This creative revolution was possible in part because so few media outlets existed, and the dollars flowing into agencies were enormous. There were few tools to effectively measure promotional effects and little pressure to narrowly target audiences. Creative directors were free to practice advertising not only as a selling tool but also as an art form.

Today, media fragmentation has profoundly altered how we consume televisual messages, especially because email, texts, mobile devices, and computers all have the capability of presenting video and offering interactivity. DVRs and other on-demand services have made what is known as "interruption" advertising far less effective. Interruption advertising is the 30-second spot that stops the action on your program with an intrusive selling message.

What these different media have in common with traditional television advertising is the need for action as an integral part of the design. That may sound obvious, but too many video commercials are inert, dull, or just bad storytelling. They don't show people in interesting and surprising ways. They don't capture our attention quickly enough, present engaging dramas, entertain us, or involve us in the onscreen action.

Drewniany and Jewler suggest that sight, sound, and motion are at the heart of a video spot and that storytelling adds motion to the best spots: "Stories are natural ways to give your commercial movement." (4)

Felton advises that in planning to create video advertising, you should consider the following questions: "What part of the . . . product story moves? What motion is inherent in my client's product? Does it go around like a can opener, splash through water like a bike, squirt like a tube of toothpaste?" (5)

In the article "Toyota IQ Font Wins Design Grand Prix" we see a spot that brings together the old and new in graphic design (A8; http://adage.com/article?article_id=144626). Toyota's strategy was to promote the agility of the Toyota iQ microcar. To dramatize that agility, the production crew filmed an iQ driving various routes around a hangar. Software translated the car's tracks into an original typeface and the spot became a hit with design, technology, and auto blogs. The typeface was downloaded 24,000 times and generated 2,300 requests on the Toyota website for a test drive.

This is the kind of initiative that hews to the important success factors for video: the product is the hero of the spot, the action dramatizes a key product benefit, and the unusual production gains attention.

Here's another example. Imagine a television spot for the world's dominant Internet company that tells an affecting story, incorporates movement and action, makes the product and its benefits the hero of the spot, *and* does it with few pictures and no video.

That's the Google Super Bowl ad of 2010 that consists of watching someone's Internet searches to the accompaniment of a spare but lovely soundtrack of music and sound effects. The search terms tell the story, as *Ad Age*'s Bob Garfield writes in "Finalement, Our Long-Awaited Take on Google's Super Bowl Ad" (A9; http://adage.com/adreview/post?article_id=142107). Beginning with a query for study abroad, an unknown Internet guy searches for Paris, cafes, ways to impress French girls, chocolate shops, translations, churches, jobs in Paris, and finally, how to assemble a crib. It's the story of a search-powered romance told in 30 seconds.

The Creative Brief: A Template for Teamwork

As we discussed in Chapter 12, the creative brief is a document that should help everyone focus on outcomes desired from a campaign or a promotion. If done right, a template such as the one below aligns everyone behind the client's goals, with each person fulfilling different roles and functions. Ideally, the brief provides both direction and inspiration to the creative team in developing the Big Idea and the most effective way to tell the product's story.

Each agency organizes its teams somewhat differently, and each uses different formats for the creative brief. However, except for very small or boutique agencies, almost all agencies use a brief to develop creative executions.

As we saw in the W+K example, team members on the Old Spice account worked quickly to respond to one person's creative insight. "Working Fast and Brilliant Is the Challenge for Creatives Today" suggests that the age of the loner artistic genius is gone, and the author writes, "Surely the true thrill and reward today is working hell for leather alongside others with different but complementary skills" (A10; http://adage.com/agencynews/article?article_id=134398).

"The Era of Creative Empowerment" argues that creative processes of the past can't be effective: "The difference is in your attitude and willingness to be open to inputs that may help you get to that final idea" (A11; http://adage.com/digitalnext/post?article_id=141473).

"Collaboration Increasingly Crucial to Way We Do Business" suggests that firms need teamwork to accomplish an integrated approach to brand promotion in part because the advertising business no longer just does advertising (A12; http://adage.com/smallagency/post?article_id=141683). Paid space and time, as we traditionally define advertising, is only one element of the integrated plan. According to Bart Cleveland, "Understanding and effectively working in a larger group with diversified expertise is something we must embrace if we are to survive the evolution our industry is undergoing." "Creative Evolution: Making the Process More Relevant to Our Time" points out just as technology has transformed advertising and promotion, collaborative tools can link teams around the world (A13; http://adage.com/digitalnext/post?article_id=134379).

Creative Evolution: Making the Process More Relevant to Our Time

Some people think that the creative process involves a lonely genius who's seized with inspiration. And while some creative people do seem to operate that way, today's advertising and promotion generally involves collaboration—teams of two or more who work together. Traditionally, that's been the art director, responsible for design and visuals, and the copywriter, responsible for the text or copy of a print or television commercial.

This article by a director of digital strategy identifies how technology is fostering creativity by using group decision-making tools and harnessing the power of an internal social network. The author writes that the technology allowed distant and even international team work and "the communication between creative teams became more quick and fluid, cultural adjustments to ensure creative worked globally . . . and we stated benefiting from large groups of people (30+) collaborating on concepts for a single plan."

If we unpack the creative brief, it becomes clearer how teamwork is increasingly critical to the success of the final product. Traditionally, an account manager or planner was the link between the client and the agency. Account managers and planners prepared the creative brief with input from the client. Today, however, account planners may call on a range of people including the creatives in honing and sharpening the creative brief.

Why are we advertising? and **Who are we talking to?** call on the planners and researchers to work with the client to clarify objectives and distill what's known about the marketing situation and the target audience. As the template suggests, it's critical to be specific about the target and avoid trying to cast too wide a net. Trying to communicate with everyone often results in failing to communicate with anyone.

Key consumer insights and the answer to **What do we want them to take away?** can emerge from both qualitative and quantitative research, observations about how people use similar products, and quotes from users. If the insights are concrete, the creatives can begin to see the story unfold. "What Are You Packing Into Your (Creative) Briefs" uses the example of the "Got Milk?" campaign built around a simple and truthful insight: "People wait until they're out of milk to buy more" (A14; http://adage.com/smallagency/post?article_id=136711). The message that food's better with milk could be and was dramatized in highly visual spots. Those spots provided the evidence by showing the humorous consequences of forgetting to buy milk.

Similarly, the key copy points, tone, or personality will help the copywriters, the art directors, the interactive specialists, and the media experts to apply creative thinking to the assignment. Based on knowledge of the target audience, the team must consider what stories they can tell through different media. For example, if the target audience of 18- to 24-year-old males uses mostly social media, texts, and mobile apps and games, what kind of verbal and visual storytelling will be persuasive?

Elements of the Creative Brief

Why Are We Advertising?
What do we want the advertising to accomplish? Pick one main objective, not a laundry list of things that will be unrealistic to achieve.

Who Are We Talking To?
Clearly identify the target audience. Resist the temptation to talk to everyone. Make a strategic decision about the best prospect. This is not about demos. The demos may or may not be relevant to the creatives. But clearly identifying the target is.

What Do We Know about Them That Will Help Us? (Key Consumer Insights)
Isolate the one consumer insight on which the creative will be based. Bring that insight to life in an inspiring way. There will be many insights. Which one is relevant to this strategy?

What Do We Want Them to Take Away? (Main Message, Promise)
What do we want the advertising to communicate? Should be based on a benefit or consumer value that is relevant to the insight/target. One sentence.

Support (Reason Why)
One or two ideas that give the promise credibility—give the consumer a reason to believe.

Key Copy Points (Optional)
May be some critical points that should be included in copy. Should be short.

Tonality
Capture the brand essence or personality. Try not to be trite. What is the image or feeling this advertising should evoke that reinforces the brand?

Mandatories
If there is something mandatory, such as a legal disclaimer or logo, be sure the team knows about it. Keep this list short, but don't surprise the creative team later with something that will affect copy or layout.

Creative Sparks
Nuggets gleaned from research (or clients) that could spark a creative idea. Relevant quotes from qualitative research can provide rich creative fodder. (6)

One Device to Rule Them All?

Media and communication devices increasingly share characteristics and capabilities. Think of what you can do with your mobile phone: It's a customized music player, gaming platform, television, restaurant finder, and map. Technology will continue to expand the boundaries of creative design. Designers will need new skills in visual storytelling deployed in media and on devices unimagined today.

We can experience the same media through many different spaces. In the next few chapters, we'll consider the changing definitions of media and ask, "Will media be the new creative?"

Notes

1. W+K Platform. Available at: http://blog.wk.com/
2. Messaris, P. *Visual Persuasion*. Thousand Oaks, CA: Sage, 1997.
3. Newman, M. *Creative Leaps*. Singapore: John Wiley & Sons, 2003.
4. Drewniany, B. L., & Jewler, J. *Creative Strategy in Advertising*. Boston: Thomson Learning, 2008.
5. Felton, G. *Advertising Concept and Copy*. New York: Norton, 2006.
6. This rendition of the ideal creative brief is courtesy of Barbara Ifshin, a professor of Strategic Communication at the Missouri School of Journalism and Account Manager for Mojo Ad at the School. She was a top executive at Y&R and Disney. Prof. Ifshin said she drew on the ideas of many advertising experts, including Jon Steele in developing the framework.

Articles

(A1) Laurel Wentz. "Old Spice's Manly Body Wash TV Spot Takes Film Grand Prix." Published June 26, 2010. Available at: http://adage.com/article?article_id=144688

(A2) Kate Macarthur. "Crispin Gets Fat on BK Chicken." Published July 10, 2006. Available at: http://adage.com/article?article_id=110370

(A3) Jack Neff. "Are Those Designer Diapers You're Wearing?" Published July 19, 2010. Available at: http://adage.com/article?article_id=144989

(A4) Peter Madden. "Is Copy Dead or Just Evolving?" Published August 2, 2007. Available at: http://adage.com/smallagency/post?article_id=119664

(A5) Al Ries. "The Visual Hammer and the Verbal Nail." Published July 3, 2008. Available at: http://adage.com/columns/article?article_id=128160

(A6) Rita Chang and Rupal Parekh. "Verizon vs. AT&T: Blistering Battle Raging Over Map Coverage Fight Is Good News for Shops, Media as Wireless Giants Square Off." Published November 30, 2009. Available at: http://adage.com/article?article_id=140748

(A7) Anthony Vagnoni. "Imagemakers Impart Advertising with Style, Special Effects and 'Shaky Cam.'" Published March 29, 1999. Available at: http://adage.com/article?article_id=62917

(A8) Teressa Iezzi. "Toyota IQ Font Wins Design Grand Prix." Published June 23, 2010. Available at: http://adage.com/article?article_id=144626

(A9) Bob Garfield. "Finalement, Our Long-Awaited Take on Google's Super Bowl Ad." Published February 15, 2010. Available at: http://adage.com/adreview/post?article_id=142107

(A10) Mark Wnek. "Working Fast and Brilliant Is the Challenge for Creatives Today." Published February 9, 2009. Available at: http://adage.com/agencynews/article?article_id=134398

(A11) Conor Brady. "The Era of Creative Empowerment." Published January 21, 2010. Available at: http://adage.com/digitalnext/post?article_id=141473

(A12) Bart Cleveland. "Collaboration Increasingly Crucial to Way We Do Business." Published January 25, 2010. Available at: http://adage.com/smallagency/post?article_id=141683

(A13) Freddie Laker. "Creative Evolution: Making the Process More Relevant to Our Time." Published February 6, 2009. Available at: http://adage.com/digitalnext/post?article_id=134379

(A14) Howard Margulies. "What Are You Packing Into Your (Creative) Briefs?" Published May 18, 2009. Available at: http://adage.com/smallagency/post?article_id=136711

Media Planning

Kurt LaTarte's last high school hockey game almost ended in tragedy when another player's skate accidentally sliced his neck and he almost bled to death. The injury halted a fiercely fought game between the Trenton Trojans and the Detroit Catholic Central Shamrocks, archrivals in a city that loves hockey.

After the accident, the teams stopped play and rivalry was forgotten as players gathered to pray while emergency technicians worked to save LaTarte's life. He fully recovered from the 1999 accident. The game was never finished but the team got a do-over eleven years later.

Ad agency TBWA and client Gatorade brought the Trojans and the Shamrocks together for a rematch. Gatorade offered coaching and fitness for the thirty-something players and filmed them preparing for the game as well as broadcasting the game itself. The video highlighted the players' friendships and the joyful camaraderie of sports.

The players' training for the rematch was an inspiring reality show and documentary that garnered significant results.

The catalyst for the promotion was Gatorade's finding that seven in ten people over thirty don't exercise and thus don't use Gatorade. Their goal was to "reignite the athletic spark among this 30+ age group." To do that, they sought to dramatize Gatorade's claim to fuel athletic performance in a heartwarming video that was likely to attract significant publicity.

Fox Sports Net produced and aired "REPLAY the Series, Fueled by Gatorade," to over ninety million households. The campaign won two awards at the Cannes Lions International Advertising Festival in 2010 in promotion and public relations. Its digital strategy featured a website (http://www.replaytheseries.com/pages/about_series2) with a five-part documentary series that told the Replay story in order to inspire other former athletes from around the nation.

Gatorade's submission to the Cannes judges reported that the promotion "created news, not advertising" with almost $3.5 million in earned media (publicity). CNN, *Men's Health Magazine,* and other media outlets featured the program, and regional Gatorade sales increased by 63 percent (A1; http://adage.com/cannes2010/article?article_id=144568). (1)

Are Media the New Creative?

"Replay" shows the evolution of media strategies from traditional paid-space-and-time advertising to a fusion of publicity, long-form branded television, live events, and digital strategies. This is an integrated approach to media planning that responds to the new reality of technology-enabled consumer behavior.

We used to think of media as channels—conduits through which messages flowed carrying news, information, and advertising messages. At one end of the conduit, ad agencies created television commercials, radio spots, and print ads. At the other end, the conduits split into different channels as media buyers placed the creative ideas—the commercials—in television programs, radio stations, newspapers, and magazines. Viewers or readers usually received the commercials as part of their consumption of news and entertainment and often as an interruption. Communication was mostly one way and people had relatively fewer choices.

Today, almost anything can be a medium and people are able to choose when and how they'll view programs and messages. That's partly why media planning is changing so rapidly and growing in importance. Once the creatives were the dominant force in agencies. Now some of the most visionary people in marketing are redefining media and creativity. Their jobs aren't simply to find the most efficient and effective ways to transmit the creatives' concepts through the various conduits. Instead, they're imagining new ways to touch consumers with brand messages that are relevant, meaningful, and effective. As we discussed in the last chapter, this new media planner is a key player in the creative team. "Digitas' Kenny: Give Media Shops More Input in Creative" reveals this change (A2; http://adage.com/mediaworks/article?article_id=125553).

> ### Digitas' Kenny: Give Media Shops More Input in Creative
>
> Not too many years ago, media buyers and planners were relegated to secondary roles while the creative folks ruled the agency world. But Daniel Kenny, CEO of the Publicis Groupe's interactive arm, argues that the media experts are crucial to success. In fact, Kenny points out that a campaign that starts "with media at its center . . . marketers can focus on a particular media outlet and how consumers use it, then plan a creative appeal that works well in that venue." The article goes on to point out that the media planners' focus on research and analytics can help them choose effective strategies and measure how well campaigns are working.

In this chapter, we'll introduce you to some media planning terms and discuss some of the ways planners analyze audience segments. Next, we'll look at a model that can help us better understand people's media choices and how they respond to innovations. As you'll see, the job of the media planner was never easy but has become even more complex as consumers control their media environment, choosing content and times as they wish.

Think of your own media consumption. At different times of the day you may be updating your Facebook profile, sending texts, watching network television, listening to your MP3 player, leafing through a magazine, playing games on your mobile or your Wii, searching for a bargain on Google, checking your RSS feed, watching a funny video a friend sent, *sending* a funny video, and watching "The Office" on Hulu. You might even be having in-person experiences in stores, sports venues, and restaurants.

A media planner's goal is to get the right message to the right person at the right time and do it as cheaply as possible. The most brilliant creative spot won't ring up sales if your best prospects don't see it, hear it, or interact with it.

The checklist for media effectiveness is deceptively simple:

- Find the best prospects for your product and service and segment them as precisely as possible.
- Identify the media, old and new, that they prefer.
- Identify other influences on their buying behaviors such as word-of-mouth recommendations or consumer-driven rating services such as Yelp.
- Identify the times when they use those media.
- Identify how often they use different media.
- Match consumer segments with available preferred media—at a price you can afford.

Then, all you have to do is get the person's attention with your message, get him to stick with you during the pitch, and get him to remember and act on the message. As we said, it isn't easy.

Media planners also must consider where their messages appear since a medium itself communicates. When Dillard's department store advertises a line of contemporary bedding in *Architectural Digest*, the products themselves take on some of the patina of the luxury orientation of the magazine. Target launched a digital music campaign promoting John Legend's "Live From Philadelphia" in both DVD and as downloadable audio with interactive billboards in New York City subways. People could plug in their ear buds and hear the album in a busy and exciting urban atmosphere, as *Advertising Age* reported (A3; http://adage.com/post?article_id=123271).

The "Replay" campaign also showed attention to context and was a good fit for ESPN's audience and vibe. As you can see, another piece to the planning puzzle is understanding the milieu in which the customer sees, hears, or engages with the promotion.

Measuring Media

Planners use the term *reach* to refer to the percentage of the target audience that has the "opportunity to see" or hear your message. Unfortunately, we currently don't really know if our prospects actually saw an ad except in certain Internet or direct marketing promotions where we can count clicks or purchases. Even worse, we have no guarantees that the spot was persuasive to the target.

Of course, just reaching someone doesn't mean you've persuaded her. A student may come to class, but that's no guarantee she's paying attention or learning. She may be distracted by a personal issue, bored with the teacher or content, or uninterested in the topic. These same factors can affect your target audience and deflect their "learning" from your promotion.

Frequency is another planner term that refers to the number of times a target audience sees or hears your message within the planning period. Although these metrics are helpful in pricing and evaluating traditional media such as television, they're less applicable to digital media, especially online or mobile video. As we see in "New Nielsen Ratings Combine Shows' TV and Online Views," the industry is working hard to develop new metrics for a new age (A4; http://adage.com/article?article_id=141675).

New Nielsen Ratings Combine Shows' TV and Online Views

Millions of dollars hinge on the size and makeup of audiences for television programs, traditionally measured only for "live" television or programs recorded on digital video recorders within the past three days (known as the "C3" measurement). The article points out that the television industry "desperately wants to show that more people watch its programming than those captured in Nielsen's current measures." Founded in 1923, Nielsen Media Research is the main audience measurement resource in more than 100 countries. As traditional television viewing audiences and ratings shrink and online options grow, the Nielsen company is trying to develop mixed media measures that give media buyers a more complete picture of who's watching what, and thus, what a 30-second spot on a given program is worth. The story reports that ad buyers are wary: "The cost of reaching one thousand viewers . . . is very different online than it is for TV. Creating a blended measure of the audience may not be a solution advertisers will want to use to determine pricing."

We can categorize the media consumers may choose by three main types: owned, paid, and earned. Forrester Research (2) and *Advertising Age* offer explanations of the advantages and disadvantages of each.

Owned media are those channels that you (mostly) control, such as your website, mobile site, games, corporate blogs and Twitter accounts, and branded social network sites. Of course, the best owned media offer opportunities for interactivity, comments, posting, and the like. Done right, many owned media sites create communities of users such as Starbuck's community effort that asks consumers to offer ideas and suggestions for improving Starbuck's products or services (see http://mystarbucksidea.force.com/). These communities can help build ongoing relationships with current and prospective customers and can be rapidly updated to take advantage of new opportunities.

Earned media is a form of publicity that also includes both legacy and digital media. It's "earned" because it's not paid for like advertising. With traditional media, a company generated news releases resulting in stories in broadcast and print, or sponsored events resulting in publicity and word of mouth. In the digital world, earned media includes viral messaging and videos, social networking brand mentions, bloggers' commentary about your brand, and votes on such sites as Digg or Delicious.

Earned media can cut both ways and emerge with messages you'd prefer not to "earn." For instance, a cable company earned a column from *Advertising Age* columnist Bob Garfield, "Comcast Must Die" (A5; http://adage.com/article?article_id=122094). Admittedly, as an advertising journalist, Garfield has a more prominent voice than most people. But he points out that the Internet enables anyone with a computer to publicize their unhappiness with comments and even video.

Comcast Must Die

Bob Garfield Crusades Against the Cable Provider

Long time *Ad Age* columnist Bob Garfield felt he was victimized by the cable giant, Comcast—and he talked about it: "Since personally being victimized by the company I call Qualmcast, I have read hundreds and hundreds of similar horror stories, so I will therefore not afflict you with the details of the arrogant, highhanded, dishonest, incompetent, inhuman and fundamentally asinine treatment I suffered at the hands of the cable monstrosity's 'customer service.'"

Garfield wrote on his blog and in his column and heard from lots of people whose experience with Land Rovers, Dell computers, and other products put them in customer service hell. His entertaining column points out that "Listenomics" offers the technology that empowers disgruntled, unhappy customers. They can now publicize their rage, create communities of angry consumers, and become part of an "e-mob." As Garfield put it, people can "blogmail" companies into submission "exerting the leverage the digital age has bestowed upon consumers to make lemonade out of lemons." As you can see, "earned" media can cut both ways.

Although there's a definite loss of control with earned media, the most forward-thinking strategists are continually looking for ways to create content that is so fun, interesting, or compelling that people want to engage with it and share it. Such shared messages also have considerable credibility with consumers: A recent study suggested that customers from word-of-mouth (WOM) referrals are more loyal and profitable than those acquired by traditional means. (3) Earned media may be highly effective and less expensive than paid, but they require delivery on a brand promise. For example, companies offering excellent customer service can be the primary drivers of "online love," as Pete Blackshaw puts it. "Setting up shop on Facebook is the easy part. Developing the brand business processes that increase odds of advocacy or favorable earned media is quite a different thing, but it's essential" (A6, http://adage.com/digitalnext/post?article_id=135965).

Paid Media Still Dominate

Paid media is still by far the most prominent category of promotion with billions of dollars going to traditional and digital media, though digital advertising dollars are still a tiny fraction of the total. For instance, a buying period known as the upfront marketplace happens each May when advertisers try to negotiate the best prices for national television advertising. The networks, including cable, try to squeeze the maximum fees out of advertisers especially for popular programs or new programs that seem to have a lot of promise. In 2010, advertisers committed almost $9 billion to the five broadcast networks as outlined in the article "Broadcast Upfront Finishes Between $8.1B and $8.7B" (A7; http://adage.com/upfront2010/article?article_id=144374).

Clearly, paid media are expensive but they still provide broad reach to mass marketers. In addition, media such as television, billboards and other out-of-home media, magazines, and newspapers can kick-start and support WOM and viral strategies as we saw with the Old Spice and Replay campaigns.

Paid media also include digital space and time such as paid search marketing, banners, and online display ads. Besides great reach, these media offer the advertiser control over the message and the context in which it's presented.

Figure 14-1 graphically shows the complexity of the media market as compared with the past. The mashed-up slide on "Home Media Capacity—Today" is purposely messy to depict the messiness of media planning in today's environment.

Why Do People Choose Different Media?

The best media planners learn everything they can about their target audience and its use of various media.

One way to look at why people choose different media at different times is through the *Media Choice Model* developed by Thorson and Duffy (see Figure 14-2). This model suggests that people have communication needs that vary from time to time and from person to person, and fulfilling these needs drives behaviors.

As you can see in Figure 14-2, people have four basic communication needs. *Connectivity* is the need to relate and communicate with others face-to-face or through media. We need friends, family, love, and relationships. When we're texting, posting on Facebook, or just hanging out with our buddies, that's connectivity. Of course, we're now able to make connections in new ways thanks to technology.

The *Information* need has to do with knowledge that helps us accomplish our goals, protect ourselves from harm, or find opportunities. It can be as important as about learning

Figure 14-1   Media Market

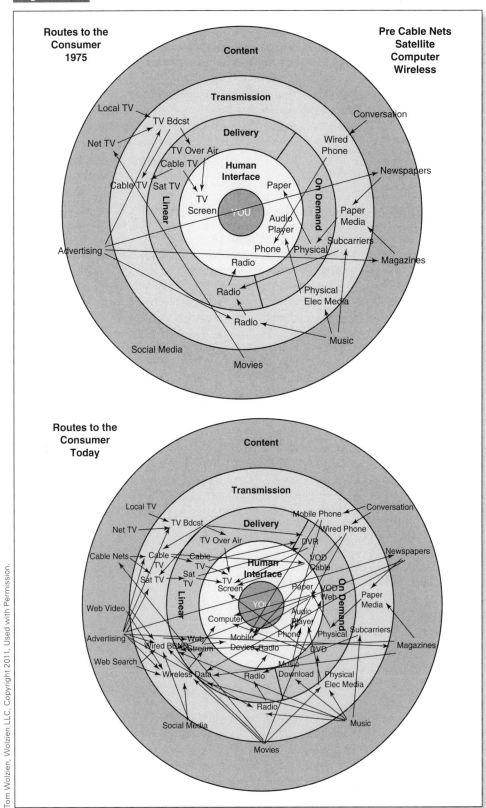

Figure 14-2   Media Choice Model

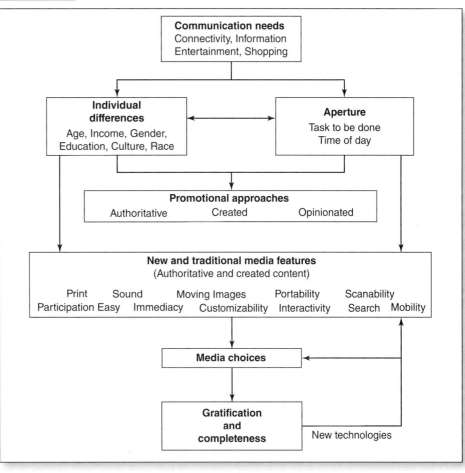

about a dangerous storm or as casual as finding a new restaurant in town or mapping directions to a party. We have lots of options for getting information today, including turning to the Internet searching for online experts, bloggers, and information clearinghouses. When we're choosing movies, books, or clothes, we may trust online reviewers such as ourselves more than experts such as newspaper columnists.

The *Shopping* need involves the processes we use to get goods and services. In the past, customers had few choices of what to buy and where to buy it. Now their choices are vast and growing. Consumers don't need newspapers and television to lead them to a purchase. Craigslist and directories and listing sites have decimated newspaper classified advertising, for example. Consumers don't even need stores, as options for buying online proliferate.

Finally, the *Entertainment* need refers to our psychological needs for diversion and fun. How people express that need is again filtered through the variables in the media choice model—one person's entertainment may be decidedly not entertaining to another. We know, however, that people are spending increasing time with media for entertainment.

Individual Differences

Who we are affects our choices, too, including age and education. A twenty-something and a thirty-something are different not only because of their ages, but also because of their life stage. At twenty-five, a person may be working at his first job, looking for a place to live, and spending his money and time in ways consistent with that life stage. At thirty, he may have other priorities, such as kids and a mortgage.

Media planners can't assume what people's media behaviors are likely to be based only on age or even life stage. For instance, many people assume that older consumers are technophobes and will be resistant to adopting new media formats and behaviors. Instead, our research has revealed that Baby Boomers are embracing Internet technologies at almost the same pace as the next youngest generation, as described in "Drop the Oatmeal and Forget What You 'Know' About Boomers" (A8; http://adage.com/article?article_id=145006).

Aperture—The Perfect Opening

Aperture is an opening or opportunity to deliver a message to a consumer at the very best time to get a sale or other action. It's based on the concept that for each customer there is an ideal moment when she can be reached with an advertising appeal.

Marketers try to take advantage of apertures for time of day, day of the week, and even seasons. If it's 11:45 A.M., you may be especially open to a message from Taco Bell. If it's November in Minnesota, you may respond to a reminder that snow tires are on sale. There are generation-specific apertures such as the responsiveness to messages about goods and services relevant to marriage, to child care, or to retirement.

Voice

You can see in the model that another aspect of media choice is what we call "voice." This refers to source of the communication we're receiving. The authoritative voice in news, for instance, would be the anchor and reporters on network or cable television and in advertising might be the traditional broadcast or print advertisement created by an agency and distributed in various media. The created voice is user-generated content, sometimes solicited by advertisers to get advertising ideas from ordinary people. Examples include Pepsico's Doritos snack and Pepsi Max 2011 Super Bowl ads that were consumer-generated with the company offering $5 million in prize money. One humorous consumer-generated Doritos ad shows an office worker finishing up his snack while a coworker watches greedily. The ad closes with the coworker going after the crumbs and seasoning on the first characters fingers. Viewers found it memorable if somewhat disturbing.

The referred voice seeks to harness the desire of consumers to recommend products and services to others and to use recommendations in their own selection decisions. Social media, comments, blogs, videos that go viral, product ratings and services like Yelp are all vehicles for consumer opinion sharing. As mentioned above, many people place more credence in recommendations from others over traditional ads even if they don't know the recommenders.

Media Features

What's so appealing to so many about the iPhone and other smartphones? Consider what they can do. Their features include the ability to store and play thousands of songs, share photos, watch videos, play games, and download audiobooks and podcasts. The iPhone

In Praise of the Original Social Media: Good Ol' Television

While monitoring and updating his Twitter account, Simon Dumenco noticed that most of the conversation focused around what was happening on television in entertainment, news and politics. Although people may be atwitter about social media and other innovations, he writes, "television still rules our lives." What's on TV right now provides the greatest fodder for social media as people share their thoughts about the funniest lines on SNL, the most exciting final moments in the NCAA finals, or the most outrageous outfit at the MTV awards. Although we now have the ability to shift the times when we consume programming, we still want to watch television together. People want to share experiences with their friends and family and with the larger culture and television still fills that powerful communication need.

Certainly broadcast audiences skew older than they used to and all audiences are more fragmented. But a recent Nielsen study pointed out that the number of hours per month people spent watching TV in the home went *up* in the first quarter of 2010 to over 158 hours a month representing a consistent trend: "In fact, TV viewing has increased more than an hour a day in the last decade, far outpacing any other major media option." (1)

We may be collectively enchanted with the potential of social and other digital media, but our enchantment shouldn't blind us to the utility of old media. In fact, a good deal of social media is about news and entertainment found in traditional channels. They're the stuff of Facebook posts, texts, and tweets.

A study that further suggests live television is robust and healthy found that there's an enormous difference between how people watch television and how they *think* they watch television. A study analyzed almost one hundred thousand hours of videotape of people in the UK watching television. Researchers found that 85 percent of programs were watched live, including those households with Sky+ boxes, the British version of DVRs. The study points out that most people underestimate how much live television they watch and significantly overestimate how much they watch videos in other forms and on other devices. (2) This is not to say that online promotions aren't important, but they may not be the best choice for a particular promotion. In addition, online and digital tactics are often more effective when linked with traditional tactics. In a study of the effectiveness of direct-to-consumer drug advertising, Nielsen found that the combination of television ads plus online promotion was highly successful. (1)

Of course, life stage and age will make a difference in media choice. Older audiences watch more broadcast news or entertainment "live" as opposed to younger viewers, as *Advertising Age* reports in "Broadcast's Youth Market Starts at 44" (A4; http://adage.com/upfront2010/article?article_id=144040). However, even among the 18 to 44 demographic, viewers watch three-and-a-half hours of live TV every day out of about eight-and-a-half hours of total media time.

Many people also assume that nobody's watching television commercials because devices enable bypassing or deleting them. But observational research revealed that users were exposed to about seventy-two minutes of TV advertisements daily. (3) Again, viewers are not zapping ads or finding ways to avoid them in great numbers.

Will technology-enabled televisions be larger versions of PCs bringing in customized content from many sources? Will viewer behaviors become more like computer behavior? Some people think so. Microsoft's Steve Ballmer suggests that monitors, slate devices, and pads will be driven by computer software. "My TV is powered by a PC," he commented, arguing that new media software will allow people to record and send television programming to their computers (A5; http://adage.com/digital/article?article_id=141336). For now, it appears that we are consuming television in pretty traditional ways and that people are using television to fulfill social needs as well as needs for entertainment, information, and shopping. Stay tuned.

Newspapers—A Dying Medium?

There's no question that legacy news companies are under severe stress, largely because of the proliferation of free content and the ubiquity of search. The current state of newspaper revenue and profits looks even worse when viewed historically since newspapers were once near monopolies and immensely profitable. Many newspapers took on too much debt when times were good. When circulation, advertising, and profits began to fall, they slashed reporting staffs and other expenses, often at the expense of a higher quality news product.

Despite the stressors, newspaper companies continue to offer significant opportunities for advertisers, especially in local and hyperlocal markets. Because the ads come bundled with information about people's communities and the world, readers are receptive to news and information in the form of sales, local store offerings, and special events. As a local advertising medium, it's still hard to beat the power of local newspapers. (4)

In a precursor to behavioral targeting online, newspapers have long provided zoned print editions so advertisers could reach the most attractive customers defined demographically and geographically. Newspapers also have sections that appeal to different types of readers so advertisers can match readers and product interests.

Contrary to what many assume, newspapers were quick to adopt digital technologies. However, they were also quick to give away their online content, content that can be aggregated by search companies such as Google, blogs such as *The Huffington Post* or *The Drudge Report,* or content farms such as Demand Media and Yahoo. Although some companies such as *The Wall Street Journal* and *The (Little Rock) Arkansas Democrat* have had success erecting pay walls for their online content, most have feared pay walls would result in drops in traffic to their sites thus making their sites less attractive to digital advertisers.

It's certainly a commentary about the state of the business when slower losses are a positive news story like this one: "Newspapers' Paid Circulation Losses Shrink" (A6; http://adage.com/mediaworks/article?article_id=143509). Despite the bad news, however, research shows that some one hundred million adults read a print newspaper and many more access newspaper websites. Newspaper websites attract more than a third of all web users, but competition for readers and advertisers continues to be fierce. Still, newspapers can and do charge more for ads on their sites and are doing more to enhance usability and news partnerships. Two articles highlight the challenges news companies face online and from search: "Mounting Web Woes Pummel Newspapers" (A7; http://adage.com/mediaworks/article?article_id=144684) and "Google Exec: We're Here to Help Newspapers" (A8; http://adage.com/digital/article?article_id=141788). The stories identify the problem not only of shrinking print revenues, but also of lower shares of online ad revenues. The so-called content farms run by AOL, Demand Media, and others generate thousands of stories using armies of freelance writers who charge little for the content they provide. This cheap content may not have the authoritative sourcing and writing provided by professional journalists, but it may be perceived as good enough by some audiences.

Search creates additional problems for newspapers in that advertising for cars, classifieds, and travel have been scooped up by category specific sites such as Edmunds.com, Craigslist.com, and Travelocity.com.

Magazines—A Publication for Everyone

Advertisers like magazines because they offer valuable audiences in terms of income and education and high-quality images and printing. In addition, magazines are not nearly as ephemeral as a TV spot or a newspaper—people tend to keep them around longer, linger over them, and pass them on to others. Some studies suggest that four different readers may see a monthly magazine. (5)

The sheer numbers and varieties of magazines are also surprising. Do you like boats? In just this category, you can choose *Sailing World, Motorboat, Cruising World, Yachting Power, Motoryacht,* or *Salt Water Sportsmen.* They're just a few of the titles listed on *Advertising Age*'s top two hundred magazines (A9; http://adage.com/datacenter/article?article_id=144979). As you can see, magazines can offer consumers publications targeted at very narrow interests and advertisers can match appeals to reader interests with some precision. SRDS offers data on over ten thousand business and consumer magazines, and you can access information at http://www.srds.com.

Like newspapers, magazines depend on multiple revenue streams—subscriptions, newsstand sales, and advertising. Magazines charge advertisers based on the size of the publication's readership whether it's paid circulation, newsstand purchases, or, increasingly, pass-along readers. Much of this is difficult to measure. Although magazine sales have slipped, the biggest hit they've taken is based on advertisers reducing their ad budgets and allocating remaining dollars elsewhere.

However, as *Advertising Age* reports, consumers' appetite for magazines is strong: Mediamark Research & Intelligence reported that over 189 million adults have read a magazine within the past thirty days (A10; http://adage.com/article/mediaworks/magazines-ad-pages-fully-return/138131). Research also shows that readers trust magazine ads more than those in other media and don't find them intrusive. (4)

Nevertheless, it appears that publishers must restructure the magazine business model significantly. In a surprising way, magazines suffer from the same problem that some websites have faced: even though they build robust audiences, advertising or subscription dollars don't necessarily follow in amounts large enough to support and grow the publication.

Some have suggested that devices such as the iPad can offer magazine-like aesthetic and tactile experiences. Many publications, including *Sports Illustrated, Popular Science,* and *O, The Oprah Magazine,* offer iPad apps (A11; http://adage.com/mediaworks/article?article_id=144927). All charge consumers for apps and for individual issues and seek advertising.

Oprah is an example of magazines' digital expansion beyond their core business into other capabilities. Because Oprah Winfrey is known for her television program's book club and recommendations, the app allows readers to access and read books within the *Oprah* app. With greater readership along with targeted behavioral advertising, Hearst, *O*'s publisher, is demanding and getting higher and higher digital ad rates.

Radio

Again, many people have predicted the end of radio, but radio advertising offers some distinct advantages. Most importantly, it offers a huge range of programming options including talk, country, top 40, alternative, classical, oldies, and so on. Media planners can connect the buying characteristics and locations of their target customers with their preferred formats.

Aperture, the optimal time to reach a particular audience, plays an important role here as well since radio is ideal for reaching commuters at "dayparts," such as the morning and evening commutes. Radio media planners price commercial time based on the desirability of the audience for advertisers. The commuting dayparts are usually the most expensive media buys, offering the most ears for commercials.

Radio offers flexibility in that the buyer can change messages relatively easily for special offers and sales. Though it doesn't have the richness of sight and movement that video offers, radio can be extremely creative and effective in triggering listeners' imagination and mind's eye through music, drama, humor, and story. "How to Make Better Radio Ads" points out that radio audiences continue to grow and that smart creative strategies can offer effective brand building (A12; http://adage.com/mediaworks/article?article_id=136781).

Radio advertising is relatively inexpensive, and recent research indicates that listeners find personal relevance and enjoyment in radio and tend to have good recall of ads. (5) Like other media, new formats, Internet radio station access, and programmable digital stations such as Pandora are altering the business model.

Ambient Media

Because of the creative revolution in what counts as media, ambient media can include an astonishing variety of vehicles. *Ambient* is defined as something that surrounds and encircles and that exists in your environment. You might simply observe an ambient message such as a poster, or use an item for another purpose. For example, the bottoms of the security trays at Denver International Airport (and others) feature large printed messages from Zappos, the online shoe retailer. As all air travelers know, the security line is clearly a captive audience. Most of us have also seen ads on napkins, on public restroom doors, and even on drinking straws. We're seeing them pop up on eggs (a CBS programming promotion), on pizza boxes, manholes, and even on flower petals (A13; http://adage.com/article?article_id=144829).

In the past, ambient media usually meant outdoor—that is, billboards. It still most often includes familiar signs with giant messages lining interstate highways and city streets. Of course, advertisers like to place their messages in high traffic areas where lots of prospects are likely to see them. Even though drivers and walkers are likely to glimpse the message for only a moment, advertisers hope that the constant reminder (frequency, in media lingo) will stick with them. Similar to other media trends, advertisers are seeking better metrics as to how many people saw an ad. The Traffic Audit Bureau uses actual traffic counts, surveys, and other measures to provide solid reports and data that could indicate effectiveness.

Another advantage is that drivers and walkers can't zap a message as they can with a DVR, nor can they change the station or channel. However, the brief moments of exposure require that the messages, especially those targeted at drivers, be very simple and eye catching.

But today's outdoor and ambient efforts aren't your father's billboards. Advertising creative expert Pete Barry points out that ambient marketing has evolved into almost any promotional execution that's unexpected. (6) Sometimes this is known as guerilla marketing that often includes stunts, product giveaways, and interactive tactics that involve and surprise audiences who may spread news of the promotion to others. For example, Volkswagen got behind an effort to encourage people to take the stairs by transforming subway steps into working piano keys in Stockholm, Sweden (A14; http://creativity-online.com/work/volkswagen-fun-theory-piano-staircase/17522).

"Inside Outdoor Advertising's Digital Makeover" shows how new digital ambient media can include an array of tactics such as bus shelters that interact with your mobile phone or 3-D installations such as a Mini Cooper with real working headlights embedded in an Albuquerque board (A15; http://adage.com/mediaworks/article?article_id=144347). A unique promotion touting a bank's friendliness to small business posted billboards featuring the services of *very* small businesses such as babysitters and dog walkers.

Inside Outdoor Advertising's Digital Makeover
Old Billboard Medium Embraces Technology, Creativity

This isn't your grandpa's billboard. Out of home or ambient advertising offers some of the most innovative ideas in advertising. This article points out that the "old as the ages" medium has become interactive and can point you to URLs, alert you to sales on your mobile phone, and spark word-of mouth and social media buzz. It can be hyper local, right down to the city block it occupies. Technology-enabled displays offer extraordinary creativity and are deployed on the sides of buildings, in bus shelters, on stair steps, on sidewalks and plazas. For media buyers and sellers, technology is enabling significant changes in how out-of-home media are measured and valued. In the past, advertisers had to rely on estimates of how many people had the chance to see a display. Today, they can measure how many really saw the ad.

As you can see, it's critical for media planners to operate from facts and research, not from common knowledge or the latest fads. Traditional media are often good solutions to marketing problems—it's all based on analysis of your target audience, your product, and your strategy. Those traditional media are often morphing into less traditional forms and ideally are part of a media strategy wherein each element is carefully constructed to support other elements.

Notes

1. Shimmel, S., & McKinley, S. "Data Integration Optimizes Advertising Media Mix," *Nielson Wire* (blog), July 1, 2010. Available at: http://blog.nielsen.com/nielsenwire/online_mobile/data-integration-optimizes-advertising-media-mix/.
2. "The Lazy Medium," *The Economist* 395 (May 1, 2010). Available at: http://www.economist.com/node/15980817?story_id=15980817.
3. "Ground-Breaking Study of Video Viewing Finds Younger Boomers Consume More Video Media Than Any Other Group," Council for Research Excellence (June 2010). Available at: http://www.researchexcellence.com/news/032609_vcm.php.
4. Shimp, T. A. *Advertising Promotion and Other Aspects of Integrated Marketing Communications*, 8th ed. Mason, OH: South-Western Cengage Learning, 2007.
5. Katz, H. *The Media Handbook*. Mahwah, NJ: Lawrence Erlbaum Associates, 2007.
6. Barry, P. *The Advertising Concept Book*. New York: Thames & Hudson, 2008.

Articles

(A1)   Brian Steinberg. "To Get LeBron, ESPN Cedes Control Over Ads, News." Published July 7, 2010. Available at: http://adage.com/mediaworks/article?article_id=144826

(A2)   Rich Thomaselli. "How LeBron's Entourage Got His 'Decision' on ESPN." Published July 12, 2010. Available at: http://adage.com/article?article_id=144882

(A3)   Simon Dumenco. "In Praise of the Original Social Media; Good Ol' Television." Published May 17, 2010. Available at: http://adage.com/mediaworks/article?article_id=143875

(A4)   Brian Steinberg. "Broadcast's Youth Market Starts at 44." Published May 24, 2010. Available at: http://adage.com/upfront2010/article?article_id=144040

(A5)   Brian Steinberg. "Future of TV: Microsoft's Ballmer Sees Content Everywhere." Published January 7, 2010. Available at: http://adage.com/digital/article?article_id=141336

(A6)   Nat Ives. "Newspapers' Paid Circulation Losses Shrink." Published April 26, 2010. Available at: http://adage.com/mediaworks/article?article_id=143509

(A7) Nat Ives. "Mounting Web Woes Pummel Newspapers." Published June 28, 2010. Available at: http://adage.com/mediaworks/article?article_id=144684

(A8) Tasneem Raja. "Google Exec: We're Here to Help Newspapers." Published January 28, 2010. Available at: http://adage.com/digital/article?article_id=141788

(A9) "Magazine Ad Page Leaders 2nd Quarter 2010." Published July 15, 2010. Available at: http://adage.com/datacenter/article?article_id=144979

(A10) Nat Ives. "Why Ad Pages Won't Ever Fully Return to Mags." Published July 27, 2010. Available at: http://adage.com/article/mediaworks/magazines-ad-pages-fully-return/138131

(A11) Nat Ives. "Oprah Magazine's iPad Edition Will Sell and Display E-Books." Published July 14, 2010. Available at: http://adage.com/mediaworks/article?article_id=144927

(A12) Andrew Hampp. "How to Make Better Radio Ads." Published May 21, 2009. Available at: http://adage.com/mediaworks/article?article_id=136781

(A13) "Petal Advertising." Published July 8, 2010. Available at: http://adage.com/article?article_id=144829

(A14) Creativity Online. Available at: http://creativity-online.com/work/volkswagen-fun-theory-piano-staircase/17522

(A15) Abbey Klaassen and Andrew Hampp. "Inside Outdoor Advertising's Digital Makeover." Published June 14, 2010. Available at: http://adage.com/mediaworks/article?article_id=144347

Media Planning for the Internet and Other Digital Media

In January 2009 Tourism Queensland embarked on a global search to find an Island Caretaker to explore the Islands of the Great Barrier Reef in Queensland Australia and report back to the world about their experiences. We like to call this the 'Best Job in the World.' On offer was a salary of AUD $150,000 for a six month position with live in luxury accommodation on Hamilton Island and the opportunity to explore all that the region has to offer.

—From the website IslandReefJob.com

Would you apply for this job?

Who would have thought that such an old medium as classified ads would launch an award-winning digital and integrated marketing campaign? An Australian agency, CumminsNitro, created "The Best Job in The World" for Queensland Tourism. Anna Bligh, Queensland's premier, said the program was "the most successful tourism marketing campaign in history." (1)

Nitro's goal was to "create international awareness of the islands of the Great Barrier Reef and execute a global tourism campaign on a classifieds budget."

With a total campaign budget of $1.2 million (tiny by traditional media standards), the agency placed classified ads in newspapers all over the world, ads that pointed interested people to IslandReefJob.com. Overwhelming traffic briefly crashed the site: On the first day of the promotion, it received more than four million hits in just an hour.

IslandReefJob.com invited applicants to upload a sixty-second video showing how they were right for the job. Queensland Tourism received almost thirty-five thousand applications from some two hundred countries.

The campaign launch video explained that the "Island Caretaker" would feed the fish, collect the mail, explore the Great Barrier Reef islands, and blog about the experience. In addition, the winner would collect $8,800 a month for six months and live rent-free in a luxurious villa.

Further campaign tactics invited the public to vote for their favorite job seeker, and the agency brought sixteen finalists to the island. More than six thousand news stories around the world covered "Best Job," and the agency calculated that the campaign received over $80 million worth of coverage.

> Notably, CumminsNitro won awards in three categories at the 56th International Advertising Festival: cyber website/interactive, PR, and direct marketing. As *Advertising Age* reported, a contest judge said, "What we really loved about ['Best Job in the World"] was that digital tied everything together" (A1; http://adage.com/cannes09/article?article_id=137551).
>
> By the way, 34-year-old British adventurer and charity worker Ben Southall won the job.

That "Best Job" won awards in three categories tells us a lot about what's going on in media. The cyber website/interactive category refers to the digital strategy of using a website, interactivity with applications and voting, and video. The public relations or publicity component garnered millions of dollars worth of earned media with news stories about each aspect of the contest. The direct marketing elements brought potential tourists to a site where they could plan their Australian vacations.

We'll discuss public relations and publicity in greater detail in an upcoming chapter. In this chapter, we'll look at various uses of interactive and digital content and customer motivations to use them. As we've seen in previous chapters, the lines between different types of media are blurring. And, as the vignettes for Old Spice and The Best Job show, today's promotions are often hybrids of many media, old and new.

When online advertising emerged in the mid-1990s, it looked a lot like print promotion expressed in pixels. Websites featured static display ads and banners, and media buyers tried to match site users to ads in very similar ways to newspapers and magazines. Marketers and media producers were still mostly in the one-to-many mindset: informational and entertainment programming were produced by networks, magazines, newspapers, and agencies and delivered to mass audiences.

Third-party online ad networks emerged to help advertisers connect with publishers (and vice versa) and other platforms mostly by selling placements in blogs, websites, social networks, and emails. The network takes a slice from each ad sale for its revenue stream and includes firms such as Izea.com, Advertising.com, and Ad-Ly.com.

The Consumer Power Shift

Few people anticipated the profound power shift between consumers and media, a shift that put consumers in control of their media consumption and even made them media producers. You may recall from our earlier discussions of the media choice model that people use media to fulfill certain communication needs: connectivity, information, entertainment, and shopping.

In addition, different media offer different features, including easy participation, customizability, time shifting and flexibility, mobility, interactivity, search, immediacy, images, and sound. Online media offer all of these features as opposed to traditional media that usually offer only a few. Today's consumers have the power of easy-to-search information to make product comparisons, check prices, find coupons, and get reviews from others who may have bought a product.

As the number of media options balloons, consumers eagerly take advantage of the choices available to them. They can often avoid the interruption model of advertising if they wish, so innovative marketers are constantly creating ways to invite consumers into brand involvement and engagement. Entrepreneurs are inventing new genres of media that fulfill people's communication needs. For instance, blogs provide self-publishing; Amazon is a giant mall with built-in recommendations and easy online buying; Facebook offers friends, some of whom the users have never met; eHarmony dating services promise love; Twitter enables microblogging; YouTube serves up silly and serious videos; and Foursquare rewards people who report on their locations.

According to eMarketer, some 221 million people were online in the United States in 2010 or about 71 percent of the population, and the average age of users is increasing. (2) In fact, the percentage of older users continues to rise, as Pew reported. (3)

	Millennials Ages 18–33	Gen X Ages 34–45	Younger Boomers Ages 45–55	Older Boomers Ages 56–64	Silient Generation Ages 65–73	G.I. Generation Age 74+	All online adults Age 18+
% who go online	95	86	81	76	58	30	**79**

Researchers predict that the growth of online audiences will fuel even more online promotions, and improved technologies and connection speeds will create a rich environment for innovation in the digital space. (3)

The challenge for Internet entrepreneurs and digital marketers is finding ways to make money and avoid irritating users with persuasive messages. The Holy Grail of interactive marketing is brand engagement—developing a relationship and a conversation with choosy consumers or prospects that result in brand loyalty and purchases.

The Internet Advantage

Internet promotion offers distinct advantages to marketers. First, it's relatively easy to measure, at least in comparison with most traditional media. Clicks tell advertisers how many people are accessing their sites or clicking through to get more information. When consumers search for or are exposed to a persuasive message for a product, they can act to make a purchase almost immediately.

Second, advertisers can target messages much more effectively through behavioral targeting. With behavioral targeting, marketers monitor web activity using tiny computer files or "cookies," and based on that activity they learn your actual or potential interest in types of products. Automated computer programs then place ads likely to be relevant to you. These "interest-based ads" are highly controversial because of the potential for privacy issues (A2; http://adage.com/adnetworkexchangeguide09/article?article_id=136003).

On the other hand, many consumers like the customization that targeting brings and are willing to sacrifice some level of privacy for convenience and functionality. If marketers have information about you and your preferences, and if they can match those preferences and purchase behavior to their product offerings, you're a more valuable prospect and they're willing to pay more to reach you.

Third, marketers can enable what author Pete Barry calls "the self sell" by creating rich online experiences that are not only targeted and relevant but also absorbing and enjoyable. (4) Burger King's famous Subservient Chicken (http://www.bk.com/en/us/campaigns/subservient-chicken.html) featured a person dressed up in a chicken suit who would respond to a user's typed commands (jump, lay an egg, sit down, etc.). The strategy dramatized BK's "have it your way" theme, and it was a huge viral success for the brand, though some critics argued that it didn't really sell chicken sandwiches (A3; http://adage.com/post?article_id=39935).

Web e-commerce sites can offer customized products such as Nike iD's "You Design It, We Build It" shoes. Users can choose different colors, materials, and performance characteristics, as well as a personal ID. E-commerce sites can let users test drive different products, an especially useful tool for games and software sellers. Book buyers can preview selected readings from a publication they're considering. The web for many consumers comes with high expectations that the information and entertainment they access is personalized for their needs and desires.

Fourth, marketers can quickly tweak or replace campaigns or ads that don't appear to be achieving their objectives. Rather than being locked into television or print commercials and schedules, they can act on results and on customer feedback. Internet advertising is also much cheaper than television and most print publications.

Although the advantages are clear, many marketers have made missteps in the digital world. Walmart's "The Hub" was a social marketing effort aimed at teenagers that tried to mimic MySpace. However, the site's rigid corporate control of content didn't ring true with the target market or their expectations for social media. Only 91,000 unique users accessed the site compared with 55.8 million unique visitors to MySpace during the same month. The company shut the site down in less than three months. The Walmart strategy led with a social media tactic rather than a good understanding of the nature of web authenticity and consumer control (A4; http://adage.com/article?article_id=112288).

In short, Internet marketing requires the same research-driven strategic thinking to achieve success that applies in any promotional activity.

Internet Marketing

Marketers have an increasing array of online promotional tools, but banner and display ads are the "old" media of the Internet and produce the second biggest revenue stream behind search. In the past, they were usually static banners positioned somewhere on a web page. Advertisers designed them so web surfers would click on the ads and go to specific sites for purchases or additional information. Click through rates (CTRs) were low then—and are low today—in the 1 to 2 percent range. Nonetheless, properly done these ads can be effective for raising brand awareness and for selling certain types of products.

Since the early days of the web, designers and data experts have experimented with rich media ads. Greater bandwidth and faster Internet speeds allow dynamic formats with video, animation, and audio. Research suggests that interactivity increases brand recall 63 percent more than noninteractive ads. (5)

Nevertheless, there are few hard-and-fast rules for effective online advertising. Again, a combination of creative factors, analytics, and testing appear to be the best routes to success. "Online Ads Not Working for You?" cites a study by Millward Brown showing that creative elements such as consistent branding and calls to action are significant in recall and brand awareness (A5; http://adage.com/digital/article?article_id=139795). In "Making Online Ads Suck Less in 8 Easy Steps," John Young proposes a rigorous approach of testing different formats and creative executions (A6; http://adage.com/digitalnext/post?article_id=143368). He advocates evaluation of each banner against alternatives and a disciplined schedule of testing. In direct marketing, this was often called "beat the champ" and the principle is the same: change the offer, the creative, the design, or the color and compare it with the original. As much as is possible, test each element and learn which delivers the best sales.

> **Online Ads Not Working for You? Blame the Creative**
> *Latest Dynamic Logic Study Finds Obsession Over Optimization,*
> *Placement Is Less Important*
>
> Advertisers and agencies constantly tinker with campaign strategies to develop right mix of elements to reach their audiences for maximum effect. As this article explains, among the most challenging questions involve determining how targeting, placement, and creative executions can work together to maximize effectiveness.
>
> There will never be a definitive "right" answer to such questions but the article emphasizes the role of research in getting to the best solutions. Findings of an online research firm suggest that crucial creative elements such as "persistent branding, strong calls to action and even human faces—and not super-targeted or high profile ad placements—make for better ad recall, brand awareness and purchase intent." Of course, this doesn't mean that advertisers can ignore the importance of smart, careful targeting— but the traditional imperative of great creative executions is still alive in the online ad world.

As mentioned above, online advertising is increasingly targeted, sometimes with results that some might find not so much personalized as kind of creepy. "The Pants That Stalked Me on the Web" recounts an *Advertising Age* writer's experience with his online purchase of a pair of shorts (A7; http://adage.com/digitalnext/post?article_id=145204). He soon noticed that the recommendations he received from Zappos.com were following him around the Internet and appearing on many different websites unrelated to apparel. He suggests that many consumers might find this type of targeting to be intrusive and disturbing.

Search

What's known as paid search or search engine marketing is still the biggest kid on the block. Advertisers pay search engines to locate ads or links near your search results. Let's say you have dog and you're planning a vacation that doesn't allow your best friend to go along. You might try searching dog boarding, kennels, or pet sitters in your area. At this point, what's known as "natural search" results will show up ranked according to the search engine's algorithm that tries to find the most relevant results for your query. If you're using Google (and more than 70 percent of searchers do), you'll likely see a list of results and a Google map.

On the top of the page, you'll see sponsored links that advertisers have bid for and bought through Google's AdWords service. (Keep in mind that Google is known to frequently change up its formulas *and* the way it positions links on the page and that it is famously secretive about its methodologies.) Advertisers buy certain search terms and pay a cost per click (CPC) based on complex algorithms. These "algos" create a "quality score" that Google defines this way:

> It looks at a variety of factors to measure how relevant your keyword is to your ad text and to a user's search query. . . . Quality Score helps ensure that only the most relevant ads appear to users on Google. (6)

Advertisers who use key words that score well pay less per click and get more desirable placements of their links on a page. One way to think of Google's quality score service is a kind of matchmaking for consumers and advertisers. Consumers who are looking for certain goods and services want results that are highly relevant to them. Advertisers, of course, want to connect with searchers who want to buy what the advertiser offers. Google watches how successful an advertiser's ads are based on how frequently searchers click on them and calculates the score accordingly.

The quality score was one of the tactics Google adopted to try to make searches more relevant and satisfying after Google had been criticized for delivering search results that weren't on target. In fact, Bing, Microsoft's search engine, launched with advertisements that emphasized Bing's superior search results.

Companies use search engine optimization (SEO) to improve natural search results and move their links higher on the results page. Optimization involves an understanding of how people search, using words and phrases that drive traffic and testing different content to identify how results might change. Another aspect of SEO is measurement of how many links a site has with other popular sites. The revenue stakes are enormous: in just three months in 2010, Google took in $5.09 billion in advertising revenue, including search and display (A8; http://adage.com/digital/article?article_id=144977).

In a related development, Facebook has partnered with Microsoft to use an individual's social preferences and links as key elements of new algorithms. Google's Social Search appears to use a similar strategy. These moves again highlight the dynamic and interconnected nature of online marketing.

Email Marketing

Although Americans are spending less time with email and more with social networks, email is still a powerful sales tool. If you access the Gilt.com or JCrew.com sites for the first time, you may be asked if you'd like to receive emails about new products and sales. This is opt-in email marketing versus spamming, the unsolicited messages you get for everything from prescription drugs to Nigerian inheritance scams. A survey found that 42 percent of consumers like to get promotional messages via email as opposed to only 3 percent for social networking sites (A9; http://adage.com/digital/article?article_id=145285). Email is also a form of social marketing, and networking websites offer email opportunities as well.

> ### Hot or Not: Email Marketing vs. Social-Media Marketing
>
> *Which Is Stronger in the Fight to Woo Consumers?*
>
> The rise of social networking and firms' efforts to figure out how they can use it as an advertising medium has tended to marginalize email marketing. This article describes that although social marketing is a hot trend, email marketing is still a valuable tool in building relationships and in increasing marketers' ROI (return on investment) for their promotional dollars. The author predicts that email marketing will become more social over time and will be increasingly linked with social media as all of the delivery platforms evolve.

Social Networking

Increasingly, people are fulfilling their needs to connect with other people on social media sites, especially Facebook. Gaming is spilling into social media and mobile. *Advertising Age* reports that the online time Americans spent with social media from June 2009 to June 2010 grew by more than 43 percent over the previous year. Americans spent almost 15.8 percent of their online time with social networks, 9.3 percent with online games, and 11.5 percent on email (A10; http://adage.com/digital/article?article_id=145207).

More than seventy million people per month play the Facebook game "Farmville" where members can farm with their friends, build stables and barns, and take care of the cows. Microsoft's Bing promised "farm cash" in Farmville ads and garnered 425,000 new fans who signed up for Bing's Facebook page. (7)

Advertising on social networks is tricky because many users are resistant to commercializing their site. Facebook's earlier foray into monetizing its site, Beacon, created huge user resentment (A11; http://adage.com/article?article_id=122463). However, a redesigned advertising strategy and a new self-serve advertising platform have garnered impressive results. Media experts estimate that Facebook's ad sales will reach $2 billion in 2010. (8) Most of these sales are local and are likely robbing dollars that once went to Yellow Pages advertising. Facebook's display ads are inexpensive in comparison with other online display ads (less than half the costs per impression), and some speculate that their low rates are suppressing overall online display revenue. In addition, display ads that mentioned friends who'd fanned a brand had significantly higher recall by viewers (A12; http://adage.com/digital/article?article_id=143381).

Although Facebook is currently the colossus of social networks, advertisers have other options, and another colossus is clearing space for its own social network: Google. Google Buzz currently offers connections and online conversations, and the giant search network acquired Zynga, a gaming provider, and Slide, a social media company. This suggests that Google, as usual, has big plans to make a splash in the social networking pool. In addition, smaller affinity sites built around hobbies and professional interests may be good plays for certain targeted campaigns.

Similarly, with "social buying" consumers can get discounts by being part of an online community or by recommending products to friends on social networks. Companies such as LivingSocial, Groupon, and Eversave are at the forefront of this trend and continue to expand at astonishing rates.

Gaming

Once considered the exclusive realm of teenagers and twenty-something guys, everyone seems to be a gamer today. New types of games emerge daily and are frequently played on game consoles, the Internet, social networks, and phones. Today, most consumers engage in some kind of game activity and, at least potentially, can be reached with associated advertising (A13; http://adage.com/article/digital/digital-marketing-guide-gaming/142227/).

Massively multiplayer online (MMO) games allow thousands of players to compete simultaneously in fantasy worlds such as "World of Warcraft" and "Lineage." Some games have a form of product placement or ads such as billboard-like signs. As players navigate the game, they may experience ads or brand-related items. Research suggests that if players see the ads as appropriate for the game's atmosphere and storyline, they're more likely have positive attitudes toward the brand. (9) Some games insert brand name merchandise such as cars, beverages, or even guns, and these are known in the business as "in-game" ads.

Companies often install games on their websites in order to make sites "stickier" to users meaning that they'll stick around longer and perhaps engage more fully with the brand. Spicyside.com is the snack food Slim Jim's branded game site with a vibe that reflects the teenage boy target market. Orbitz, the travel site, offers quick and fun travel- and leisure-themed games that are saturated with the Orbitz brand.

Mobile

With the advent of phones that are smart and getting smarter, many Americans are walking around with powerful computers in their pockets. In addition, netbooks, laptops, and tablets such as the iPad and Dell's Streak have untethered people from their wired constraints. Mobile technology continues to change how we navigate our physical worlds, shop, dine, and play. According to Pew, 83 percent of American adults have cell phones or smartphones, and more than half of all adults connect to the Internet wirelessly. Thirty-five percent have accessed the Internet using their mobile device. (10)

Nevertheless, marketers face considerable obstacles in harnessing mobile devices, especially smartphones, in their promotions. First, the screens are small and different phone providers have different screen sizes, touch pads, and capabilities. Second, mobile users are resistant to intrusions, and even minimal uninvited messages could be an irritant on a tiny screen. Third, mobile websites based in browser technology as opposed to applications or apps, tend to be clunkier and harder to use so formats are limited, at least for now.

Texting would seem to be a fruitful mobile advertising option, especially in the 18- to 34-year-old age group where it's much more popular than talking. But advertisers haven't been very successful using texted ads, as the article "Texting Trumps Talking in U.S., Just Not as Ad Platform" shows (A14; http://adage.com/digital/article?article_id=142180). Some companies have built branded apps that have been cool enough or have sufficient utility for users. For example, Kraft has built a menu app called "Big Fork Little Fork" aimed at young parents and kids. (11) At some Starbuck's, you can pay for your latte with the Starbucks card mobile app.

Other apps offer shoppers coupons and price comparisons while the consumer is in the store. An app called ShopSavvy allows shoppers to scan a product's bar code with their camera phones. It then reports online pricing as well as pricing at nearby stores. Such apps can make for radically transparent buying experiences and underscore the power shift between marketers and consumers discussed earlier.

Video and Branded Entertainment

Three former PayPal friends founded YouTube in 2005 when they observed how difficult it was to upload videos for friends and others to see. The video sharing website quickly became a media and cultural phenomenon. Some estimates suggest that YouTube viewers access some two billion videos daily worldwide. (12) Google bought YouTube in 2006 for $1.65 billion.

Online video is big. In March 2010, comScore reported that U.S. Internet users watched 31.2 billion videos in that month alone. Video is a good play for marketers in that it can be deployed in many media formats—on social networking sites, blogs, mobile, and so on. But just because videos and video sites get a lot of hits doesn't mean that managers have found ways to make money. The Internet is littered with darkened sites that attracted lots of traffic, but little revenue. Hulu.com, a video site that offers full episodes of television programs, movies, video clips, and trailers seems to be getting that figured out. Although YouTube attracts far more views, Hulu has been able to charge high rates for its video ads and to sell out its advertising inventory.

How did they do it? They recognized that online consumers want choices and developed a "choose your own" pre-roll ad program. A pre-roll is a brief ad that runs before programming. In addition, Hulu offers high-quality professional material as opposed to the user-generated and short-form clips seen on YouTube (A15; http://adage.com/digital/article?article_id=144968).

Another video option is creating a web series by building a branded and original entertainment program. Successful examples include Procter & Gamble's "Buppies" and Ikea's "Easy to Assemble." A reality-based web program was "The Real Women of Philadelphia" created by Kraft foods. It invited cooks to submit recipes and ultimately participate in a cook-off with celebrity chef Paula Deen of the Food Network (A16; http://adage.com/article?article_id=145276).

Viral videos in marketing are a form of publicity or earned media that advertisers place on sites such as YouTube hoping that millions of email forwards raise the brand's profile. Keep in mind that you can't make a viral video—making a video is a communication tactic. Having a video go viral is the desired outcome. A great viral video will feature the brand enough to make it effective, but not so much as to make it appear blatantly commercial. It will surprise and delight viewers and give them a reason to share and give other media reasons to comment on and highlight it (A17; http://adage.com/article?article_id=145240).

Interactive and web-based television has been an elusive piece of the online puzzle. Like Apple TV, Google TV seeks to turn your television set into an interactive monitor with web-like capabilities. According to Google's promotional video, new televisions will be equipped with interactive and web surfing capabilities or existing sets can be connected with a new separate box. The company claims that Google TV will transform the television into a complete entertainment device with your photos, music, games, and Android apps—all packaged in a personalized and customizable format (A18; http://adage.com/digital/article?article_id=144014).

Some advertising experts think that this rich and personalized service will offer the opportunity to develop new ad formats, browser advertising optimized for the larger screen experience, and links between mobile devices. As you can see, Google TV and similar products combine formerly distinct media channels. Aside from offering significant advertising opportunities, these offerings require careful coordination of media channels so your brand sends powerful and consistent messages.

Notes

1. O'Loughlin, T. "Briton lands 'world's best job' as caretaker of Australian island," *The Guardian*, May 6, 2009. Available at: http://www.guardian.co.uk/uk/2009/may/06/briton-wins-best-job-australia.

2. "U.S. Internet Users, 2010," eMarketer. Available at: http://www.emarketer.com/Reports/All/Emarketer_2000670.aspx.

3. "Generations Online in 2010," Pew Research Center. Available at: http://pewresearch.org/pubs/1831/generations-online-2010.

4. Barry, P. *The Advertising Concept Book*. New York: Thames & Hudson, 2008.

5. Barnum Sully research 2010.

6. Google AdWords Help. Available at: http://adwords.google.com/support/aw/bin/answer.py?hl=en&answer=10215.

7. Vranica, S. "Brands Friending Social Gaming Amid New Web Craze," *Wall Street Journal*, August 8, 2010.

8. Womack, B. "Facebook 2010 Sales Said Likely to Reach $2 Billion, More Than Estimated," *Bloomberg.com* (blog), December 15, 2010. Available at: http://www.bloomberg.com/news/2010-12-16/facebook-sales-said-likely-to-reach-2-billion-this-year-beating-target.html.

9. Wise, K., Bolls, P. D., Kim, H., Venkataraman, A., & Meyer, R. "Enjoyment of Advergames and Brand Attitudes: The Impact of Thematic Relevance," *Journal of Interactive Advertising* 9(1), 2008.

10. Rainie, L. "Internet, broadband, and cell phone statistics," Pew Internet, January 5, 2010. Available at: http://www.pewinternet.org/Reports/2010/Internet-broadband-and-cell-phone-statistics.aspx?r=1.

11. Silverstein, B. "Kraft Craftily Builds Menu App for iPad," brandchannel, July 13, 2010. Available at: http://www.brandchannel.com/home/post/2010/07/13/Kraft-iPad-App-Big-Fork-Little-Fork.aspx.

12. Chapman, G. "YouTube Serving Up Two Billion Videos Daily," Google News, May 16, 2010. Available at: http://www.google.com/hostednews/afp/article/ALeqM5jK4sI9GfUTCKAkVGhDzpJ1ACZm9Q.

Articles

(A1)   Ann-Christine Diaz. "Tourism Queensland's 'Best Job' Picks Up Its Third Grand Prix." Published June 24, 2010. Available at: http://adage.com/cannes09/article?article_id=137551

(A2)   Rich Karpinski. "Will Using Behavioral Data Lead to Smarter Ad Buys?" Published April 20, 2009. Available at: http://adage.com/adnetworkexchangeguide09/article?article_id=136003

(A3)   Bob Garfield. "War & Peace and Subservient Chicken." Published April 26, 2004. Available at: http://adage.com/post?article_id=39935

(A4)   Mya Frazier. "Walmart Shuts Down the Hub." Published October 4, 2006. Available at: http://adage.com/article?article_id=112288

(A5)   Kunur Patel. "Online Ads Not Working for You? Blame the Creative." Published October 20, 2009. Available at: http://adage.com/digital/article?article_id=139795

(A6)   John Young. "Making Online Ads Suck Less in 8 Easy Steps." Published April 19, 2010. Available at: http://adage.com/digitalnext/post?article_id=143368

(A7)   Michael Learmonth. "The Pants That Stalked Me on the Web." Published August 2, 2010. Available at: http://adage.com/digitalnext/post?article_id=145204

(A8)   Edmund Lee. "Google Profit Surges as Marketers Return to Search." Published July 15, 2010. Available at: http://adage.com/digital/article?article_id=144977

(A9)   Steve Rubel. "Hot or Not: Email Marketing vs. Social-Media Marketing." Published August 9, 2010. Available at: http://adage.com/digital/article?article_id=145285

(A10)   Jack Neff. "Time Spent on Facebook, Gaming Surges." Published August 2, 2010. Available at: http://adage.com/digital/article?article_id=145207

(A11)   Abbey Klaassen. "Why Lying, Not Beacon, Was Facebook's Biggest Blunder." Published December 6, 2007. Available at: http://adage.com/article?article_id=122463

(A12)   Jack Neff. "Nielsen: Facebook's Ads Work Pretty Well." Published April 19, 2010. Available at: http://adage.com/digital/article?article_id=143381

(A13)   Matt Story. "Digital Marketing Guide: Gaming" Published February 22, 2010. Available at: http://adage.com/article/digital/digital-marketing-guide-gaming/142227/

(A14)   Michael Bush. "Texting Trumps Talking in U.S., Just Not as Ad Platform." Published February 18, 2010. Available at: http://adage.com/digital/article?article_id=142180

(A15)   Michael Learmonth. "New Data Shows Hulu Serves More Video Ads Than Google." Published July 15 2010. Available at: http://adage.com/digital/article?article_id=144968

(A16)   Andrew Hampp. "If You Build a Web Series Around It, Will They Come?" Published August 9, 2010. Available at: http://adage.com/article?article_id=145276

(A17)   Michael Learmonth. "Levi's Walking Man Strides Onto Viral Chart." Published August 5, 2010. Available at: http://adage.com/article?article_id=145240

(A18)   Kunur Patel. "Google TV: What Does It Mean for Advertisers?" Published May 20, 2010. Available at: http://adage.com/digital/article?article_id=144014

CHAPTER 17

Promotions and Their Relationship to Advertising

© MACON VALERIE/SIPA/Newscom

Every fan of "The Simpsons" knows the Kwik-E-Mart, the animated series' send up of convenience stores that looks suspiciously like the 7-Eleven chain. At Kwik-E-Mart, you can find Apu (the Indian-American owner), Buzz Cola, Krusty-O's cereal, the Slurpee-like Squishee, and nonsense promotional signs such as "These things won't be gone until <u>you</u> buy them!"

The Simpsons: The Movie joined with the real 7-Eleven for an imaginative and gutsy co-marketing promotion. The big idea? Transform eleven of the chain's 6,400 stores into mock Kwik-E-Marts complete with outdoor signage, goofy products, and even graffiti, courtesy of the Simpson family brat, Bart.

Moviemaker Twentieth Century Fox and the convenience chain also stocked the other U.S. 7-Elevens with Simpsons products, including collectible cups, temporary tattoos, magnets, and comic books. Other food items featured members of the Simpson family on the package. Another aspect of the promotion was a contest to find the best "real" Springfield, the Simpson's hometown. The winning town, Springfield, Vermont, hosted the movie's premiere.

People lined up to experience the Kwik-E-Mart stores, generating thousands of stories in local and national media and capturing the attention of a key demographic, 18- to 28-year-old men. (1)

Advertising Age reviewer Bob Garfield wrote that the 7-Eleven executives' willingness to lampoon themselves was "one of the most courageous acts in marketing history. The courage will be rewarded" (A1; http://adage.com/post?article_id=119062).

In this chapter, we'll look at sales promotion, cross marketing, coupons, loyalty programs, giveaways, and in-store promotion. We'll see examples of some of the most creative efforts to spur an immediate purchase, foster brand loyalty and repeat purchases, encourage people to try a product, or give them a financial incentive to buy an item they might not otherwise have chosen.

As you've seen in previous chapters, the lines between categories of promotion are blurring. The *Simpsons* movie promotion scored in many categories: first, it publicized the movie *and* the chain, getting millions of dollars worth of earned media. Second, it highlighted a brand objective for 7-Eleven in making it a cooler, hipper choice for a young demographic. Third, the contest, the store visits, and the merchandise all provided incentives and raised awareness of the movie and the series. Traditional advertising on television and in print featured the movie and the promotion.

Sales Promotion

The key words in understanding sales promotion are *short-term* and *incentive*. Marketers use sales promotion when they're willing to provide price cuts, gifts, or rewards to a target audience in hopes of getting an immediate but likely temporary sales boost. Their three main targets are a manufacturer's sales force, the trade (resellers including wholesalers and retailers), and consumers. (1) For instance, if Coca-Cola wants to increase sales of VitaminWater, it may create a contest offering cash awards or prizes to its top salespeople. For the retailer, Coke may offer reduced prices so the store can sell VitaminWater at a discount. Or, Coke might provide free displays or other in-store materials known as point-of-purchase or point-of-sale promotions. For the consumer, the retailer and Coke may co-market to offer prizes or premiums, cents-off coupons, or points the consumer can accumulate for other benefits.

As with other elements of advertising and promotional planning, marketers need to weigh the risks and benefits of each initiative. "How to Balance Brand Building and Price Promotion" suggests that, especially in economic downturns, marketers need to frequently update analytics by monitoring customer behaviors, sales, and the larger marketing environment (A2; http://adage.com/cmostrategy/article?article_id=141232).

> ### How to Balance Brand Building and Price Promotion
> *As the Economy Improves, the Debate Will Intensify:*
> *Don't Be a High-Stakes Gambler*
>
> This article explains how the "great recession" that began in 2008 intensified marketers' discussions about how to properly allocate their resources between what's known as "long-term brand building" and "short-term price promotion." Put simply, the long-term strategy seeks to establish a brand in customers' minds as preferable to competitors and to position the brand as top of mind awareness for consumers. Marketers usually accomplish this through consumer advertising. However, especially in economic turndowns, marketers eager to pump up sales emphasize price promotions with coupons, big price cuts, and the like. This usually results in quick sales upticks—but has a dark side for the companies. Consumers quickly develop the "buy only on the deal" mindset. This puts firms in the position of competing only on price and in suppressing their margins of profit, a combination that can be disastrous in the fiercely competitive consumer package goods category.

Researchers must analyze what's known as price elasticity, the study of how consumer demand for a product changes when the price changes or when the price of a competitive product changes. In addition, companies need to be mindful of the danger of training consumers to "buy only on the deal," thus potentially damaging not only profits but brand reputation. It sounds complicated, but it's important for marketers to understand the impact of a price reduction or increase on sales, repeat sales, and future consumer behavior.

Companies using sales promotions also risk disappointing customers through insufficient planning or preparation. Pepsi offered New York Yankees fans the promise of free baseball tickets. After standing in long lines, people learned that Pepsi was giving away fewer tickets than it promised and a near riot ensued with chants of "Pepsi Sucks" (A3; http://adage.com/adages/post?article_id=136057).

Coupons and Samples

More than one hundred years ago, the Post Company issued what were likely the first coupons to consumers for the venerable Grape Nuts cereal. "Coupon" sketches the history, benefits, and pitfalls of coupon programs (A4; http://adage.com/article?article_id=98604). From the traditional coupons snipped out of newspaper circulars to evolving online and outdoor executions, coupons are a major element in sales promotion. Leo Burnett Advertising in Toronto created a unique distribution for client James Ready beers with the theme of allowing beer drinkers to save up to buy more James Ready beer (A5; http://creativity-online.com/work/james-ready-billboard-coupon/19864).

The agency placed coupons on billboards and invited people to use their mobile phone cameras to take photos of the offers to be redeemed at local retailers. The "coupons" could be redeemed for quirky drinkers' necessities such as "15% Off Couples Hair Removal." Of course, this tactic functioned mainly as a traditional outdoor advertisement, but it also co-marketed with local businesses and offered a new way of coupon distribution.

QR codes are also finding their way into many advertising and promotional applications. The QR, or quick response, code is a two-dimensional figure that contains data and can be read by mobile devices. For instance, a consumer can scan a QR code on a window decal, sign, or other medium and receive a mobile coupon, link to a website, or get sale information. Even better, the consumer can redeem the coupon directly from her phone with no need for printing (A6; http://adage.com/digitalnext/post?article_id=140932).

Young parents who also want text alerts about promotions and deals are adopting other forms of mobile coupons. "Study Says More Parents Embracing Mobile Coupons" reveals changing patterns of usage with services such as Groupon (A7; http://adage.com/digital/article?article_id=145355). Smartphone innovations will likely further change the face of coupon distribution and redemption.

Sampling is mainly aimed at encouraging consumers to try out a new product. Traditional in-store programs let people taste a food manufacturer's snack, try out a new perfume, or get a trial-sized sample. Other distribution methods include perfume strips and packets of cosmetics bound inside of magazines, mass mailing of trial sizes of products, restaurant samples of new beverages, and distribution at sports and entertainment venues.

The stampede toward social networks attracted Splenda artificial sweetener with its Splenda Mist prototype. Using it, diners can spritz foods using a pocket- or purse-size spray bottle. The company's campaign on Facebook invited users to register for a first look at Splenda Mist. Those who registered delivered up their email and shipping addresses as well as demographic information. The company asked for feedback from those trying the product and obtained fifteen hundred completed surveys. In just two weeks, Splenda gave away more than sixteen thousand samples (A8; http://adage.com/digital/article?article_id=137851).

Premiums, Frequent Shopper, and Loyalty Programs

Premiums are usually defined as gifts offered to consumers as a way to encourage them to make a purchase decision. They overlap with other aspects of sales promotion in that they are often also intended to encourage a trial of a product or service. eBay, the online auction and retail site, partnered with Delta Airlines in a promotion to offer free WiFi to Christmas holiday passengers. The passengers used a promotion code that linked to eBay's holiday website thus accomplishing several goals: first, Delta could showcase its new service and offer an incentive to holiday fliers. Second, eBay could introduce many new users to its services during a peak pre-Christmas and Hanukkah shopping window (A9 http://adage.com/article?article_id=140315).

The Gap combined a publicity stunt with a customer loyalty and premium program called "Sprize yourself today" (A10; http://creativity-online.com/work/gap-sprize/18063). A Gap store in Canada literally turned a store upside down—signage, fixtures, and display—to highlight their Sprize loyalty program. Many news stories featured amazed shoppers encountering the store whose transformation dramatized the loyalty concept that The Gap was turning shopping on its head. Sprize members received "splurge insurance" that promised if a purchased item went on sale within fifteen days, shoppers would automatically get a credit to their account. Members also received notice of private sales and 15 percent off merchandise on a day of their choosing.

Sponsorships

Sponsorships are become increasingly important in the integrated marketing communication mix. Typically, a brand can align itself with an event such as the World Cup or Olympics, or a sport such as NASCAR or professional football. This usually involves acquiring the rights to be identified as a sponsor in the venue and its identifying materials. Marketing planners look for sponsorship opportunities that are a good fit for their brand image, target audience, and goals. For instance, a staid insurance firm probably wouldn't want to link its name to an edgy sport such as World Wrestling Entertainment, unless of course the goal was to drastically change the audience the insurance company was trying to reach.

Companies also sponsor cultural events such as concerts, art museum shows, charitable events, and festivals. (2) Often this type of sponsorship is aimed at burnishing companies' reputations as good corporate citizens. This is known as cause marketing, and companies provide support for not-for-profit organizations dedicated to education, literacy, health matters, children's issues, and the like. Pepsi's Refresh campaign redirected marketing dollars from Super Bowl ads to a social media initiative that solicits consumers' ideas for community projects. Visitors to refresheverything.com vote and decide on the winning projects that receive grants ranging from $5,000 to $250,000. Categories include health, arts and culture, food and shelter, the planet, neighborhoods, and education (A11; http://adage.com/digital/article?article_id=141973).

Whether this departure from Pepsi's tradition of fun and entertaining ads will be effective is unclear. However, Coke fired back with a Facebook charity promotion linked to its Super Bowl advertising. For every bottle of Coke users virtually give to others on Facebook, the company donated $1 to Boys & Girls Clubs and offered sneak previews of Super Bowl ads (A12; http://adage.com/superbowl10/article?article_id=141777). But the lure of the Super Bowl is very strong: on September 15, 2010, *Ad Age* reported that Pepsi was back for the 2011 Super Bowl with three ads (A13; http://adage.com/article?article_id=145898).

Anheuser-Busch also reallocated some marketing dollars when it moved a portion of its online budget to big event sponsorships and successfully bid to become the NFL's official beer. The NFL sponsorship cost a reported $500 million for a five-year commitment. This deal plus A-B's "official beer" sponsorships of the NBA, the PGA, the LPGA, ML Soccer, and others is a significant strategic move and likely an attempt to wall off such events from major competitors. Such arrangements allow the advertiser to use game footage and league logos in their creative executions, something marketing executives think is a significant advantage (A14; http://adage.com/article?article_id=143774).

Sponsorships may be vulnerable to ambush marketing, a practice that flouts regulations against using an event to promote a product without paying for the rights. Nevertheless, major brands often try to use measures to piggyback on major events such as the World Cup held in June 2010. Both Nike and Carlsberg deployed highly successful viral videos to gain consumers' attention. Nike's "Write the Future" spot pulled more than twenty-two million views, as the article "Nike, Carlsberg Ambush Way to World Cup Buzz" describes (A15; http://adage.com/article?article_id=144396).

Challenges for sponsorship campaigns include the difficulty in measuring the investment's return on investment (ROI). "Why Brands Need to Better Optimize the Value of Their Sponsorship ROI" notes that companies need to identify their marketing objectives and use research to quantify the sales or other metric resulting from a sponsorship. The article offers this useful example of the decision making that should take place:

> A Nascar team sponsor was evaluating how a change to a less popular driver would affect the sponsorship's ROI. By understanding the chief factors that determine Nascar ROI—the popularity, success and likability of the driver—it was projected through research that, although incremental sales might drop in the short run, the lower price the marketer would pay would actually raise the ROI (A16; http://adage.com/sportsmarketing10/article?article_id=145070).

Another issue with sponsorships is managing the potential risks of linking a brand to a celebrity, league, or event. "What to Do When Your Sponsorship Agreement Goes Sour" (A17; http://adage.com/article?article_id=142247) suggests that companies carefully consider the relationship between their target markets and the sponsored individual or organization. It argues that it's unwise to "put all your eggs in one basket" by having only one or two celebrities or organizations in their portfolios. If a sponsorship goes really sour as Accenture's sole partnership with Tiger Woods did following the sex scandal, the marketer has few options except to end the relationship.

Still, sponsorships are growing in importance with their ability to deploy many tactics and consumer experiences. Coke hired Chinese pop music sensation Leehom for a 2009 program called "Open Happiness" and developed outdoor and print advertising, promotions, and a remix of a Leehom song written for Coca-Cola. Consumers downloaded the "Open Happiness" video via Bluetooth on interactive bus stop signs and could opt in for a mobile ringtone. The campaign even included a cause marketing component with 10 percent of ringtone download revenues going to the Coca-Cola Yunnan Aids Orphan charity (A18; http://adage.com/article.php?article_id=137935).

Point of Purchase

If you're like most of us, when you're standing in the checkout line at the gas station or supermarket, a display of candy bars, a rack of magazines, or breath mints catches your eye and you put it on the counter. These are point-of-purchase (POP) or point-of-sale (POS) efforts and are generally categorized under trade promotions. They can include in-store displays such as celebrity cardboard cutouts, custom display shelves, posters, and increasingly, digital displays. The goal of POP strategies is to encourage an impulse buy whether the displays are placed around the store or at the crucial checkout point.

Retail marketing is a huge aspect of many companies' strategies, especially for the categories of consumer packaged goods (CPGs). These are items such as cosmetics, beverages, clothing, food, and other "consumables" that people use regularly and have to replace, as opposed to durable or hard goods that may last several years, such as appliances or furniture. "Trade Marketing Finally Gets Some Respect (Well, at P&G)" describes consumer packaged goods company Procter & Gamble's restructuring to ensure that it receives the same level of analysis as other tactics. The article reports that P&G's investment in trade marketing is estimated at $2 billion annually (A19; http://adage.com/article?article_id=117379).

As for other aspects of the marketing mix, planners are continually searching for the most effective tactics in attracting consumer dollars. An example is a study that compared the effects of price reductions versus in-store displays as sales tools. The research found that low-tech cardboard units drove more sales than price reductions (A20; http://adage.com/article?article_id=132767).

Trade Marketing Finally Gets Some Respect (Well, at P&G)

Most consumers don't give much thought to "trade marketing" or the many strategies and tactics marketers deploy to get their attention and dollars. This article points out how the traditional organizational structure of most consumer products firms have had trade promotions as part of the sales force. In the past, the silos of advertising, sales, public relations and other marketing elements discouraged all of these divisions from working together. But when P&G, the world's biggest and most influential CP firm, drastically changes its strategy, the world's marketing experts take notice.

In assigning over $2 billion of its trade marketing money to the brand marketing teams, it's a sign that trade promotions should and must be part of each brand's marketing strategy based on research and sales results: "Once the new system is introduced, general managers or marketing directors who find a brand responds better to trade marketing than consumer marketing will be able to shift more funds in-store. This should make for a more genuinely discipline-agnostic P&G."

Digital marketing is pushing its way into POP strategies as well. You may recall that one of the elements of the media choice model is aperture, or the optimal time when a consumer is mostly like to make a purchase. Innovations in location-based marketing are giving companies new ways to take advantage of potential consumer receptivity to a purchase. Mobile technologies now allow consumers to opt into location-based mobile marketing. "Geo-fencing" or "geo-triggers" allow stores to communicate with customers once they go into a defined geographical area.

Innovations in this technology are emerging every day. The Minneapolis-based Ovative Group is fostering a product that places small hardware devices in stores that detect smart phones and uses apps to enable the customer to have a personalized experience. The app detects the store, offers coupons, and reviews and recommends products. It also gathers information about your purchases and movements in the store. For example, if you spent some time looking at a flat screen television, the retailer could send you follow up emails for sales and other promotions. (3)

Consumers can choose to follow a brand or retailer and get personalized offers via SMS (texts) or other technology. This can prompt action since the message is likely to be relevant and timely, key aspects of aperture-based selling. "Forget Foursquare: Why Location Marketing Is New Point-of-Purchase" quotes a Borrell Associates research executive who says, "What used to be called point-of-purchase is now called mobile advertising" (A21; http://adage.com/digital/article?article_id=142902). The same executive went on to say that "the buckets that were so nicely separated between advertising and promotions starting to fade." Borrell predicts that location-based mobile spending will grow to $4 billion by 2015.

> ### Forget Foursquare: Why Location Marketing Is New Point of-Purchase
>
> *Ad Age* offers some intriguing possibilities in this article about the potential for mobile advertising. Consider this paragraph: "It's the ad served while you are reading the news in the morning on an e-reader that knows you're at home and three blocks from a Starbucks. It's a loyalty program on your phone that, through a hotel-room sensor, sets the lights and thermostat and turns the TV to CNN when you walk in the door. It's finding a restaurant in a strange city on a Tuesday night, discovering that a store nearby stocks the TV you're looking for, or that a certain grocery on the way home has the cut of meat you need."
>
> As a consumer, you can enjoy the feeling that your likes (and dislikes) matter to a firm, you can be reminded that a latte just now would be especially welcome, and that you can save time with a mobile update about the product you're looking for right now. The article reveals that about a third of searches have "local intent" or the desire to fulfill some purchase need at a retailer near the consumer. Surging innovations in mobile apps and other technologies will likely spur the development of even more sophisticated mobile advertising.

As appealing as these geo-based technologies may be, persistent problems regarding privacy remain. This applies especially to children, who are considered to be more vulnerable to marketing messages.

Debates about how best to allocate marketing dollars will continue to rage as metrics for each tactical approach become more precise. Although traditional advertising, especially on television, has always been the most glamorous part of the business, trade and consumer promotion have the biggest budgets—a phenomenon explained in the article "In Push for Digital Dollars, Look Beyond CPG's Big TV Budgets" (A22; http://adage.com/article?article_id=142078). Consumer packaged goods (CPG) companies spend vast amounts of money on their marketing efforts in part because shoppers need to be reminded of brands and preferences and in part because the competition is so fierce. CPG sales in 2008 were over $1 trillion. In addition, the vast numbers of brands and products create a cluttered consumer environment that many believe requires substantial promotional and in-store investment. The numbers tell the story: In 2008, manufacturers spent 25 percent of revenues on marketing and 78 percent of that was allocated to promotions.

Notes

1. Grossberg, J. "Cowabunga! 7-Elevens Get Kwik-E Makeover," *E! Online* (blog), July 2, 2007. Available at: http://www.eonline.com/uberblog/b55532_Cowabunga_7-Elevens_Get_Kwik-E_Makeover.html#ixzz0y1PjXymx.

2. Shimp, T. A. *Advertising Promotion and Other Aspects of Integrated Marketing Communications*, 8th ed. Mason, OH: South-Western Cengage Learning, 2007.

3. Kim Garretson, Ovative principal, Forum on Digital Innovation, personal communication May 3, 2011.

Articles

(A1) Bob Garfield. "7-Eleven's Simpsons Movie Stunt: Brilliant Cross-Promotion." Published July 9, 2007. Available at: http://adage.com/post?article_id=119062

(A2) Doug Brooks. "How to Balance Brand Building and Price Promotion." Published December 29, 2009. Available at: http://adage.com/cmostrategy/article?article_id=141232

(A3) Ken Wheaton. "Pepsi Promotion Ends with Chants of 'Pepsi Sucks.'" Published April 17, 2009. Available at: http://adage.com/adages/post?article_id=136057

(A4) "Coupon." Published September 15, 2003. Available at: http://adage.com/article?article_id=98604

(A5) "James Ready Beer." Creativity Online. Available at: http://creativity-online.com/work/james-ready-billboard-coupon/19864.

(A6) Allison Mooney. "Google Bets (Again) on QR Codes." Published December 7, 2009. Available at: http://adage.com/digitalnext/post?article_id=140932

(A7) Kunur Patel. "Study Says More Parents Embracing Mobile Coupons." Published August 12, 2009. Available at: http://adage.com/digital/article?article_id=145355

(A8) Natalie Zmuda. "Facebook Turns Focus Group with Splenda Product-Sampling App." Published July 13, 2009. Available at: http://adage.com/digital/article?article_id=137851

(A9) Natalie Zmuda. "EBay Gets Onboard with Delta for Holiday Promotion." Published November 4, 2009. Available at: http://adage.com/article?article_id=140315

(A10) "Sprize." Creativity Online. Available at: http://creativity-online.com/work/gap-sprize/18063)

(A11) Natalie Zmuda. "Pass or Fail, Pepsi's Refresh Will Be Case for Marketing Textbooks." Published February 8, 2010. Available at: http://adage.com/digital/article?article_id=141973

(A12) Natalie Zmuda. "Coke Ties Facebook Charity Promotion to Super Bowl Ads." Published January 27, 2010. Available at: http://adage.com/superbowl10/article?article_id=141777

(A13) Natalie Zmuda. "Pepsi Storms Back Into the Super Bowl." Published September 15, 2010. Available at: http://adage.com/article?article_id=145898

(A14) Jeremy Mullman. "A-B's Return to NFL Signals Bet on Big-Event Sponsorships." Published May 10, 2010. Available at: http://adage.com/article?article_id=143774

(A15) Jeremy Mullman. "Nike, Carlsberg Ambush Way to World Cup Buzz." Published June 11, 2010. Available at: http://adage.com/article?article_id=144396

(A16) John Rowady. "Why Brands Need to Better Optimize the Value of Their Sponsorship ROI." Published July 26, 2010. Available at: http://adage.com/sportsmarketing10/article?article_id=145070

(A17) Jim Andrews. "What to Do When Your Sponsorship Agreement Goes Sour." Published February 22, 2010. Available at: http://adage.com/article?article_id=142247

(A18) Normandy Madden. "Coke Partners with Pop Star Leehom for Summer Promotion." Published July 15, 2009. Available at: http://adage.com/article.php?article_id=137935

(A19) Jack Neff. "Trade Marketing Finally Gets Some Respect (Well, at P&G)." Published June 18, 2007. Available at: http://adage.com/article?article_id=117379

(A20) Jack Neff. "In-store Displays Are More Effective Than Price Cuts." Published November 24, 2008. Available at: http://adage.com/article?article_id=132767

(A21) Kunur Patel. "Forget Foursquare: Why Location Marketing Is New Point-of-Purchase." Published March 22, 2010. Available at: http://adage.com/digital/article?article_id=142902

(A22) Gian Fulgoni. "In Push for Digital Dollars, Look Beyond CPG's Big TV Budgets." Published February 15, 2010. Available at: http://adage.com/article?article_id=142078

18 CHAPTER

Public Relations and Advertising

Sitting aboard a United Airlines jet waiting to deplane, Dave Carroll was horrified to see the company's baggage handlers crashing guitar cases into the ground. He alerted flight attendants who ignored him. Carroll soon learned that the baggage handlers broke his $3,700 Taylor guitar (A1; http://adage.com/adages/post?article_id=137817).

Later, he contacted numerous customer service employees at United who repeatedly passed him along to others, told him that his claim was unreasonable, and treated him with bored disdain. They denied his claim.

His response after he couldn't get any satisfaction from United? He wrote and performed a song, posted it on YouTube, and the negative publicity for the airline poured in. The song, entitled "United Breaks Guitars," goes like this:

> I've heard all your excuses
> and I've chased your wild gooses
> and this attitude of yours I say must go.
> United, you broke my Taylor guitar.
> United, some big help you are.
> You broke it, you should fix it.
> You're liable just admit it.
> I should have flown with someone else
> Or gone by car.
> Because United breaks guitars. (1)

United finally responded after the YouTube video received more than two million views—and even used some social media to do it. (2)

United's stonewalling and ignoring what appeared to be a legitimate customer complaint demonstrates how inadequate planning, poor employee training, and consumer-unfriendly policies can blow up into genuine crises. Regardless of your business, paying attention to customers and other publics on whom you depend has never been more important. Every contact a customer has with your company defines your brand, including employee attitudes and behaviors, the look and cleanliness of your stores, your product performance, your web presence, and of course, your advertising and public relations messages.

This chapter focuses on the evolving role of public relations and how PR practices relate to advertising and other forms of corporate and marketing communication. We'll discuss the concept of controlled and uncontrolled media, publicity and earned media, different roles of public relations, crisis communication, and public relations' growing importance in the marketing mix.

When people hear the term *public relations*, many different activities and functions come to mind. For some people, it's the glib, glad-handing fellow who charms people into going along with his views or "spins" the facts to change people's minds. For others, it brings to mind a glamorous job that mostly requires expense account lunches and schmoozing skills.

In reality, public relations is a complex set of communication approaches to all of a brand's stakeholders, including consumers, government regulators and elected officials, interest groups, employees, retailers, investors, and even vendors. Missouri Professor Glen Cameron, one of the world's most highly regarded PR researchers, defines public relations as "the strategic management of competition and conflict for the benefit of one's own organization—and when possible—also for the mutual benefit of the organization and its various stakeholders or publics." (3)

This definition suggests a mindset that not only emphasizes dialogue over one-way communication and the importance of strategic versus tactical thinking, but also acknowledges that conflict is an inevitable part of doing business. It further suggests that responsible public relations should serve the organization *and* contribute to the well-being of publics. This may seem to be an idealized view, but many companies espouse the view that being a good corporate citizen is not only the right thing to do, it's also good for business.

Controlled and Uncontrolled Media

As you've seen in earlier chapters, traditional advertising is usually defined as persuasive messages placed in paid space and time. It's often described as controlled media, meaning that the advertiser can specify when and where a message is deployed, at least initially. Other types of controlled media that are considered part of the public relations function include a firm's website, public speaking events, RSS feeds, emails, and special events. Publicity and other forms of public relations communication are usually uncontrolled media. For example, the originator of a news release can distribute a new product story to traditional news outlets, blogs, or online publications. However, she can't specify if, when, or how the publication will use it or how it will be presented. (4) When publicity efforts using controlled or uncontrolled media result in news coverage, viral success, Facebook fans, website hits, or purchases, it's considered to be "earned media." We refer to it in that way because marketers "earn" the publicity when the PR activity is exciting or interesting enough to attract others' attention. If it attracts the attention of opinion leaders or influencers, the marketer gets even bigger bang for the buck. Earned media placements are very attractive to marketers in that they are often far less expensive than paid advertising, and consumers frequently find them more credible than advertising.

With the rise of digital media, even "controlled" media can take off in ways unexpected by the creators. Some offended parents interpreted a television ad for the pain reliever Motrin, manufactured by Johnson & Johnson, as implying that babies were little more than fashion accessories for moms. J&J pulled the ad from its schedule and its website after social media backlash that included a funny and biting parody (A2; http://adage.com/adages/post?article_id=132738). On sites such as YouTube, parodies and mashups of traditional ads can take on lives of their own. For example, Apple's "I'm a Mac" and "Silhouette" campaigns sparked hundreds of videos including a copycat ad from a Mexican advertising agency. "Mexican Riff on Apple Advertising Has Locals Crying Plagiarism" describes an ad that, while not a parody, clearly borrows its format from the Apple "I'm a Mac" spots (A3; http://adage.com/article?article_id=138095).

Uncontrolled media such as crowd-sourced efforts or online contests can also have unintended consequences. When GM invited consumers to create their own commercials for the Tahoe SUV, the company received more than twenty-one thousand entries. Unfortunately, three thousand of the spots mocked SUVs in general and the Tahoe in particular. These gained far more attention than the many positive ads, as described in the article "Consumer-Made Commercials Blast Chevy" (A4; http://adage.com/article?article_id=108317). One ad says, "We paved the prairies, we deforested the hills, we strip-mined our mountains and sold ourselves for oil to bring you this beautiful machine." Chevy decided not to filter the negative spots. Some observers thought that the strategy brought even more attention and visits to the Tahoe site without doing significant damage to the brand. However, brands need to think carefully about what kinds of reactions such strategies might elicit.

Ever-expanding communication capabilities present other challenges to brands' reputations. A few influential bloggers blasted a new version of Procter & Gamble's Pampers Cruisers diaper and even started a Facebook group dedicated to bringing back the old design. "Can One Bad Tweet Taint Your Brand Forever?" highlights how a few outspoken dissatisfied customers can stir waves of negative postings and publicity (A5; http://adage.com/digital/article?article_id=142205). Real time tracking of the blogosphere and other digital media helps companies monitor what's happening in the social media sphere, but deciding on appropriate responses is still a complicated problem. Unlike United in the example above, P&G responded swiftly to the original complaint, but that didn't appease the original unhappy customer. Even though it's important for companies to be responsive and vigilant, the article suggests that well-planned strategies can't always be successful against a few disgruntled and vocal individuals.

Even fans of a product can get a company into hot water. BrosIcingBros.com appeared to be a site that poked fun at Smirnoff's Ice Malt Beverage and featured a viral drinking game. The website showed young guys being "iced" or caught without a Smirnoff Ice and thus required to chug a bottle on one knee. The mocking tone notwithstanding, many observers believed Smirnoff began the website as a viral marketing stunt. But it soon appeared that enterprising college kids had hijacked the brand. Smirnoff evidently threatened legal action and the site went dark (A6; http://adage.com/article?article_id=144493).

Examples like these show that PR practitioners and marketers must work together to deal with potential problems and crises. Blogging and social media can be a double-edged sword for companies and for news organizations. They can be wildly successful in raising interest and awareness and incredibly damaging to a company's reputation if somebody highlights shortcomings or problems.

Different Roles for Public Relations

Public relations can be loosely separated into two main areas. The first plays a role in marketing support, a role that is growing in today's media world. The second involves fostering and building relationships with key stakeholders and maintaining a brand's or corporation's reputation. In both areas, public relations practitioners use a variety of tools and approaches.

Let's consider each of these general areas. *Marketing public relations* (MPR) involves programming that's aimed primarily at driving sales. It includes tactics such as publicity, traditional media coverage, special events, social media efforts, company-sponsored blogs, and publicity stunts. It frequently overlaps with tools thought of as sales promotion. MPR objectives may include generating interest in a company's products or services, helping the sales force get leads and close deals, and driving store or e-commerce traffic. It's part of the marketers' toolbox that we've discussed in previous chapters.

Gap's Piperlime brand deployed a website complete with a blog, a widget that lets users experiment with different looks, a Facebook page, and Twitter feed. Traditional advertising, YouTube videos, and a "pop-up" store in New York City are all part of the mix. Pop-up stores are short-term retail spaces usually open for no more than a month that act both as sales promotion and as publicity vehicles. The Piperlime vibe is a bit pushy and edgy and features posts that say things such as "Every time you wear sweatpants in public, a single guy leaves New York." "Is Piperlime a Mean Girl?" examines the edgy brand personality that churned up complaints and also a lot of interest and traffic (A7; http://adage.com/article?article_id=145411).

Ad Age reported on another MPR approach in "Small Agency of the Year, Campaign of the Year: Definition 6's 'Happiness Machine'" (A8; http://adage.com/smallagency10/article?article_id=145066). The article describes an agency's imaginative strategy when it installed a Coke machine at St. John's University in New York. It looked completely normal but offered students happy surprises. The hollowed out machine hid a real person. When a customer paid for a bottle of Coke, he or she might receive multiple sodas, pizzas, balloon animals, huge sub sandwiches, and even flowers. The resulting videos, shot over two days, depicted delighted and amazed customers enjoying their unexpected gifts. As the agency hoped, the videos went viral on YouTube.

As we've seen, marketers are increasingly drawn to earned media such as these campaigns achieved because they tend to be less expensive and often are more trusted by consumers. Although we still have many news media and entertainment outlets, PR managers are relying less on reporters and news organizations and more on creating content that's aimed directly at consumers (A9; http://adage.com/article?article_id=139864). The article says that even though PR professionals and agencies are still using pitches to reporters and editors, companies such as realty giant Coldwell Banker developed its own YouTube channel, "Coldwell Banker On Location," that's aimed at helping brokers and potential buyers learn about the housing market. While promotional in nature, it provides needed information to first-time buyers and others who have questions about the home-buying process. Procter & Gamble also bypassed traditional media and created its own branded print magazine, "Rouge," that looks and feels like a high-end women's fashion and beauty magazine, but features ads only for P&G products.

Best Buy's Geek Squad is upfront and funny about its goals. The PR person in charge of the initiative is known as "mistress of propaganda." However, the videos the Geek Squad created are less promotional than you might expect and are mainly tutorials answering questions buyers might have about their computers and mobile devices. The program is strategically smart in that it underscores the Geek Squad's authoritative and friendly role in guiding customers through complex technology purchases.

Although these direct-to-consumer channels and strategies offer opportunities for marketers, those creating the strategies must keep in mind that what's offered to consumers has to be relevant, interesting, and engaging for consumers. They'll be walking a fine line between being useful or edging into territory that's too hard sell or too obviously real propaganda.

Another challenge for MPR is the pressing need for metrics to show results for investments in campaigns. "PR Metrics Evolve to Show How Discipline Drives Sales" explains how publicity and other aspects of PR have always been difficult to measure (A10; http://adage.com/article?article_id=139430). Even though an event or product announcement may earn a huge number of impressions in print or broadcast media, it's harder to link those impressions with desired consumer behaviors.

But clients are insisting on accountability for their PR investments, and technologies are playing an important role. Because most campaigns are part of an integrated strategy, marketers try to determine how results from different channels may push traffic to others. Agencies and clients must be clear as to their objectives whether they relate to sales, attitudes toward the brand, brand image, or other measurable criteria.

> ### PR Metrics Evolve to Show How Discipline Drives Sales
>
> Attempting to evaluate the impact of PR has always been a tough job, but in the past clients tended to accept "softer" metrics such as brand awareness. Today, as this article explains, clients now demand to see the effects of campaigns on sales and other business measures. This includes such activities as lead generation (giving sales people contacts of those who might be likely buyers) as well as actual sales. *Ad Age* reports that the trade organization for PR, the Public Relations Society of America, is asking practitioners for their input in developing best practices for metrics of success. Marketers continue to seek accountability and returns on their spending in order to get maximum efficiency. Another trend reported in this article is the demand for "more integrated measurement solutions." This means that clients are asking agencies to show how new media and traditional media work together to contribute to a campaign's success. The measurement issues are tricky. As reported in this article, the agency learned that interest in entertainment and paid and earned social media appeared to drive traffic to the campaign sites. Search was much less effective. This led to revisions in campaign strategies and also revealed the importance of timely data and information about what's working and what isn't. The article concluded with three keys to success:
>
> 1) The client and agency must clearly determine campaign goals and expectations of what factors are important and thus understand what's important to measure: Sales? Awareness? Numbers of impressions or appearances of stories in media?
> 2) The client and agency must determine how much they can and should invest in measurement of results, an activity that can be expensive.
> 3) The client and agency must establish a communication plan to assure that they are in agreement about how and when metrics are communicated and shared.

Managing Relationships

The second major area involves developing and nurturing relationships that will help the organization survive and thrive in its environment. (4) Typical activities include conducting research, monitoring public opinion, and advising management about policies and publics. PR or public affairs activities often include these functions as well:

- government relations, public affairs, and lobbying, including work with government regulatory bodies and efforts to impact public policy for the benefit of the firm

- internal communication and employee relations

- issues management and relationships with special-interest groups such as environmental organizations, child advocacy groups, or health organizations
- industry relations communicating with others in the same business category
- philanthropy through donations of money, employee time, or organizational resources to charitable causes
- development or fundraising campaigns and efforts to encourage individuals, foundations, and corporations to contribute to not-for-profit organizations such as hospitals, museums, and other charities

Public relations practitioners are also responsible for anticipating, averting, or managing crisis situations that put a corporation or an industry at risk.

Complexity of PR Campaigns

An example of a controversial effort by the Corn Refiners of America, an industry trade group, illustrates the complexity of PR campaigns. The Corn Refiners launched an extensive initiative after high-fructose corn syrup (HFCS), an ingredient in hundreds of food and beverage products, came under fire from numerous health advocates and consumers. The critics said HFCS contributed to obesity and diabetes and was hidden in products ranging from soft drinks to ketchup. Food manufacturers like corn syrup because it's usually significantly cheaper than sugar. The association spent $30 million in 2008/2009 for advertising and PR efforts to convince consumers and policy makers that people metabolized HFCS just like sugar (A11; http://adage.com/article?article_id=142788). Despite the extensive campaign by the Corn Refiners, major brands such as Heinz, Gatorade, and Mountain Dew are switching to sugar for at least some of their products because of persistent consumer demand.

The HFCS controversy reveals two important aspects of public relations practice. First, efforts for corporate image enhancement, advocacy campaigns, or attempts to influence policy are generally thought of as public relations even if they use paid advertising or other tools in the mix. For instance, after the disastrous oil spill in the Gulf, BP used paid advertising, media relations, and other crisis communication in what most think has been an expensive but mostly ineffective attempt to repair its image.

A second and related point is that most people overestimate the power of positive public relations and brand messaging and often overestimate the negative impacts of bad publicity. Communication research for the past fifty years has shown that persuasion itself has relatively limited effects on individuals. Many people assume that a persuasive message will have uniform direct effects on audiences. But in fact, effectiveness is limited by many factors. People are different from each other with different attitudes, beliefs, experiences, and peer groups. We're also inundated with thousands of messages of all kinds, so we're unlikely to pay a great deal of attention especially to things that have limited perceived personal effect on us. Good or bad, publicity can be powerful, but rarely can it overcome strong public opinion or the weight of events. Thus PR practitioners must use careful research and planning and be realistic about likely outcomes.

More on Crisis Communication

Crises that threaten an organization can take multiple forms. Some crises are natural disasters such as the aftermath of a hurricane or tornado, accidents such as fires or chemical spills, or criminal behavior such as workplace shootings. Some crises are rooted in corporate or government misdeeds or carelessness: financial meltdowns based on greed and bad management decisions, manufacturing or operations that prove to be unsafe for workers and consumers, and poor decisions that inadvertently offend key publics or consumer groups. Still others are hoaxes or deliberate and malicious attacks on an organization.

Toyota's worldwide recall of millions of vehicles mostly due to faulty accelerators was particularly painful since the company built its brand on trusted reliability. When the reality of a company's behavior is jarringly different from what it says about itself, public opinion is likely to be harsh in its judgments.

As described in an earlier chapter, the explosion of BP's Deepwater Horizon well in the Gulf of Mexico began with the tragic deaths of eleven employees, and the well continued to gush oil and bad news for the company over the course of many months. But as *Advertising Age* columnist Bob Garfield wrote, BP's problems began with what's known as greenwashing, or attempting to paint a company as environmentally responsible when in fact its "green" behaviors were mainly cosmetic.

Reports showed that BP had a long history of cutting corners, using unsafe practices, and taking unreasonable environmental risks. "Greenwashing to Godwashing, BP and Obama Fail at Image Control" points out that some years ago, the company changed its logo to the "helio," a cheerful and gentle symbol reminiscent of the sun or a flower (A12; http://adage.com/article?article_id=144553). Because BP's practices have been shown to be so different from its public image, many people automatically dismiss their public pronouncements and advertising as propaganda. People feel betrayed and manipulated. As Garfield writes, "Words matter. Images matter, and when you contaminate them you despoil your own communications environment."

A sense of betrayal also surfaced when Minneapolis-based Target Corporation donated $150,000 to Minnesota Forward, a political action committee. A PAC is a federally sanctioned organization that is allowed to solicit and collect money for candidates and legislative issues. The point of contention was that Minnesota Forward also supported a gubernatorial candidate with outspoken anti-gay viewpoints.

Target's contribution was entirely legal—yet gays, a valuable customer segment for the company, were outraged and began to organize boycotts. For many years, Target has presented itself as a friend of the gay community and supporter of gay rights. This apparent reversal of its views was the flashpoint for social media and other backlash.

The article "Key Issue in Gay Community's Target Boycott: Sense of Betrayal" points out that companies must be proactive and consider the implications of involvement in controversial issues (A13; http://adage.com/bigtent/post?article_id=145436). It's likely that Target didn't imagine the kind of reaction its donation would elicit. Certainly companies can't operate risk-free. But in building relationships and reputations, they need to consider how some actions may portray them as insincere and hypocritical, even if they're unintended.

Hoaxes and malicious attacks are particularly difficult for companies. Two Domino's Pizza employees videotaped themselves apparently contaminating foods in particularly disgusting ways, an incident described in a previous chapter. The YouTube video received tens of thousands of views. Although the Domino's crisis team responded fairly rapidly with media interviews, its own apology video from the company president, and a Twitter account to respond to questions, the event was damaging. The Domino's employees, who claimed the video was merely a prank and that no customers consumed the foods, were fired and later arrested. Domino's reviewed its hiring practices after the incident (A14; http://adage.com/article/news/domino-s-youtube-nightmare-continues/136015/).

What can companies do to prepare for and respond to criticism and crises? Most importantly, they can put in place intelligent and responsive customer service and operational policies. In any PR situation, a predesignated team should respond quickly, accurately, and fairly. Even in the olden days before the web enabled instant communication, it wasn't good business to hide mistakes or problems, even if the problems weren't an organization's fault.

The bottom line? Whether companies plan for it or not, social media and other digital services and devices have accelerated communication whether it's negative or positive. Communicators must imagine themselves in the situation and how they would wish others to respond to problems, questions, or complaints. As media become more social, people, enabled by technology, are able to respond quickly and with high impact.

A company's public relations success isn't dependent only on its public relations officers or even its top management. Firms need to ensure that operations managers are thoughtful and sensitive to the implications of policies and actions that have the potential for negative or unethical outcomes. The PR practitioners in an organization are often the internal voices that insist on aligning company practices with company communication.

Public Relations' Growing Importance

PR practitioners have always focused on the many audiences and stakeholders on which organizations depend, whereas advertisers and marketers often had a narrower frame of reference around segmented target consumers. "How PR Chiefs Have Shifted Toward Center of Marketing Departments" discusses how public relations leaders, usually with titles such as chief communication officers, are becoming top executives for the marketing function (A15; http://adage.com/cmostrategy/article?article_id=139140). It cites Intuit's Harry Pforzheimer, an executive who serves as the company's chief communication and marketing leader. Intuit provides small business software including the tax preparation program, TurboTax.

The article suggests that the growth in the importance of PR relates in part to its role in generating earned media. "It's a little harder to measure, but when you know that roughly eight out of 10 customers bought your product because of word-of-mouth, that's a pretty powerful tool," Pforzheimer said in the *Advertising Age* interview. He further commented that the PR communications programs reach "three to four times more people than its advertising does."

The article also quotes American Airlines' Roger Frizzell, vice president of corporate communication and advertising, who said that the merging and integration of communication functions is rooted in consumers' increased awareness of social, environmental, and diversity issues and corporations' role in them. Trends indicate that corporations are recognizing the growing importance of holistic and integrated communication programs that build relationships with stakeholders using a range of strategies.

How PR Chiefs Have Shifted Toward Center of Marketing Departments
Specialists Helm Ad Efforts too at Intuit, IBM, and American Airlines

Many people think PR is limited to crisis communication or churning out news releases. But comments from top PR people show that new technologies and communication trends have made PR skills more important than ever and are calling on their skills in developing strategy within short time frames. The growing importance of word of mouth and direct engagement with customers are among the factors driving the changes. As research reveals that publicity and relationship management efforts are reaching more customers and potential customers than advertising, firms are deciding to integrate both functions under a single control. Other factors include PR's traditional broad and deep knowledge of customers and potential customers, and practitioners' understanding of how to nurture and enhance a firm's corporate reputation.

The article cites a top software executive who says that selling a company perspective is crucial. *"Selling that perspective to consumers and the media, he said, has always been important externally, but internally wasn't always acknowledged as part of the marketing puzzle by the gatekeepers."*

Marketing public relations has become much more than creating news releases for media. It's a strategic function rooted in audience research that helps marketers understand how to reach the right person at the right time with the right message in the most efficient way. It seeks the optimum mix of tactics including viral video, social marketing, word of mouth, events, product trials, blogs, and media relations. Most importantly, it seeks to create content and experiences that will delight customers.

Public relations' role in fostering relationships among stakeholders will likely continue to grow as well, as publics' expectations of organizations grow. With social media, people are empowered to communicate their complaints and cheers regarding company practices and their experiences with a brand. For PR practitioners, that means that they must be well integrated into top decision making to ensure that company policies and products meet high standards for performance, ethics, and social responsibility. Further, practitioners should develop well-researched response and action plans that are ready if and when problems or crises occur.

Notes

1. Available at: http://www.youtube.com/watch?v=5YGc4zOqozo http://www.youtube.com/watch?v=T_X-Qoh__mw.
2. Available at: http://twitter.com/UnitedAirlines/status/2577748677.
3. Cameron, G. T., Wilcox, D. L., Reber, B. H., & Shin, J.-H. *Public Relations Today.* Boston: Pearson, 2008.
4. Cutlip, S. M., Center, A. H., & Broom., G. M. *Effective Public Relations.* Upper Saddle River, NJ: Pearson, 2006.

Articles

(A1) Ken Wheaton. "United Is Happy to Answer Your Complaints After You Humiliate Them." Published July 9, 2009. Available at: http://adage.com/adages/post?article_id=137817

(A2) Marissa Miley. "Angry Moms Parody Motrin Ads." Published November 20, 2008. Available at: http://adage.com/adages/post?article_id=132738

(A3) Valentina Vescovi. "Mexican Riff on Apple Advertising Has Locals Crying Plagiarism." Published July 23, 2009. Available at: http://adage.com/article?article_id=138095

(A4) Marc Graser. "Consumer-Made Commercials Blast Chevy." Published April 5, 2006. Available at: http://adage.com/article?article_id=108317

(A5) Jack Neff. "Can One Bad Tweet Taint Your Brand Forever?" Published February 22, 2010. Available at: http://adage.com/digital/article?article_id=142205

(A6) Kunur Patel. "Smirnoff Says It Took 'Measures' to Stop Icing Site." Published June 16, 2010. Available at: http://adage.com/article?article_id=144493

(A7) Natalie Zmuda. "Is Piperlime a Mean Girl?" Published August 16, 2010. Available at: http://adage.com/article?article_id=145411

(A8)   Ann-Christine Diaz. "Small Agency of the Year, Campaign of the Year: Definition 6's 'Happiness Machine.'" Published July 26, 2010. Available at: http://adage.com/smallagency10/article?article_id=145066

(A9)   Michael Bush. "As Media Market Shrinks, PR Passes Up Reporters, Pitches Directly to Consumers." Published October 26, 2009. Available at: http://adage.com/article?article_id=139864

(A10) Michael Bush. "PR Metrics Evolve to Show How Discipline Drives Sales." Published October 5, 2009. Available at: http://adage.com/article?article_id=139430

(A11) Natalie Zmuda. "Major Brands No Longer Sweet on High-Fructose Corn Syrup." Published March 15, 2010. Available at: http://adage.com/article?article_id=142788

(A12) Bob Garfield. "From Greenwashing to Godwashing, BP and Obama Fail at Image Control." Published June 21, 2010. Available at: http://adage.com/article?article_id=144553

(A13) Steve Roth. "Key Issue in Gay Community's Target Boycott: Sense of Betrayal." Published August 18, 2010. Available at: http://adage.com/bigtent/post?article_id=145436

(A14) Emily York. "Domino's Posts Apology Video on YouTube." Published April 15, 2009. Available at: http://adage.com/article?article_id=115184

(A15) Michael Bush. "How PR Chiefs Have Shifted Toward Center of Marketing Departments." Published September 21, 2009. Available at: http://adage.com/cmostrategy/article?article_id=139140

Integrated Marketing Communication

The headline might read, "Ad Agency Takes On Ruthless Dictator." The story begins in Zimbabwe with its leader, Robert Mugabe. Mugabe, who was once a freedom-fighting hero to many Africans, became increasingly tyrannical over the years, rigged elections, instituted disastrous economic policies, and through his militia, committed terrifying atrocities.

The Mugabe regime exiled *The Zimbabwean*, a newspaper that reported on the offenses of the government and the suffering of the Zimbabwean people. Relocated to neighboring South Africa, the paper continued to report on events in Zimbabwe using in-country correspondents. But the publication struggled to keep its presses running, especially after Mugabe slapped a 55 percent "luxury" tax on importing the paper from South Africa to Zimbabwe, thus making it far too expensive for the country's impoverished citizens.

The Zimbabwean asked ad agency TBWA Hunt Lascaris, located in Johannesburg, South Africa, to help them gain enough new customers, advertising, and revenue to continue its work.

TBWA took note of the outrageous currency inflation resulting from Mugabe's policies. How outrageous? The government printed a $100 *trillion* dollar note worth about $300 in U.S. currency. CNN reported that a loaf of bread cost $300 billion Zimbabwean dollars. (1)

The agency saw that the piles of almost worthless banknotes offered an opportunity for an entirely new medium. The campaign printed messages directly on to the bills such as "Thanks to Mugabe This Money Is Wallpaper," "Fight the Regime That Has Crippled a Country," and "It's Cheaper to Print This on Money Than Paper."

The agency distributed banknote flyers and mailed wads of cash to media outlets and reporters. They attracted worldwide coverage and millions of website hits. The campaign also featured billboards and murals composed of the real bills. The upshot? Sales of *The Zimbabwean* skyrocketed.

Why was the "The Trillion Dollar Campaign" so successful that it won the Outdoor Grand Prix award at the Cannes Lions International Advertising Festival *and* the Integrated Campaign prize at the CLIO Awards? In part, because of the key insight of the integrated campaign: printing the campaign on real but worthless bills dramatized Zimbabwe's plight, showing that the money was literally not worth the paper it was printed on.

Moreover, despite a tiny budget, the campaign carried its highly focused theme through multiple channels using outdoor media, mail, publicity strategies, and digital media. Thus each element of the campaign supported and amplified the other elements (A1; http://adage.com/cannes09/article?article_id=137519).

As you've seen in earlier chapters, marketing communicators have an ever-expanding array of choices available to them in deploying persuasive campaigns. The challenge for agencies and clients is putting the right combination of elements together to get the maximum effect for the minimum cost. Ideally, they will construct a plan that uses the optimal strategies, media, and creative message for the target audience.

In this chapter, we'll discuss the concept variously known as integrated marketing communication (IMC), integrated brand promotion, or strategic communication. (2) Though these phrases are used in somewhat different contexts, they share important similarities. Here we'll refer to IMC. In simplest terms, IMC "is the process of using a wide range of promotional tools working together to create widespread brand exposure." (3) We'll consider the philosophy behind using IMC, discuss the primary components of successful IMC programs, and look at the challenges to implementing them.

In previous chapters we've noted that marketers shouldn't start with the assumption that certain tactics will be effective in any particular assignment. In the past, many advertisers built campaigns on the premise that television or print promotions were the default choices. Today we start with the marketing communication problem or opportunity and try to identify how to get the most persuasive message to the target audience at the right time and in that audience's preferred media. In some cases, we might use traditional paid space and time exclusively; in others, we might use them in combination with social media or publicity.

As we've seen, what people think of as media has vastly expanded. In fact, many persuasive campaigns don't use media at all in the traditional sense, but are based on giving the consumer a memorable and positive experience. "The Last Campaign: How Experiences Are Becoming the New Advertising" suggests that digital and peer-to-peer experiences are increasingly more appealing than traditional media messaging (A2; http://adage.com/digitalnext/post?article_id=140388). The article cites a study reporting that 65 percent of U.S. consumers said that their digital or web-based interaction with a brand affected their beliefs and attitudes and 97 percent said this interaction was a deciding factor in their purchase behavior.

The Last Campaign: How Experiences Are Becoming the New Advertising

Red Bull, Virgin America, Uniqlo and Guinness Lead the Way

The article takes on the question, "is advertising dying?" and cites numerous statistics that reveal that consumers are shifting away from traditional media and are looking to their technology-enabled peers for recommendations and suggestions. In addition, the author argues that "digital brand experiences" are becoming very influential in developing consumers' relationships with brands and in driving purchases. The findings of the survey support the importance of firms' creating positive online experiences. They use a remarkable array of tactics, including iPhone apps, calendars, micro-sites, blogs, sponsorships, and cause marketing. He concludes: "experience is the new advertising."

Red Bull, manufacturer of the popular energy drink, is known for its quirky animated television commercials and such off-the-wall events as Flugtag, which invites competitors to build homemade, engine-free flying machines and launch them off docks over water to see how far they "fly." This combination of advertising, digital media such as the Red Bull blog, and unusual events is a highly successful strategy in communicating with its mostly Gen Y audiences. The article cites Amazon's Jeff Bezos, who comments about his own e-commerce philosophy: "We are not great advertisers. So we start with customers, figure out what they want, and figure out how to get it to them." This is a nice simple description of how IMC works.

Elements of IMC

Planning and implementing an IMC program involves several steps: researching and identifying target audiences, identifying the brand/product beliefs or position the audiences have, developing strategies to reach them (including media choices), setting objectives, planning budgets, and implementing tactics.

Identifying the audience is critical. As discussed in the chapter on research, planners will use a wide range of approaches in trying to gain deep and significant understandings of their best potential customers. In this process, planners also will try to understand what position the product can or should occupy in the consumer's mind. For example, a Rolex and a Swatch watch both tell the time pretty well, but the social and cultural meanings and gratifications buyers derive from their purchase and use are quite different. Therefore the IMC strategies and tactics will also be different.

Planners also are tasked with setting objectives—clarifying what's supposed to happen as a result of the IMC plan. Is the goal to raise awareness? Introduce a new product? Increase sales? Once they find the answers to these questions, they're better able to develop implementation strategies and tactics, including the best media mix, messages, and budgets. This relates to our earlier discussions of theory that provides a solid basis for decision making.

Evian began a recent campaign by allocating almost all of its resources to a digital strategy. The viral blockbuster "Evian Babies" featured special effects stunt babies roller skating, leaping fences, and break dancing under the theme "Evian: Live Young" (A3; http://adage.com/digital/article?article_id=143256). The video attracted 102 million views, 130,000 comments, and 500,000 Facebook fans. The company used what was referred to as "minimal" paid promotion on YouTube.

But Evian turned its digital strategy on its head by bringing the YouTube babies to television, thus integrating traditional media into the promotional mix. The article suggests that the company determined that in order to gain wider audiences and increased sales, a digital-only strategy wasn't sufficient.

This underscores the concept that planners need to be "medium agnostic." This means that they try to discard prejudices or preferences toward any particular communication channel, whether it's television, mobile, or social media. It's too easy to fall in love with certain media, especially when excitement about a particular approach is high.

Marketers often get infected with the excitement and preferences of other agencies or clients who want to try the newest and hottest tactics. But if those tactics aren't right for your target customer or product, the effort is likely to fail. Both *The Zimbabwean* and Evian campaigns used combinations of traditional media with creative twists along with digital strategies rather than going "medium first."

The trend toward IMC has been accelerating for some years. MasterCard's iconic marketing theme built around "There are some things money can't buy. For everything else, there's MasterCard," was mostly TV centric. The brilliant theme was also highly "campaignable," meaning that it could be translated into almost unlimited creative treatments and promotions for products, vacations, and even small business needs.

In 2009, MasterCard extended the "priceless" effort with an iPhone app and website that encouraged users to post their favorites to a networked community sharing products, stores, deals, and other things they've found (A4; http://adage.com/digital/article?article_id=138151). The company also created MasterCard Marketplace "to find the things you want for less." Some critics thought the concept of sharing deals was too promotional and didn't jibe with the sentimental charm of the television spots. The takeaway is that some messages may not work in different media where expectations of the experience are different.

IMC Gains Momentum

Although many in the business world seem to think that IMC is the most efficient and effective approach to today's marketing, many firms struggle to implement it. A 2009 survey showed that almost three-quarters of companies indicate that they're using IMC, but only about one-quarter reported their IMC programs as "excellent" or "very good." "Essentials for Integrated Marketing" identifies some of the obstacles they face and suggests some "imperatives" to improve results (A5; http://adage.com/article?article_id=127599). The article points out the need for consistency in communicating a compelling consumer insight. Barriers to consistency can emerge from process, structural issues, and employee issues. If each tactical or media team (television, digital, etc.) develops its own brand messaging and media, they're unlikely to achieve synergy with other elements.

The article describes how Kraft, Procter & Gamble, and MasterCard all use different but related approaches to break down the traditional silos and the budgets allocated to each silo. Kraft assigns a cross-functional team that's focused on strategic goals for each Kraft brand. The objective is to move programming development from traditional organizational chart assignments and budget categories toward customer-focused problem solving. Political and organizational cultural factors can also get in the way as power and budget reallocations change internal relationships.

The article offers the notion that IMC calls for pervasive reorganization and for "renaissance marketers." These renaissance employees are individuals with a variety of skills and interests. They have relentless customer focus and understand the range of marketing and public relations tools and capabilities. Renaissance marketers should also have the ability to conduct and interpret research and data.

Industry awards programs mirror trends in marketing. The growth in IMC and in new formats is clear. An *Advertising Age* headline in 2009 proclaimed "Cannes Swept by PR, Integrated, Internet Winners" and had the subhead: "Tally Suggests Ad Age is Over—or, at least, It's Evolved to a Higher Plane" (A6; http://adage.com/cannes09/article?article_id=137630). The writer notes that "the age of interruption is over" in the light of the top

Advertising's Future

"When the going gets tough, the tough innovate."

—Andrew Razeghi,
Marketing Professor,
Northwestern University

The star of an online video series is a perky insurance agent in Maple Grove, a fictional town somewhere in the Midwest. That star is Gayle, the go-to person for Maple Grove's quirky residents who want advice about chili cook-offs, marital harmony, newfound wealth, and the daily challenges of a guy who's a plumber by day and a rock star by night. The program is "In Gayle We Trust" and it's part of American Family's new branding strategy.

When most people think of cutting-edge innovation and high-risk strategies, they don't usually think of the insurance business. But when the company brought in Lisa Bacus as vice president of marketing, she saw an opportunity for brand building by emphasizing the company's caring customer service—a much different strategy from the competition, which mostly focuses on low-price appeals. Gayle's character reinforces the message that American Family's agents are supportive and reliable.

When big changes are afoot and it's unclear where a business is headed, it's usually good advice to "follow the money." The story of American Family's big strategy shift begins in 2009 when the firm began to reallocate a portion of its marketing dollars from thirty-second television spots to branded entertainment, social media, games, a radio advice program, and a microsite.

A second phase of "In Gayle We Trust" launched in 2010 complete with lead generation software that tracks when customers request price quotes or ask for more information about American Family products. The array of digital tactics got results with significant increases in web traffic, price quotes, and requests to find an agent—and in consumers' unaided recall of the branded programs. Following the money gives us insights into the future of advertising and brand promotion (A1; http://adage.com/madisonandvine/article?article_id=144984; A2; http://adage.com/cmostrategy/article?article_id=141940).

How Downturns Affect Advertising

Andrew Razeghi of Northwestern University summarized what we know about business best practices during economic downturns. (1) One of his suggestions is to increase communications with customers—advertise more, not less. Evidence supporting this suggestion is a study that showed companies that increased their advertising during the U.S. recession of 1980–81 averaged higher sales growth during and after the recession. In fact, by 1985, these companies had sales over 256 percent greater than those that reduced advertising. Going back as far as the Great Depression, we have lots of support for advertising heavily during a downturn: those companies that continue to advertise or even increase their advertising reap significant sales rewards, especially immediately after economic recovery.

But there is also evidence that changes and innovations occurring during a recession can significantly change the lay of the land for lots of different industries, including advertising. Advertising was blamed, along with "greedy big business," for much of the woes of the Great Depression, and negativity toward advertising is argued to have been maintained ever since. (2) Radio emerged during the recession and gobbled up significant advertising market shares. The Wheeler-Lea Amendments to the Federal Trade Commission Act (1938) increased government regulation on advertising, including putting deceptive advertising practices under the jurisdiction of the Federal Trade Commission. James B. Arndorfer summarizes these changes further in "How the Depression Shaped Modern Ad Biz" (A3; http://adage.com/article?article_id=136262).

So what does the history of advertising and recessions tell us about what to expect in the next years, as the United States recovers from the largest economic downturn since the Great Depression?

Advertising's Financial Future

Before we take a look at the future of advertising, we should consider the current financial health of advertising. The recession that began in 2008 led to the biggest decrease in advertising ever in 2009.

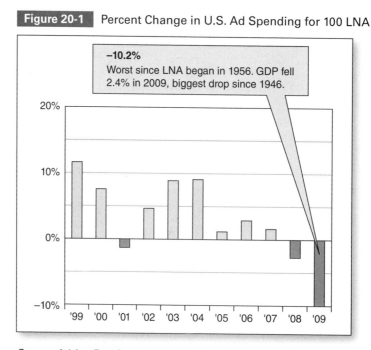

Figure 20-1   Percent Change in U.S. Ad Spending for 100 LNA

Source: *Ad Age* DataCenter (LNA); Bureau of Economic Analysis (GDP).

Media economist Robert Picard reported in a ten-year study of developed countries that advertising expenditures are closely predicted by the U.S. gross domestic product (GDP). (3) More specifically, he said that a 1 percent decrease in GDP on average is associated with a 5 percent decrease in advertising expenditures. From 2008 to 2009 there was a 2.4 percent decrease in U.S. GDP. And in fact, there was a 10.2 percent drop in advertising expenditures, as you can see clearly in Figure 20-1—the worst drop since the Great Depression.

So one thing we have to try to predict is advertising growth or decrease over the next few years. A number of American companies use a variety of research methods to make predictions about media and advertising expenditures. In 2010, Veronis Suhler Stevenson predicted that in general, consumer advertising revenues (including television, newspapers, consumer magazines, broadcast and satellite radio, Yellow Pages, and out-of-home media) would stagnate from 2010 to 2015 with an annual growth rate of just over 2 percent. (4) PricewaterhouseCoopers was also pessimistic. It predicted that although advertising spending would increase between 2011 and 2014, in 2014 it would still be 9 percent less than it was in 2007. Slightly more optimistic, research company Magna predicted growth in advertising revenue of 2.1 percent in 2010, and then an average annual growth of 3.5 percent a year from 2011 through 2015.

It's important to put these figures into context. Although predicting slow growth for advertising, the same research companies predict much greater growth in media and communications spending from 2010 to 2015. (Media and communications include revenues generated by subscription TV and on-demand services, mobile apps, and video games.) They predicted these revenues would grow more than 6 percent a year through 2015. This means that advertising's share of money spent on media will significantly decrease.

Now let's turn to the specific areas of advertising expenditures. Figure 20-2 shows how the advertising pie was divided up in 2009.

In 2009, television absorbed the lion's share of advertising dollars, with network TV still the biggest within that category. Magazines were second and newspapers third. The Internet was fourth.

PricewaterhouseCoopers predicts that by 2014 online advertising will have increased to $34 billion and newspapers will have decreased to $22.3 billion. Television is expected to remain in first with a $10 billion increase. Magazines are predicted to stay about the same or grow slowly. Thus, there's a good chance that advertising will play a smaller overall media role by 2015, and the relative importance of advertising media will shift downward.

In 2009 Forrester Research predicted a postrecession scenario in which interactive advertising would increase and traditional advertising would decrease (A4; http://adage.com/digitalnext/post?article_id=138023). The company's rationale for this prediction is that during the last few years, advertisers have observed the greater effectiveness and efficiency of digital advertising. This, however, flies in the face of other companies' predictions that television will maintain its dominance. Although the resilient strength of television is somewhat surprising, 2009 research by Joel Rubinson provides a possible explanation. (5) Rubinson, the head of research at the Advertising Research Foundation, summarized research done on television advertising effectiveness over the last fifteen years and reported that "TV has not declined in its effectiveness at generating sales lift and appears to be more effective than either online or print at generating brand awareness and recognition." Nevertheless, there are major changes afoot, and we will look at a sampling of them next.

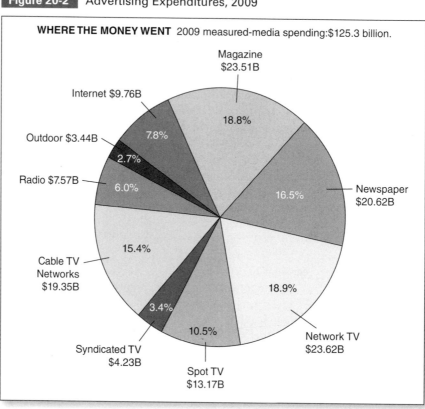

Figure 20-2 Advertising Expenditures, 2009

Source: WPP's *Kantar Media*.
Pie chart reflects 2009 U.S. measured-media spending for all advertisers including 100 LNA.

Future Challenges to Advertising

As we have seen, many experts predict a declining financial role for advertising. What are the specific challenges to advertising that threaten to reduce its importance in the marketing mix? Specific threats to advertising's share of the promotion pie include the flexibility, accountability, and targeting specificity of the Internet; increasing dollars being invested in search; and movement away from narrow segments, especially in terms of programming content segments (for example, the vast expansion of television choices with hundreds of cable channels and almost limitless on-demand opportunities). But the fragmenting is also being caused by the upswing in mobile media: smart cell phones, e-readers, and touchpad tablets. All of these give consumers more choices but make it necessary for advertisers to learn how to reach them through the new devices.

The fragmenting of audiences will mean that advertising increasingly will need to play a role in integrated marketing communication programs, often more as a supporting actor than in starring role. For example, as we saw in Chapter 18, companies are spending a larger share of marketing dollars on public relations and less on advertising. As we saw in Chapter 19 on integrated marketing communication, sales promotions are also becoming a more dominant marketing tool. The role of social media may become increasingly important, as these sites become media channels themselves. It is not yet clear how best to incorporate advertising into these sites, but the future of social media will have a major effect on the future of advertising.

Although many predict an increasing role for television advertising, it is likely that your computer and your 55-inch television are going to become one. What that means for advertising will be critically important to advertising's influence.

Changes in how advertising looks and feels are coming as well. Advertising executions are likely to emphasize more emotional messages than rational approaches. Long-form advertising may increase as well. Changes such as these will mean that the role of the full-service advertising agency will change, probably with much less long-term loyalty from advertiser clients. We look at possible changes and the challenges they create in more detail.

Challenge 1: The Competitive Impact of the Flexibility, Accountability, and Targeting Power of the Internet

The three attributes of Internet advertising—flexibility, accountability, and targeting power—suggest that it will become more and more important to the future of advertising.

Flexibility

Geo-tagged promotions are an excellent example of the flexibility the Internet creates for marketing. Geo-tagging, as Garrick Schmitt defines it, combines people's virtual and physical worlds by sending them messages directly linked with a brand they're physically close to through their smartphones, such as Apple's iPhone and Google's Android, both of which are GPS-linked (A5; http://adage.com/digitalnext/post?article_id=141069). Schmitt describes a number of examples. Foursquare is a location-based social network that allows users to connect with specific local businesses such as bars or restaurants. It is now experimenting with allowing these businesses to offer specials, coupons, or advertisements within the network to entice participation. Starbucks has an iPhone app that allows the user to tell friends on Facebook or Twitter where they are located so that those who wish can join the user for a latte.

Even more elaborate, an app called Shopkick enables users to get points for entering a store and making purchases. Once in a store, the user receives advertisements for various specials around the store. After a certain number of points are collected, the user is rewarded with credits, music downloads, or gift cards. (4) Major retailers such as Macy's, Best Buy, and American Eagle have already signed onto the program.

Imagine going into a Macy's, collecting some "Kickbucks" for just showing up, and then being lured by advertisements for shoes, jewelry, or handbags. The idea is that this kind of geo-tagged advertising will sell you more, make the store seem more like a "friend," and keep you in the store longer. As always, privacy issues will be a problem because the data on what you actually buy are so valuable to other businesses targeting you. It has long been clear that the closer a consumer is to an opportunity to purchase, the more effective the advertising, which means geo-tagging will likely join direct mail and catalogues as an unusually powerful marketing tool. Although advertising will sometimes play a role in geo-tagging schemes, money poured into promotions of this type is likely to come from what used to be extensive retail advertising.

Measurability of the Impact of Advertising

As we saw in Chapter 5, determining whether advertising causes specific purchases is difficult to ascertain when the advertising is carried in traditional media. Internet advertising does not solve all the problems of measuring the impact of advertising, but it does reduce them. When a person clicks on an online ad, the advertiser can identify that person, often specifically, and that information can be compared against a list of those who make purchases. Clicks on online ads can lead marketers to a much closer profile of who their buyer is and why they buy, and what ads prompt behavior to buy.

Often, Internet advertising provides a direct and immediate offer to consumers, so it is possible to determine exactly when the advertising causes a purchase. In the geo-tracking example above, we saw this same kind of power to assess the impact of advertising. If our Macy's shopper is offered a deal on shoes and purchases them, it is clear that the advertising made the sale. Moving more advertising dollars toward the Internet where measuring its impact is easier and more accurate is highly likely.

Behavioral Targeting

Another unique advantage of Internet-based advertising is that it can track website visitors with "cookies," which track users' behavior and then feed these users advertisements targeted at their interests. As we explained in Chapter 6 on target market segmentation, this allows far more specific targeting than is possible in any of the traditional media. We also saw that because behavioral targeting emerges from huge integrated datasets on people's behavior, the threat to personal privacy becomes greater as well, and in the next few years we will see significant conflict between advertisers and government regulatory bodies.

Challenge 2: Competition from Search

Before the Internet, planners targeted advertising messages as well as they could given that those media often reached lots of different kinds of people. Consumers searched for information about products, but it was time consuming and effortful. When Google introduced search programs, everything changed. As content on the Internet exploded, search algorithms could quickly wade through all that content and find information about comparative brand performance, price, and where purchases could be made. Consumers gained power over the information delivered to them. Marketers can now buy search terms and use them to guide consumers directly to their online stores. Advertising is left out of the loop in a pure search process.

We should also emphasize the role of "search advertising," promotional messages delivered on the Internet to a consumer who is doing a search. Marketers can purchase search terms and pay to have their advertising delivered on the first search page of the consumer's search. This provides quality targeting for the advertisement, but the consumer's search also yields many nonadvertising sources for the desired information—sites offering information or products directly. In fact, in 2010, click-through rates for search advertisements averaged only about 1 percent, meaning that consumers preferred to go directly to listed sites. (6)

Challenge 3: Advertising's Relationship with Other Promotional Tools

As we saw in Chapter 19 on integrated marketing communications, the idea of combining advertising with other promotional tools is not a new one. There is compelling evidence that messages from multiple sources are more effective than repeated messages from a single source. As traditional media advertising via television, radio, newspaper, and magazine is used less (with the possible exception of television), there are increasing numbers of new media—delivered via Internet and mobile devices that can reach consumers with or without advertising. As these media are used more for public relations or sales promotions, the portion of total marketing budgets devoted to advertising will decrease. Rather than marketers thinking first of advertising, they may become more likely to think of the cheaper and better-targeted alternatives they have through the new media.

Challenge 4: Role of Social Media

As social media such as Facebook increase the number of users and the time they spend on the sites, the social media actually become media channels. Expenditures for social media advertising are increasing. To date, however, social media advertising is less expensive than advertising in traditional media channels. This means less money invested in advertising.

Challenge 5: What Will Television Look Like When It Becomes a Computer?

Brian Steinberg writes that television will soon become a "web convergence device" that allows many more content choices for the viewer (A6; http://adage.com/article?article_id=140751). Consumers will be able to watch conventional television, select pay content, answer their email, chat on Facebook, order from Amazon, and play interactive games. A central question emerges: How can all of this merged content generate advertising revenues? We've seen that advertising revenues are likely to grow slowly overall and to be divided among more and more media. It is interesting to consider Steinberg's view of what will eventually shake out in the fight for television advertising revenues.

> ### The Future of TV
>
> *We'll Be Ordering Up Our Own Video, Ads and Products on a Web Convergence Device. But Who Will Reap the Revenue?*
>
> Everybody knows that access to programming of all kinds is coming to new devices and venues everyday. And everybody knows that somebody has to come up with the money to support the creation and distribution of content. Put simply, advertising, subscription fees, or a combination of the two will have to be achieved or there's no incentive to take the risks inherent in developing shows and films.
>
> This article points out that television throughout its history has been far more than a mere monitor—it was the single place people could access the shows that brought families together and provided the topics of conversation at the water cooler the next day. Insiders are arguing that television is becoming part of the Internet "cloud" accessible through all kinds of devices. Social media and advertiser sites offer other venues that enable consumers to buy and recommend products and services. The goals of many advertisers include intertwining consumer viewing activities and behaviors with ad messages that are contextual and thus likely to be welcomed.
>
> "Addressable" advertising sends messages to consumers based on data that media companies and marketers have gathered about them. If you're a gamer, you'll get those kinds of ads; if you're a dad AND a gamer you may get highly targeted ads tailored just for you.
>
> But big questions remain: who will control the ads and reap the benefits? Where will the consumer data come from and how will it be used? And how will consumers feel about their personal information being used to pitch them products and services?

Challenge 6: How Will Advertising Content of the Future Look?

Every year *Advertising Age* provides perspective on the most creative advertising during the year and what the trends in advertising content are. Kunur Patel offers some recent highlights in her review of the 2009 awards (A7; http://adage.com/agencynews/article?article_id=139270). It's notable that the top agencies produced both great television work and prize-winning applications for the Internet world. These two strengths will become increasingly important in the next few years.

Rupal Parekh points out that drawing audiences to advertising will become increasingly important in advertising's future, as compared with the interruption model of advertising seen in traditional television advertising (A8; http://adage.com/madisonandvine/article?article_id=143603). Thirty-minute advertorials on television pioneered the notion that people would accept advertising as programming. As Parekh points out with many examples, brands are an interesting story in and of themselves, and inviting people to hear those stories fits well with the migration toward consumer control over message delivery.

Challenge 7: Advertising Agency Changes

Large advertising agencies have traditionally focused on television advertising. Understanding how to create and place advertising in such digital environments as smartphones, e-readers, and social media are areas of expertise that advertising agencies need and are often lacking. Phil Johnson reported in *Ad Age* that there are several major changes that advertising agencies will have to navigate in order to be successful in the future (A9; http://adage.com/smallagency/post?article_id=139064). Two of these are particularly compelling.

The first is that agencies will have to focus less on target audiences and more on media channels. This is because data mining now provides such specific understanding of who buys what that the kind of expertise that advertising agencies traditionally provided is becoming less relevant. When companies harvest cookies placed on your computer and your mobile phone, they learn what products and brands you are interested in and which you purchase. As we've seen, that information can also be connected with credit card purchases.

On the other hand, even if we know your interests and buying behaviors exactly, we still have to send you the right messages through the right channel at the right time. For example, if we know you watch lots of football on television, read an online newspaper for football stories, buy football tickets by mail, and frequently go to team websites, then the question that advertising agencies must determine is what ad messages to deliver to you in each of these media.

Second, Johnson predicts that accountability will become much more important for advertising agencies. Because it is so difficult to "prove" the value of an advertising campaign, advertising agencies could often get away without doing so. But as we've seen in many examples, in digital environments human behavior toward the brand is directly measureable. An online advertisement that's delivered via email either does or does not succeed in getting a customer to a sale. People click on search ads or they don't. Some digital advertising doesn't provide immediate success indicators (the best example is online video advertising), but most do. The immediacy of this feedback is very significant for advertising agencies because they and their clients will have evidence of the effectiveness of their messages and placements.

> ### Creating the Future of Adland
> *How Agencies Can Escape the Commodity Trap*
>
> If your product is a commodity, it's something that is really difficult to differentiate from similar products. The term usually refers to such things as corn and pork bellies and their demand and pricing is based on the commodity's relative scarcity. But the problem is that one company's corn isn't different from anybody else's corn, except based on price. Clearly, if you run an advertising agency (or many other kinds of companies) you want to be able to charge higher prices because of other product characteristics such as quality, fashionability, performance, and so on. You don't want to compete as a commodity.

> This article suggests that agencies have to go beyond offering insights into audience preferences into offering access and even into creating communities. This moves agencies from only delivering messages about a product or service into creating content and communities that draw and inspire loyalty and interest. This can also mean creating new media channels through social media such as Twitter, Internet music and radio and so on. As we've suggested throughout this book, the successful agency of the future will integrate campaigns, platforms, and technology to achieve measureable results. In addition, research and analytics will drive success and the successful marketers. The author concludes by saying that the successful agencies and marketers will be collaborators in gathering and researching audience information and providing content and exciting experiences for customers.

Al DiGuido predicts three main features of advertising agencies of the future, and those features are consistent with the findings we've reviewed in this chapter (A10; http:// adage.com/agencynews/article?article_id=142257). First, he says that agencies will be smaller because of the reduced financial impact of advertising. The agency leader may not be the creative director and may instead be the person who coordinates the integrated marketing campaign. Second, data indicators of campaign success will outstrip the importance of awards for advertising creativity. Third, the successful agency will have its own technology wizards who figure out new ways to deliver messages to consumers. In fact, the creativity of new media inventions will become one of the most important determinants of which agencies win the accounts.

A Final Word

We hope this introduction to the world of advertising and promotion and *Advertising Age* gave you insights into persuasion and its tools. Further, we hope you've seen how innovations in media and advertising affect you in everyday life. Technology, marketing, media, and advertising permeate social relationships, entertainment, education, politics, news, and shopping.

Whatever your career interests, learning about advertising can help you become a better persuader. Knowing about research, evidence-based decision making, and strategy can help you be a better planner and manager. Even more important, knowing the uses and misuses of persuasion can help you become a more informed citizen and consumer.

Notes

1. Razeghi, A. J. *Innovating through Recession: When the Going Gets Tough, the Tough Innovate.* Available at: http://www.scribd.com/doc/7450921/Innovating-Through-Recession-Andrew-Razeghi-Kellogg-School-of-Management.
2. O'Guinn, T. C., Allen, C. T., & Seminik, R. J. *Advertising and Integrated Brand Promotion.* Mason, OH: South-Western Cengage Learning, 2009, p. 86.
3. Van der Wurff, R., Bakker, P., & Picard, R. G. "Economic Growth and Advertising Expenditures in Different Media in Different Countries," *Journal of Media Economics* 21 (2008): 28–58.
4. Clifford, S. "Aisle by Aisle, an App That Pushes Bargains," *New York Times,* August 17, 2010.
5. Rubinson, J. "Empirical Evidence of TV Advertising Effectiveness," *Journal of Advertising Research* 49, No. 2 (June 2009). Available at: http://www.thearf.org/assets/pub-jar?fbid=QVCujClyp9F.

6. Baker, L. "Bing Driven Ad Click Thru Rate 55 percent More Than Google," *Search Engine Journal*, July 27, 2009. Available at: http://www.searchenginejournal.com/bing-search-ads/12091/.

Articles

(A1)   Andrew Hampp. "American Family Insurance Extends Branded-Entertainment Platform." Published July 19, 2010. Available at: http://adage.com/madisonandvine/article?article_id=144984

(A2)   Andrew Hampp. "American Family Insurance Grows Its Family with Trust." Published February 8, 2010. Available at: http://adage.com/cmostrategy/article?article_id=141940

(A3)   James B. Arndorfer. "How the Depression Shaped Modern Ad Biz." Published April 27, 2009. Available at: http://adage.com/article?article_id=136262

(A4)   Josh Bernoff. "Advertising Will Change Forever." Published July 20, 2009. Available at: http://adage.com/digitalnext/post?article_id=138023

(A5)   Garrick Schmitt. "The Future of Geo-tagged Marketing, Now." Published December 14, 2009. Available at: http://adage.com/digitalnext/post?article_id=141069

(A6)   Brian Steinberg. "Future of TV." Published November 30, 2009. Available at: http://adage.com/article?article_id=140751

(A7)   Kunur Patel. "The Creativity Awards Report." Published September 28, 2009. Available at: http://adage.com/agencynews/article?article_id=139270

(A8)   Rupal Parekh. "Why Long-Form Ads Are the Wave of the Future." Published May 3, 2010. Available at: http://adage.com/madisonandvine/article?article_id=143603

(A9)   Phil Johnson. "Creating the Future of Adland." Published September 16, 2009. Available at: http://adage.com/smallagency/post?article_id=139064

(A10) Al DiGuido. "What Will Advertising Agencies Look Like in 2015?" Published February 23, 2010. Available at: http://adage.com/agencynews/article?article_id=142257